OTHER BOOKS BY

MICHAEL L. BROWN

LET NO ONE DECEIVE YOU:
CONFRONTING THE CRITICS OF REVIVAL

FROM HOLY LAUGHTER TO HOLY FIRE:
AMERICA ON THE EDGE OF REVIVAL

ISRAEL'S DIVINE HEALER

IT'S TIME TO ROCK THE BOAT:
A CALL TO GOD'S PEOPLE TO RISE UP AND PREACH
A CONFRONTATIONAL GOSPEL

OUR HANDS ARE STAINED WITH BLOOD:
THE TRAGIC STORY OF THE "CHURCH" AND THE JEWISH PEOPLE

WHATEVER HAPPENED TO THE POWER OF GOD?
IS THE CHARISMATIC CHURCH SLAIN IN THE SPIRIT
OR DOWN FOR THE COUNT?

HOW SAVED ARE WE?

*THE END OF THE AMERICAN
GOSPEL ENTERPRISE*

For more information on ICN Ministries, or for a complete resource
catalog of other books and tapes by Dr. Michael L. Brown, write to:

ICN Ministries
8594 Highway 98 West, Pensacola, FL 32506
Phone: (850) 458-6424 · Fax: (850) 458-1828
E-mail: RevivalNow@msn.com

GO AND SIN NO MORE

GO AND SIN NO MORE

A CALL TO HOLINESS

MICHAEL L. BROWN

Regal

A Division of Gospel Light
Ventura, California, U.S.A.

Published by Regal Books
A Division of Gospel Light
Ventura, California, U.S.A.
Printed in U.S.A.

Regal Books is a ministry of Gospel Light, an evangelical Christian publisher dedicated to serving the local church. We believe God's vision for Gospel Light is to provide church leaders with biblical, user-friendly materials that will help them evangelize, disciple and minister to children, youth and families.

It is our prayer that this Regal book will help you discover biblical truth for your own life and help you meet the needs of others. May God richly bless you.

For a free catalog of resources from Regal Books and Gospel Light please call your Christian supplier, or contact us at 1-800-4-GOSPEL or at www.gospellight.com.

Cover Design by Kevin Keller · Interior Design by Robert Williams · Edited by David Webb

LIBRARY OF CONGRESS CATALOGING-IN-PUBLICATION DATA
Brown, Michael L., 1955–
    Go and sin no more / Michael L. Brown.
        p.   cm.
    Includes bibliographical references.
    ISBN 0-8307-2395-1 (Hardcover)
    1. Holiness.   2. Salvation.   3. Brown, Michael L., 1955–
4. Christian life.   I. Title.
BT767.B885   1999   98-50206
234'.8—dc21   CIP

1 2 3 4 5 6 7 8 9 10 11 12 13 14 15 16 17 18 19 20 / 05 04 03 02 01 00 99

Rights for publishing this book in other languages are contracted by Gospel Literature International (GLINT). GLINT also provides technical help for the adaptation, translation and publishing of Bible study resources and books in scores of languages worldwide. For further information, write to GLINT at P.O. Box 4060, Ontario, CA 91761-1003, U.S.A. You may also send e-mail to Glintint@aol.com, or visit their web site at www.glint.org.

CONTENTS

FOREWORD

Personal holiness is the key to God's ultimate plans for us all. "Be ye holy; for I am holy" (1 Pet. 1:16, *KJV*) is a command, not a suggestion. Romans 8:29 clearly emphasizes this great truth: "For those God foreknew He also predestined to be conformed to the likeness of his Son, that He might be the firstborn among many brothers." Conformed to His likeness! That is what God's call to us to live holy lives is all about. It's the central element of God's wonderful plan for our lives.

How can we be holy? In ourselves, we cannot. We can only do so by the ministry of the Holy Spirit within us. That is why for 47 years Campus Crusade for Christ—now in 172 countries with a staff of 19,000 and 181,000 volunteers—has strongly emphasized the ministry of the Holy Spirit. "For it is God which worketh in you both to will and to do of His good pleasure" (Phil. 2:13, *KJV*). We cannot effectively do anything, even witness for Christ, without the enabling and power of the Holy Spirit.

Of course, God has given us a free will, and therefore we must be willing to cooperate with Him. We must *choose* to be filled with the Spirit. We must *choose* to allow the Holy Spirit to be in control of our lives.

In my experience, the thing I have found most essential in helping people to make right choices is a knowledge of God's attributes, to know who He really is. We need to grasp the awesome power and omnipotence with which He formed at least 100 billion galaxies out of nothing and hurled them into the far reaches of space— merely by speaking. We must grasp His great omniscience; we should know that He knows *everything*. We must better understand His great love and mercy. We must grasp the nature of His righteousness, His divine justice and His own perfect holiness. We need to realize that He is not a "Force," but a Person—the One who knows us, who loves us, who died for us.

The more we understand the nature of God, the more we will want to please, love, trust and obey Him. How can we *not* want to please and obey such a One every single moment of every day?

I *cringe* at the thought of displeasing Him. I would rather die than to be unfaithful to Him. But when I think I may have failed and grieved Him about anything, I am quick to confess it according to 1 John 1:9 and continue to walk in the light.

I like to think of life in Christ in terms of "spiritual breathing." I *exhale* by confessing any known sin. Then I *inhale*, surrendering control of my life to Christ and receiving the fullness of the Holy Spirit by faith.

Go and Sin No More is a magnificent, comprehensive work on the important but oft-neglected subject of holiness. Dr. Michael L. Brown's wonderful insights make this one of those rare life-changing books. Every Christian who reads it will be blessed and will never be the same. I believe it is God's message for this hour.

DR. BILL BRIGHT
Founder and President
Campus Crusade for Christ International

ARISE FROM YOUR SLUMBER!

For the better part of the last ten years, it has been on my heart to write a book completely devoted to the theme of holiness, and I was confident that, at some point, the Lord would enable me to write an entire study devoted to this crucially important theme. However, it came as a total surprise when, in May of 1998, the Spirit began to move me to write this book.

You see, although I have been a serious, committed believer since 1971, spending most of the last 27 years earnestly pursuing the Lord, and although my standards have been considered "high" by many colleagues, friends, and students, I felt inadequate to write on the subject of holiness at this time in my life. I had always suspected that somehow when the time came to write, I would have much more fully "arrived" in my devotion to God, being more consecrated and set apart than at any other time in my life. Yet, when the familiar, intense prompting to write this book began in May, I knew without a doubt the time to write on holiness was *now*.

How do I explain this? Really, it's quite simple: While I continue to pursue holiness and strive for greater Christlikeness in thought, word, and deed, I will never in this life reach the "final stage" of sanctification. And so, now is as good a time as any to express the burden of my heart and share the insights gained in a quarter-century of seeking to obey the Word of the Lord.

It can also be said without hesitation or doubt that *now* is a crucial time to address the subject of holiness among God's people. It is a sad but undeniable fact that the abysmal standards of our society merely reflect the abysmal standards of much of the Church, and our nation is infected with moral rot because the Church has failed to be the light, shine the light, or walk in the light. That's why the Spirit is calling us to holiness in a pronounced, emphatic, even urgent way.

Of course, there are no quick fixes to achieve holiness, something I thought about almost daily as I looked at my computer monitor and saw the "Shortcut to Holiness" icon (i.e., the icon directly linking me to the chapters of this book). As William Wilberforce once said, "There is no shortcut to holiness; it must be the business of our whole lives." And this gives us all the more reason to make every effort to please our Master by devoting ourselves to holiness. Surely, this is a key to effective service and fruitfulness.

No doubt, the battle continues to rage, especially in this terribly hedonistic era. But God's grace continues to be sufficient, and I continue to be convinced that habitual, deliberate sin has no place in the life of a believer. Being under the lordship of Jesus and walking in the Spirit means making a break with sin, being set free from the domination of sin, and living a life marked by obedience as opposed to disobedience. I believe that this is the biblical norm, in spite of the temptations, battles, and frustrations we all face. Don't let a personal history of moral and spiritual failure dissuade you from reading on. There is hope for you! If God calls us to be holy, then we *can* be holy.

It is the purpose of this book: (1) to encourage, exhort, challenge, and call you to radical, biblical holiness; (2) to present to you God's standard for holiness as clearly expressed in the Scriptures; (3) to point out common pitfalls and misunderstandings in our pursuit of holiness; (4) to show the way to being holy by the Word and Spirit of God.

Some readers will have their standards challenged or raised; others will have their standards reinforced. Some readers will be strengthened in their resolve to live for God; others will finally gain that resolve. Some will need to reevaluate some pet doctrines; others will find their beliefs fortified. (On this note I would give a word of caution: Don't allow yourself to lose sight of the whole purpose of this book because of doctrinal differences concerning "once saved, always saved." Instead, if you can agree that true believers are *called* to live holy lives and that true believers should *want* to live holy lives, you can then utilize the biblical incentives to holiness found throughout this book while evaluating doctrinal issues at a future time after careful and prayerful reflection.)

The style of this book is simple, clear, and direct. You'll see that I pull no punches. The book is also personal and honest. I write to myself as well as to you! Endnotes have been kept to a minimum, being used only when I felt it necessary to direct the interested reader to further, relevant sources or when some peripheral point deserved mention, but not in the main text. I am also not too proud to acknowledge some fine books of quotations that I have drawn from through the years, as will be evident through the endnotes.

Several years ago, after preaching one night in Kuopio, Finland, I spent the early hours of the morning with the Lord. In close communion with Him, I wrote down this simple prayer: "Lord, help me to hate sin in my life as mercilessly as I judge it in the lives of others." Would that all of us lived this out! It would change many of our lives dramatically. And when we realize that *God hates sin*— acutely, passionately, totally—we have more than enough reason to flee from that which defiles and cleave to that which is good, pure, and wholesome—in other words, to that which is holy and to Him who is holy. It is for Him, through Him, and to Him that we are holy. Let's pursue His call! Are you ready to begin?

Special thanks are due to my precious wife, Nancy, for her tremendously valuable input while I worked on this book through the summer and, more importantly, for always encouraging and challenging me to deepen my commitment to the Lord. I also want to express my appreciation for Bill Greig III and Kyle Duncan with Gospel Light and Regal Books for their very deep and real burden to see the message of holiness spread throughout the Church. And to my fellow workers in the Brownsville Revival and Brownsville Revival School of Ministry (including our wonderful student body, already more than a thousand strong in less than two years of existence), I pray that the pages that follow will help articulate our passion: that we may see God's people ablaze with the holy fire of revival, set apart to Him by life or by death. It's time for a holy Bride!

⌒

As I write the closing words of this preface, it is September 21, 1998, Rosh Hashanah, the traditional Jewish New Year, known in the Scriptures as Yom HaT'ruah, the Day of the Sounding of the Shofar (Ram's Horn). In Jewish tradition, this is the first of the "Days of

Awe," the ten days of repentance culminating with the Day of Atonement (Yom Kippur), ten days set apart for deep introspection and change. According to Moses Maimonides, the piercing blast of the ram's horn on this day had a clear and pointed significance. It said:

> Wake up from your sleep, you sleepers! Arise from your slumber, you slumberers! Examine your deeds! Return to God! Remember your Creator! Those of you who forget the truth in the futilities of the times and spend all year in vanity and emptiness, look into your soul, improve your ways and your deeds. Let each of you abandon his evil ways and his immoral thoughts (Laws of Repentance 3:4, as vibrantly translated by Avraham Yaakov Finkel).

And how pitiful—and possibly poignant—it is that today, Rosh Hashanah, explicit video discussion of the secret sins of our nation's president have been aired for the entire world to see and hear. This is certainly a perfect time for some serious reflection.

TWENTY REASONS NOT TO SIN, PART I

O miserable man, what a deformed monster sin has made you! God made you "little lower than the angels"; sin has made you little better than the devils.

JOSEPH ALLEINE

First we practice sin, then defend it, then boast of it.

THOMAS MANTON

Sin is the dare of God's justice, the rape of His mercy, the jeer of His patience, the slight of His power, and the contempt of His love.

JOHN BUNYAN

I was leaving a church meeting in Houston when a young man approached me and handed me a prayer card. "I just entered Teen Challenge," he explained, "and I'm a recovering alcoholic and drug addict. Would you please pray for my wife?" Written on the card was his wife's name with the request that the Lord would keep her safe while he was in the rehab program. I assured him that I would pray for her, and I encouraged him not to use the language of the world—referring to himself as "a recovering alcoholic and drug addict"—but to recognize that in Jesus, he was a new creation.

Later that afternoon, I took his card in my hands as I knelt in prayer and asked for God's blessing on his wife, Maria. And then I began to think: Sin just doesn't pay! Drugs promised this young man such pleasure; drink promised him such peace; both delivered destruction. Now two precious lives hung in the balance. Would sin claim another victim, another marriage, another family? Would sin destroy yet again?

And then I continued to think about our miserable, sinful human nature: Why is it that we fall into the same traps over and over again? Why is it that we believe the same lies long after they have been exposed? Why is it that we make a habit of doing wrong—even when we desire what is right? Why? Could it be that we never step back and look at the lasting consequences of sin? Could it be that sin tastes so good—even if it is only for a moment—that we forget how rotten it makes us feel when we digest it? Could it be that Satan has done such a good job of packaging the poison that we drink it because of the bright shiny label? Could it be that the beginning of the story is so alluring, so appealing, so sensual, so seductive that we are blinded to the horrible, tragic end? Could it be?

Listen to the warning of Proverbs:

> My son, attend to wisdom, bend your ear to knowledge, that caution may be your safeguard, and prudence may take care of you; keep hold of caution and sound sense, that they may save you from the loose woman: her lips drop

honied words, her talk is smoother than oil itself, but the
end with her is bitter as poison, sharp as a sword with double
edge; her feet go down to Death, her steps lead straight to
the grave (Prov. 5:1-5, *Moffatt's translation*).

But she looked so good! Those enticing lips, that inviting
smile, those beautiful curves, that captivating glance. She was just
what you wanted, just what you needed, the very thing that would
satisfy, the very thing that would fulfill. But outward appearances,
my friend, can be deceiving. In the end, the beauty bites. In the end,
she kills. In the end she is a not a gorgeous woman; she is a dagger,
sharp as a double-edged sword.

Yes, the seductress is sin personified: It never delivers only what it
promises, and it always betrays both the user and the used. You see,
the sharp sword stabs the seductress, too: Manipulated and merchan-
dised, degraded and sometimes diseased, sin spits her out when it's
finished with her. No one wins this game! When will we ever learn?

Listen once more to the wisdom of Proverbs:

Who has woe? Who has sorrow? Who has strife? Who has
complaints? Who has needless bruises? Who has bloodshot
eyes? Those who linger over wine, who go to sample bowls
of mixed wine. Do not gaze at wine when it is red, when it
sparkles in the cup, when it goes down smoothly! In the end
it bites like a snake and poisons like a viper (Prov. 23:29-32).

What a picture Solomon paints! Just look at the wine glistening in the cup, the very image of joy and celebration. It sparkles!
Aged white wine, choice red wine, set aside for this special moment.
How it enhances the night! How it charms the whole party. But
look again: Grown men are lying in their own vomit. Dignified
women have slept with crude strangers. Carpets are stained with
blood from a fistfight over nothing. The sparkling wine has fangs!
The glistening drink destroys.

And that is just the snapshot of the moment. Look at the scene again, six months later, five years later, when intoxicating drink has become a close companion: Jobs have been lost, marriages torn apart, children beaten by fathers in a drunken rage. Yes, liquor is a murderer, a bandit, a thief, even if it sparkles and shines. Ask the parents of the kids who were crushed to death by the car of a drunken driver. Ask the husband who lost the wife of his dreams to a vehicle swinging out of control—just because the driver had to have one more drink before he went home. There is nothing more hateful than sin and its fruit![1]

That's why the Word never tires of giving us warnings, showing us how to avoid the tentacles of temptation:

> My son, keep your father's commands and do not forsake your mother's teaching. Bind them upon your heart forever; fasten them around your neck. When you walk, they will guide you; when you sleep, they will watch over you; when you awake, they will speak to you.[2] For these commands are a lamp, this teaching is a light, and the corrections of discipline are the way to life, keeping you from the immoral woman, from the smooth tongue of the wayward wife (Prov. 6:20-23).

Yes, "the corrections of discipline are the way to life," and disobedience brings death. Always. Keeping this before us at all times—binding it in our hearts forever and fastening it around our necks—will help us to resist the allurement of lust and the seduction of sin, no matter how lovely the temptation appears: "Do not lust in your heart after her beauty or let her captivate you with her eyes, for the prostitute reduces you to a loaf of bread, and the adulteress preys upon your very life" (Prov. 6:25,26). This is hardly fun and games!

And so the Word asks: "Can a man scoop fire into his lap without his clothes being burned? Can a man walk on hot coals without his feet being scorched?" (Prov. 6:27,28). Absolutely not! If you play with fire, you *will* be burned. If you play with sin, you *will* be destroyed. It is never worth it in the end. Never!

Think of that young man in Teen Challenge—one of countless tens of thousands in similar straits this very hour—trying so hard to get his life back together, weighed down with care for his wife, hoping somehow to make a break with the past and begin a new life. What can end this cycle of despair?

The Word of God has given us the antidote. The Scriptures have provided the cure. There are biblical truths that can save lives from destruction. There are principles that can snatch souls from hell's grasp. But these truths must be applied. You can drown with a life preserver within your reach. You can burn to death with a fire escape right outside your window. You can die of a snake bite with the antivenin sitting in a bottle on your shelf. The solution must be put to use. The way of escape must be pursued. The helping hand must be grasped. So I urge you, my friend, to listen and learn. Do it now, before it's too late. These truths could save your life. They have certainly helped to save mine!

I give you twenty reasons not to sin, any one of which is enough to keep you holy. Twenty should keep you strong until Jesus comes! And even though a few of the examples used may seem extreme or even irrelevant to you—after all, most Christians are not involved in things like drug addiction, murder, or sexual perversion—the fact is that sin *is* extreme, its effects on our lives are extreme, and its final consequences are extreme. When we see sin for what it really is—in its most full and extreme forms—it will help us to flee from even the "smallest" sins.

#1
Sin Does Not Satisfy

Sometimes as believers we forget that sin can bring real pleasure. It often feels great to sin. That's why sin is so powerful and addictive. It can be exciting, thrilling, stimulating, and lots of fun. There are godless comedians who are hysterical to hear. There are drugs that can make you feel like a king, like you own the world. And there are plenty of people who thoroughly enjoy their sexual immorality and their partying lifestyle. Yes, in the words of Hebrews 11:25, there are pleasures of sin that can be enjoyed for a short time. But there is no lasting satisfaction in sin!

After the drugs wear off, after the high fades, after the sexual ecstasy is reached, we are left with an empty feeling, a feeling of being unclean, ungratified, discontent. It's hollow! That's why so many "stars" reach the top only to find that they are totally alone when they get there. It's not what it's cracked up to be!

And that's why when sinners really meet Jesus, they gladly abandon their sinful habits in a moment. When they encounter the Bread of Life, they no longer hunger and thirst for anyone or anything else (see John 6:35). The problem is that we—not the Bread!—sometimes get stale, failing to spend quality time in prayer, the Word, worship, and active witness and service. We forsake the fountain of life and hew out "broken cisterns that cannot hold water" (Jer. 2:13). And then sin—appealing, enticing sin—calls to us again, reminding us of those intimate moments we once enjoyed in its embrace, failing to remind us of the hell we went through when we woke up from our dream.

Expose the fantasy now! Say it out loud until it sinks in: Sin will never satisfy! In the end, the happiness becomes sadness, the thrill becomes a nightmare, the pleasure becomes an addiction. Sin never keeps its promises.

#2
Sin Leads to More Sin

According to Proverbs 5:22, "The evil deeds of a wicked man ensnare him; the cords of his sin hold him fast." When you sin, you tie yourself up, and instead of the sinner being free to "do his own thing" while the believer is bound by a set of dead rules and regulations, it's really the reverse. The sinner is a slave to sin, while the believer is free to do the will of God (see John 8:34-36). In the words of Oswald Chambers:

> Worldly people imagine that the saints must find it diffi-
> cult to live with so many restrictions, but the bondage is
> with the world, not with the saints. There is no such thing
> as freedom in the world, and the higher we go in the social
> life the more bondage there is.[3]

But don't expect sin to let you in on this secret. Instead, the voice of temptation says, "You're really struggling with lust. If you would just watch that porno flick, you would get the release you so desperately need. You'd be free from that oppression! Go ahead. It will bring relief."

What a lie! The only thing watching that filth will produce is a desire—and *need*—to watch another unclean movie. Sin leads to more sin. You can bank on it.

In the wise words of Ecclesiastes, "Whoever loves money never has money enough; whoever loves wealth is never satisfied with his income" (Eccles. 5:10). You always want more! Greed cannot be satisfied with possessions; drug addiction cannot be satisfied with a great high; lust cannot be satisfied with a one-night stand; pride cannot be satisfied with promotion and fame. Proverbs tells us that the eyes of a man are never satisfied (see Prov. 27:20), and every honest man reading this can testify that this is true. Otherwise, sir, one glance at that bikini-clad woman would have been enough, wouldn't it? Why did you have to look again . . . and again?

That's the way sin operates—in the little things as well as the large, in lying as well as lusting, whether stealing a candy bar or robbing a bank. The promised fulfillment is fleeting. Before we committed the sinful act, we made a firm resolve: "I'll do this one thing only this one time, but never again." What happened? To paraphrase the famous potato chip slogan, you can't eat just one!

At first, the temptation may come once a month, but when you give in, it's like feeding a fire. Soon it needs to be fed again. The next time, the temptation may return after two weeks. If you sin again, it will return after a week, then after a day, and then—you're bound! Just ask the heroin addict how it works. He's an expert on bondage. Unfortunately for him, it's his own bondage, and he doesn't know how to get free.

SIN ALWAYS DRAGS THE HUMAN CHARACTER—AND THE HUMAN WILL—DOWN. SIN NEVER LIFTS US UP.

If you submit to God and resist the devil (see Jas. 4:7), the power of temptation and sin is broken. If you give in to it, it wraps another cord around you, making it tougher for you to fight back the next time. And every time you sin, it becomes harder for you to resist and easier to yield. You weaken, and you lose your resolve to fight. That's why the time to say "No!" is now—before the ropes hold you fast. Otherwise, if you invite one sin to come and visit you for a night, soon enough you'll be shocked to find hundreds of other sins—transgression's "extended family"—coming to live with you on a permanent basis. So kick the intruder out!

#3
Sin Leads to Worse Sins

This principle is absolutely terrifying. It's bad enough that sin leads to more sin, that one drink leads to another, that one immoral act leads to another. But it's even more sobering to realize that *sin always drags the human character and will down; sin never lifts us up.* The child abuser was not born that way! The serial killer started somewhere—perhaps with fits of disobedience when he was a child, perhaps by being cruel to his pet cat, perhaps with a sexual fetish—before becoming a monster capable of taking innocent human lives. Sin will drag you into the mud!

I can testify to this firsthand. When I began getting high in the late '60s at the age of fourteen, I first tried smoking pot and hash, but they had no effect on me. So I decided to try something more potent—uppers, downers, possibly LSD—but I was sure I would never use anything like speed, let alone a real low-life drug like heroin. Never!

But sin quickly dragged me down, and it wasn't long before I was snorting speed, although I was still positive that I would never shoot it into my veins. I was a nice Jewish boy! Putting needles in my arms was unthinkable. Yet, it wasn't long after that I began to mainline speed, injecting it into my veins. Still, I assure you before God, I *knew* that I would never shoot heroin. Me?! Heroin was for criminals living in the inner city. I was a lawyer's son living on Long Island. Soon enough I was shooting heroin—*at the ripe old age of fifteen*. Sin leads to worse sins!

I remember hearing the testimony of a young man at a baptismal service as he gave witness to God's delivering power. From the ages of six to fourteen he was involved in sexual sin—yes, from the age of six. The door was first opened when he began taking an interest in the lingerie and swimsuit sections of his mother's J. C. Penney catalog. As he got older, that didn't satisfy, so he began to search for racier and more lewd pictures. Soon this led to outright pornography and sexual fantasy. The downward descent is guaranteed.

In fact, sexual immorality provides one of the most vivid illustrations of the slippery slope of sin. At one time, a man may find *Playboy* magazine very alluring. But after a while, it's too "soft," so he gets his hands on harder, more explicit magazines. True, they are quite graphic. "But," the deceived conscience says, "they're *hardly* perverse. That kind of stuff—kiddie porn, bestiality, sadomasochism—is gross."

Not for long! Soon "normal" pornography just doesn't do it, and the flesh cries for the next step downward, and then downward again and again. Now, the conscience is seared, and all kinds of unspeakable perversion have become a necessary ingredient to life. How treacherous sin is!

Of course, some of you might be saying, "What has this got to do with me? In no way am I even nearly that bad! I admit that I watch some movies with a little nudity and profanity, but I have no interest whatsoever in pornography, and I've held to the same standard for years. Sorry, buddy, but your examples of porno addicts and serial killers have *nothing* to do with me."

Are you sure? Satan is a lot more wily than you realize. He already has you in his grasp. In fact, you have already deceived yourself. You have abandoned God's standards and set up your own in their place.

Did you ever notice Proverbs 14:12? "There is a way that seems right to a man, but in the end it leads to death." The same verse is repeated in Proverbs 16:25. The Lord is trying to make a point! Just because you justify yourself doesn't mean that He justifies you. Just because you are "not that bad" in your own eyes—or in the eyes of society at large—doesn't mean that in God's eyes you aren't a hardened sinner.

You see, *everyone* has a stopping point, a point beyond which they will not go, even if it gets adjusted from time to time. There are terrorists who will murder soldiers but not civilians. There are thieves who will steal from their own mothers but not from their grandmothers. (Believe it or not, when I was shooting heroin, I met people like that!) There are prostitutes who will sell their bodies to men but not to women. And there are people who will watch PG-13 movies but never R. Or they will watch R-rated movies but not X, or X-rated movies but not XXX. "All a man's ways seem innocent to him, but motives are weighed by the Lord" (Prov. 16:2).

But there's something else to this "I'm-really-OK" mentality that's frightening. Consider the things you say are "not that bad." There was a time in your life when you thought that those things were *very* bad. You once judged them to be unclean and degrading. Now you're making yourself out to be a pretty good person because *that's all* you do! Who knows how long it will be before you take another downward fall? Once you depart from the clear standard of the Word, what will hold you back? Sorry, friend, but you lose.

This is the cycle: Sin doesn't satisfy, leading to more sin, which then opens the door to worse sin. And all the while the heart grows harder:

> So I tell you this, and insist on it in the Lord, that you must no longer live as the Gentiles do, in the futility of their thinking. They are darkened in their understanding and separated from the life of God because of the ignorance that is in them due to the hardening of their hearts. Having lost all sensitivity, they have given themselves over to sensuality so as to indulge in every kind of impurity, with a continual lust for more (Eph. 4:17-19).

How shocking it is to read about a highly respected CEO of a major company, a married man with family, being caught in a child pornography ring, traveling to distant points of the globe just to get his hands on a fresh little boy. How utterly perverse! Yet sin, carried to its natural extremes, always gets uglier and uglier. There is no such thing as "clean" sin. Wake up today, dear reader, before it is the terrible thud of hitting bottom that brings you back to reality. Wake up today, before the voice of your conscience becomes silent, before you get to the point where you can commit unspeakable and repulsive acts without the slightest tinge of conviction.

Somewhere in a prison cell in America—probably, in many prison cells—there sits a pretty little teenager who never planned to kill, but her drug addiction led her to prostitution, and then her pimp made her life miserable and her only way of escape was a gunshot to his head . . . and it all started with a single drink at her best friend's house. "Just one drink and that's it, OK? I'm really scared to fool around with this stuff." Not scared enough! Now she's a murderer, a victim, and a criminal, lost for life unless God intervenes. Do I hear sin cackling in the background as she sobs in her cell?

I tell you once more: Sin leads to worse sins—uglier, harder, more destructive, more despicable, more disgusting, more deadly. Make an about-face *right now* and slam the door shut in sin's face. Turn toward holiness and away from hardness. Grow in purity and not perversion. Walk in the direction *today* that you want to walk in forever.

#4
Sin Enslaves

No one wants to be a slave. Slaves have no freedom, no rights. Slaves live to do the will of another. They have no future, no ability to determine their lot in life, no hope—unless someone can liberate them. Slavery is misery, especially when the master is harsh, selfish, insensitive, cruel, and powerful. Just think of slavery to Satan! What could be worse?

This is one of the great reasons *not* to play games with sin. Sin shackles! It dances (but like a spider's web) and shines (but like silver fetters). And when you touch it, it holds fast like glue and swallows like quicksand. It's easy to step into it but so hard to step out of it! Your freedom is gone in a moment. The principle works like this: Before you got entangled with a specific sin or habit, you were free. Now you are under the power of someone or something else. But you didn't have to be enslaved!

Let me give you a relatively harmless example from everyday life. All of your friends love to go skiing, but you have no interest, having never gone skiing once in your life. You can't believe how much time your friends spend on this silly pursuit, how much money they waste, how much effort they expend. For what? You've got better things to do.

But one winter, you end up vacationing near the mountains, and skiing does seem like something fun to try. Your family would really enjoy the experience, and the snow is so beautiful and pristine—so why not give skiing a shot? After all, it will never have any kind of hold on you. Yet somehow, after that first outing, it catches your fancy, and you really think that you might be able to get pretty good at this sport, and, after all, having the wind in your face and feeling that sense of exhilaration . . . . Well, why not?

What you need are some good lessons, and some top-of-the-line ski equipment, and a few ski magazine subscriptions, and a little more vacation time . . . and suddenly you're hooked! Now you live for those monthly breaks when you can get away and fly down those hills, and not even a few broken bones will deter you. Do you get the picture? Of course, there's nothing wrong with skiing, and I imagine it can be a lot of fun and quite a neat experience. (I say "imagine" because I'm one of those people who's never gone skiing, although it seems to be a really neat sport and I have lots of Christian friends who thoroughly enjoy it.) I only use it to illustrate a point: Once you were perfectly content with your lot in life and not the least bit interested in skiing. Now it's got you in its grip. That's the way sin works!

Has it worked its way into your life? Look at your daily routine and give this some careful thought. What rules your life? Whose power are you under? Do you live to do the will of God, or are you compelled to do the will of someone or something else? To be bound by anyone or anything other than the Lord is totally unacceptable. As Oswald Chambers once said, "Make it your habit to have no habits." That is a lofty—but attainable—goal.

When I was in high school, my class was shown the classic 1930 German movie *The Blue Angel*. It was about a stiff, formal college professor whose students begin attending a local burlesque show featuring a seductive blonde dancer. (I imagine the movie was somewhat risqué for its era, but it would be considered quite tame today. Plus, I don't believe I was even saved when I saw it.) In the movie, the professor becomes outraged when his students are delinquent in class because of their late nights at the show, and he decides to attend himself, utterly turned off by the whole affair. Yet soon he is taken in! This dancer flirts with him, plays with his emotions, drags him down into her world, and then leaves him a humiliated laughingstock.

At the beginning of the movie, the college professor was the picture of academic excellence and discipline, a highly respected man. At the end, he is an alcoholic, a tragic figure, a slave to a low-life woman, a debased wretch. Yes, once he was free; now he is under the power of someone or something else. He should never have gotten entangled! Yet the swaying, seductive motion of sin sucked him right in.

Ask the compulsive gambler how powerful sin's grip can be. He never imagined that those nickel-and-dime wagers would eventually become a huge addiction that would cost him his marriage! Ask the man who has fallen prey to child molestation what slavery to sin is all about. He can no longer look at a kid playing on the street—or even at his own grandson sitting on his lap—without being aroused. How perverse! Yet once he was normal and free.

Sin enslaves, and it does so in at least three ways. First, sin enslaves to itself, a point we have emphasized again and again. Sin leads to more sin and to worse sins, each one more entrapping and more binding than the last.

Second, sin enslaves to the flesh. When we habitually sin, addictions are created and bodily cravings come alive with a vengeance. Harmful mental habits are formed and destructive patterns of living are birthed. The drug addict now *needs* another fix (whereas the very thought of drugs used to be repulsive). The kleptomaniac doesn't know how to function without stealing (even though stealing was once unthinkable). The glutton gets headaches if he doesn't cave in to yet another eating binge (and all the while, he is ashamed of his weight and lack of discipline). Once they were free. Now each one is a slave. So why start the process if it only leads to bondage in the end?

Third, and worst of all, sin enslaves to demons. What a horrific thought! Demon spirits helped inspire Nazi officers to throw

Jewish babies into blazing fires—saving them the cost of a bullet—and motivated Nazi doctors to operate on Jewish twins, mutilating them without anesthesia. Demon spirits helped to move a vicious rapist to violate and strangle and bludgeon and electrocute an eighty-year-old grandmother—and then torture her elderly husband to death. Demon spirits pushed a child abuser to commit yet another act of sodomy, and urged the racist to carry out one more hate-filled murder.

Demons are the epitome of everything ugly and destructive, yet when you give yourself to sin, you give yourself to them. Suddenly, they are harassing you, intimidating you, beckoning you, moving you, dominating you. They used to flee from you! Now, they torment and incite you. Now you heed their voice!

In fact, some of you find yourselves in dire straits. You used to gaze into the face of your wonderful Savior without fear or condemnation; now, you stare at mocking demons when you sleep—if you sleep at all. You're a captive, you're a slave, you're a prisoner. God seems to be your Master only from a distance; demons rule you where you really live. Yes, sin enslaves!

What sin could possibly be worth committing if the price you pay (or the reward you receive) is slavery—slavery to sin, to the flesh, to demons, to the devil himself? I urge you, in the words of an Old Testament prophet, consider your ways!

Maybe you've never smoked a cigarette, but so many of your friends smoke, and a cigarette really seems to calm their nerves. "Why not have a drag?" Don't do it! You're free right now. Why get entangled? Soon nicotine will pollute your lungs and it will be so hard to put those little tobacco fiends down. Stay clean, my friend, stay free.

Or maybe this is where you are today: You've never watched pornography in your life, and you would never think of renting an R- or X-rated video. But now, hardcore porn is just a mouse click away on your computer. The Internet is calling you by name. What does that stuff look like anyway? What is it like to see people living out your secret fantasies? Your heart is pounding. The temptation is real. Stop! You're free right now. Don't get ensnared! Walk away before shame overtakes you. Walk away and ask God to cleanse your mind. Fill yourself with holy thoughts. Fill yourself with worship and the Word. And breathe a sigh of relief and thanksgiving. You've escaped a very deep pit.

Or maybe it's something even more serious. You're a married woman with some problems in the home. Your husband is not the man he used to be, and it seems like he's hardly your soul mate anymore. And that handsome colleague on your job—so friendly, so courteous, so concerned—he's such a delight to work with. And he's so funny, too, not to mention that flat stomach he has and those wonderful biceps that almost jump through his sleeves. His wife left him three years ago (what a tramp she was!), and he's a little lonely. Now, you find yourself getting dressed in the morning wondering how he'll like the outfit. Coffee breaks are the highlight of your day. Tomorrow you'll be having lunch together . . . . No! Flee for your life.

Your marriage is still intact and you haven't yet committed treason against the Lord. Your home can be holy and blessed. Don't lose your freedom! Don't cross over the line. Run the other way! Divorce is not an option. Break the cycle while you have the power and don't listen to the devil's lies. *Satan has only your destruction in mind.* He's plotting to bring you down. Now is the time to consider your ways!

In fact, *right now*, even before you turn the next page, ask yourself some serious questions. *Which way are you going?* Are your standards higher today than they were in the past, or have they gradually become lower? Is your ability to resist temptation stronger now than it was before, or do you find yourself slipping more quickly, sinning more freely, yielding more easily? And are you doing things now—habitually, or with some regularity, or with little sense of conviction or guilt—that you would *never* have gone near in the past?

If your answers reveal a disturbing, negative pattern, there is reason for serious concern. You see, there is a murderer out to get you, and you are playing right into his satanic lap. So run for your life while you still have the chance. Tomorrow may be too late.

CHAPTER TWO

TWENTY REASONS NOT TO SIN, PART II

Oh, take heed, take heed, you who profess to be sanctified by the blood of the covenant, that you do not consider the covenant an unholy thing. See to it that you do not make your bodies, which you profess to be set apart for God's service, slaves of sins (see Rom. 6:6), or "your members servants . . . [of] iniquity unto iniquity" (Rom. 6:19)—lest you should hear in that hour the voice of the recording angel as he cries, "Thou art weighed in the balances and found wanting."

CHARLES SPURGEON

Sin hath the devil for its father, shame for its companion, and death for its wages.

THOMAS WATSON

To what may a sinner be compared? To one who beholds open handcuffs and places his hands into them.

A SAYING FROM
THE JERUSALEM TALMUD

When you really stop to think about it, sinning is simply insane. And as born-again children of God, we have to be somewhat insane to keep sinning. We *do* love Jesus. We *do* want to please Him. We *do* believe what the Word says—and yet we sin! Why? It makes no sense at all.

Here are some more thoughts that will help to drive the madness out and bring us back to sanity. Let's expose sin's folly here and now.

#5
Sin Degrades and Humiliates

Think about any public figure—the president, a sports star, a prominent educator, a Nobel Prize winner—who has worked for years to gain the respect of the people and establish a solid reputation. And then look at what happens to that reputation when that person commits gross sin and his sin finds him out. Everything changes! A reputation is sullied, and you now look at that person differently. He or she has been polluted, colored, stained. (You can write it down as a principle for life: Sin stains the sinner.) All the hard-earned popularity, all that individual's great accomplishments become compromised in a moment.

How do you view that great, hulking football player when you learn that he's an avid, practicing homosexual? Or that gifted author when you find out he's a wife beater? And what do you think of that outstanding Teacher of the Year after you discover that she's had five abortions? And how "anointed" does that powerful preacher now seem when you hear that he's addicted to pornography? How degraded such people become in our eyes. Their whole lives become tainted, their greatest achievements marred. The shameful reproach is never worth the sinful release. Sinning is so stupid!

In the words of the Preacher, "Dead flies putrefy the perfumer's ointment, and cause it to give off a foul odor. So does a little folly to one respected for wisdom and honor" (Eccles. 10:1, *NKJV*). Those lifeless little flies change the whole chemistry of the ointment, and that sweet-smelling fragrance becomes a foul, stinking stench. Just think of the real-life example of the Nobel Prize winner—a brilliant, influential scientist who was caught soliciting boys for sex in the Philippines. How do we view him now?

It was Solomon who warned that "a man who commits adultery lacks judgment; whoever does so destroys himself. Blows and disgrace are his lot, and his shame will never be wiped away" (Prov. 6:32,33). So why commit the act, my friend, if you will be ashamed of it the rest of your days? It only makes sense to do things you will feel good about afterwards. Don't spend the next five years (or longer) kicking yourself and saying, "What a fool I have been!" Be wise now—before you take the fall.

Ask Samson if his sexual flings were worth it. Ask the disgraced pastor if stealing money from the church offerings was something he would like to do again. Ask the pregnant teenager if her long-gone "Mr. Wonderful" was really so wonderful after all. And then ask all three how they feel about their sins. "Miserable!" they would cry out as one. Yes, sin degrades and humiliates by what it does to you and by how it makes you feel.

Satan loves to mock the human race. He loves to see men and women, the pinnacle of God's creation, putting needles in their arms, committing sodomy, shooting and stabbing each other, begging for money for another drink, dressing as transvestites, dying of sexually transmitted diseases, tossing and turning in their guilt, wallowing in their shame, drowning in their embarrassment. The devil loves to humiliate us.

Think again of Samson—the mighty deliverer, one of the most supernaturally anointed men in the Word—shackled in bronze fetters with his eyes gouged out, grinding at the prison mill, a laughing-stock to the enemies of God—enemies whom he was called to defeat, enemies who once ran from him in terror. And it was lust that brought him down! (It has often been pointed out that Samson's first recorded words in Scripture were, "I have seen a . . .

woman" [Judg. 14:2]—and a Philistine woman at that.) The devil delights in turning our existence on earth into a living hell.

But Jesus loves to shower us with glory and honor. He not only redeems our lives from the pit, but He crowns us with love and compassion (see Ps. 103:4). He washes us with His blood, frees us from our sins, and makes us a kingdom of priests to serve His God and Father forever (see Rev. 1:5,6). He takes us into His family, and He is not ashamed to call us brothers and sisters (see Heb. 2:11). That's what our Savior does! He upgrades, not degrades our lives.

So, the next time you're tempted to sin, think of the Savior instead. As you resist the enemy of your soul, your Friend will be there to fortify you and help you stand.

#6
Sin Steals Joy

Don't underestimate the importance of joy! The Bible tells us the joy of the Lord is our strength (see Neh. 8:10) and that in His presence is fullness of joy (see Ps. 16:11).[1] The book of Proverbs says:

A cheerful heart is good medicine, but a crushed spirit dries up the bones (Prov. 17:22).

A man's spirit sustains him in sickness, but a crushed spirit who can bear? (Prov. 18:14).

We can endure almost anything when our spirits are up. But when we are wounded, crushed, depressed, and down, even a bright, sunny day looks bleak.

Sin bursts the bubble of joy and breaks communion with the Source of all true happiness.[2] (It was Teilhard de Chardin who commented that, "Joy is the most infallible sign of the presence of God." Sin drives that presence away!) Sin steals something that all the money in the world can't buy. The lift from your heart is gone; the feeling that "all is well" has departed. Where there was fullness, there is a gaping hole; where there was peace, there is turmoil.

Tell me, honestly, what fleshly pleasure is worth such loss?

#7
Sin Steals Our Confidence Before God

Before I was saved, I often traveled around with drugs in my pockets, riding the buses and hitchhiking through town with heroin, or speed, or mescaline right on my person. (I was pretty slick, huh?) And where I grew up, hitchhiking was illegal, and that meant that every so often, a policeman might stop me and have a talk with me, even taking down my name or threatening me with arrest. And I was hitchhiking with narcotics in the pockets of my pants and coat! Every time I saw a cop car in the distance, I would quickly scoot off the road and onto the sidewalk, my heart pounding. (I know what you're thinking, and you're right. I was a total fool.) Even when I would get on the bus for a nice, legal ride, if I saw the police, I got nervous. After all, I was a lawbreaker, guilty of possession of drugs.

When I got saved, the drugs went in a matter of days, and when I would travel around town and see the police go by, I noticed my heart wasn't pounding anymore. I almost invited their scrutiny, since I was "straight" and the illegal junk was gone. I could ride the buses and walk the streets without a moment's fear. I had confidence before God and man. My conscience was clean.

But sin steals all purity and innocence, making us uneasy with people and uncomfortable with God. Think of the man who just betrayed his best friend for the sake of a big business deal. He can no longer look him in the eye. Or consider that new believer who got falling-down drunk last night. He looks lethargic in church today. His head is down, his shoulders sag, he's silent during prayer time. The boldness is gone, the enthusiasm has vanished. That spark is missing. And what about that older sister, attacked by a serious affliction that she knows is demonic, but with no power to rebuke it, because months of watching soap operas and perverse talk shows have drained her authority dry? Why should the devil flee from her? She's not submitted to God and she knows it. Satan knows it, too (see Acts 19:13-17).

The good news is that we *can* live in such a way that makes us confident before the Lord:

And now, dear children, continue in Him, so that when He appears we may be confident and unashamed before Him at His coming.

Dear friends, if our hearts do not condemn us, we have confidence before God and receive from Him anything we ask, because we obey His commands and do what pleases Him.

In this way, love is made complete among us so that we will have confidence on the day of judgment, because in this world we are like Him.

This is the confidence we have in approaching God: that if we ask anything according to His will, He hears us. And if we know that He hears us—whatever we ask—we know that we have what we asked of Him (1 John 2:28; 3:21,22; 4:17; 5:14,15).

Jesus is the key to our confidence, having already made a way for us, and being determined to keep that way wide open:

Therefore, since we have a great high priest who has gone through the heavens, Jesus the Son of God, let us hold firmly to the faith we profess. For we do not have a high priest who is unable to sympathize with our weaknesses, but we have one who has been tempted in every way, just as we are—yet was without sin. Let us then approach the throne of grace with confidence, so that we may receive mercy and find grace to help us in our time of need (Heb. 4:14-16).

Therefore, brothers, since we have confidence to enter the Most Holy Place by the blood of Jesus, by a new and living way opened for us through the curtain, that is, His body, and since we have a great priest over the house of God, let us draw near to God with a sincere heart in full assurance of faith, having our hearts sprinkled to cleanse us from a guilty conscience and having our bodies washed with pure water (Heb. 10:19-22).

I don't know about you, but I'd rather be confident than cowering, pressing forward than shrinking back, living clean than standing condemned. I'd rather breathe fresh air than inhale smog and would much rather get a good report from the Great Physician than hear bad news. I'd rather choose purity instead of pollution. How about you? Don't let sin steal your confidence.

#8
The Wages of Sin Is Death

There is only one way in which sin is faithful: Its reward is always death. Unfortunately, sin never shares this secret with you, instead promising you riches, fame, pleasure, fulfillment, and power. And, while you may experience some of these along the way, they are only fleeting, lasting at best a few short decades. And then the real payday comes, and the results are always the same: death, both natural and spiritual.

It is true that sin brings death right from the start, always killing something in us when we transgress. It assaults our sensitivity, trashes our conscience, mauls our willpower, and defiles our soul. You could almost say that every time we sin, something in us dies. (That's why there can be no sin in heaven, since heaven is a place of perfect life.) Then, at the end of the road, sin pays up with death—and that means separation from God, now and throughout eternity.

For this reason Paul strongly warned the Galatians, "Do not be deceived: God cannot be mocked. A man reaps what he sows. The one who sows to please his sinful nature, from that nature will reap destruction; the one who sows to please the Spirit, from the Spirit will reap eternal life" (Gal. 6:7,8).

It may seem for a while that sin is bringing happiness, gratification, and promotion, and that God's very honor is being mocked. After all, if sin is so bad and if God is so strongly against it, why do there seem to be no consequences to show for it? Why does it appear that people are getting away with such foul, fleshly acts? Well, you need not trouble yourself or worry over this, since the Lord will not be mocked. (Remember Psalm 37!) He has set up eternal, infallible principles, and what we sow we will reap. For the godly, it means that in due time we will reap a harvest of life if we don't faint and cave in (see Gal. 6:9; Jas. 3:18; Luke 18:1-8). But the godless will most certainly reap death.

#9
God Will Punish Sinners—
In This World and the World to Come

It is enough that God has established immutable laws of sowing and reaping, so that everything we do has consequences for better or for worse. Cigarette smoking leads to lung cancer. Alcoholism leads to cirrhosis of the liver. Promiscuity leads to STDs. Obesity leads to heart disease. The consequences alone should keep us from sin.

But there is more to sin's rotten reward than the outworking of God's "passive" principles. (By "passive" I mean principles that work on their own, without outside intervention.) God Himself actively judges sinners. The Lord cuts them down! Just look at some of His promises. (I doubt you have claimed any of these lately.)

First, consider God's warnings to Israel. This is a lengthy passage, but it is worth reading carefully:

If you will not listen to Me and carry out all these commands, and if you reject My decrees and abhor My laws and fail to carry out all My commands and so violate My covenant, then I will do this to you: I will bring upon you sudden terror, wasting diseases and fever that will destroy your sight and drain away your life . . . .

Those who hate you will rule over you, and you will flee even when no one is pursuing you. If after all this you will not listen to Me, I will punish you for your sins seven times over. I will break down your stubborn pride and make the sky above you like iron and the ground beneath you like bronze . . . .

If you remain hostile toward Me and refuse to listen to Me, I will multiply your afflictions seven times over, as your sins deserve. I will send wild animals against you, and they will rob you of your children, destroy your cattle and make you so few in number that your roads will be deserted . . . .

When you withdraw into your cities, I will send a plague among you, and you will be given into enemy hands. When I cut off your supply of bread, ten women will be able to bake your bread in one oven, and they will dole out the bread by weight. You will eat, but you will not be satisfied. If in spite of this you still do not listen to Me but continue to be hostile toward Me, then in My anger I will be hostile toward you, and I Myself will punish you for your sins seven times over. You will eat the flesh of your sons and the flesh of your daughters. I will destroy your high places, cut down your incense altars and pile your dead bodies on the lifeless forms of your idols, and I will abhor you . . . .

I will scatter you among the nations and will draw out My sword and pursue you. Your land will be laid waste, and your cities will lie in ruins (Lev. 26:14-33).

Now, consider Jesus' warnings to the Church (don't just skim these words either):

If you do not repent, I will come to you and remove your lampstand from its place.

Repent therefore! Otherwise, I will soon come to you and will fight against them with the sword of My mouth.

I have given her time to repent of her immorality, but she is unwilling. So I will cast her on a bed of suffering, and I will make those who commit adultery with her suffer intensely, unless they repent of her ways. I will strike her children dead. Then all the churches will know that I am He who searches hearts and minds, and I will repay each of you according to your deeds.

Remember, therefore, what you have received and heard; obey it, and repent. But if you do not wake up, I will come like a thief, and you will not know at what time I will come to you.

I know your deeds, that you are neither cold nor hot. I wish you were either one or the other! So, because you are lukewarm—neither hot nor cold—I am about to spit you out of my mouth (Rev. 2:5,16,21-23; 3:3,15,16).

I never want to hear such words spoken to me! I never want to be the object of God's wrath. (Even writing such words is frightening.) If the whole world was against me and God alone was for me, I would have nothing whatsoever to fear. But if the whole world was for me and God Himself was against me, I would be in mortal terror. The most frightening sentence a created being can hear is the Creator saying, "I am against you!" That is the ultimate nightmare. The Almighty, Sovereign Lord against *me*. (Dear reader, put your own name here and say it out loud for effect.) May it never be!

I want to live in harmony with my Father, encouraging Him to kindness by my dependent, obedient walk and not provoking Him to wrath by my irreverent, casual, or even flagrant sins. There are lots of consequences to our misdeeds, like prison sentences, broken homes, and sick bodies. But all those pale in comparison with God's holy judgment.[3] Who can stand when His gavel falls?[4] Well did the psalmist write, "Who knows the power of Your anger? For Your wrath is as great as the fear that is due You. [So] teach us to number our days aright, that we may gain a heart of wisdom" (Ps. 90:11,12). Grant us that heart, Lord God, that we may be wise all our days.

#10
Sin Hurts the Lord

Maybe the image of an angry, vengeful God doesn't mean much to you. After all, you're saved! That's your Father I'm speaking of, the one you call "Abba." You revere Him, but not with servile fear; you honor Him, but not groveling in terror. He's your best Friend, your most intimate Companion, your hope, your joy, your life. Hell's flames do not threaten you. Fiery judgment doesn't scare you. You're a committed believer, and you certainly hate the thought of sin. Still, sometimes you struggle.

Then maybe this will help. When you sin, you wound your Savior and spit in His face, making a mockery of His love and denying your very words of devotion and praise. Your sin stings Jesus! Is He really "all you need," the very "reason you live," as you love to sing and proclaim in worship? Is He really the one in whom your soul delights? Then why are you hurting Him with your persistent sin?

When you have some time for quiet reflection, read through all of Ezekiel 16, where the Lord finds baby Israel abandoned in the desert, kicking in her blood, and takes her in, caring for her until she is a beautiful woman ready for marriage. Shockingly, she turns away from her Husband and prostitutes herself to other lovers, to peoples who never did anything for her at all. Look at how personally God takes this:

I bathed you with water and washed the blood from you and put ointments on you. I clothed you with an embroidered dress and put leather sandals on you. I dressed you in fine linen and covered you with costly garments. I adorned you with jewelry: I put bracelets on your arms and a necklace around your neck, and I put a ring on your nose, earrings on your ears and a beautiful crown on your head. . . .

Your food was fine flour, honey and olive oil. You became very beautiful and rose to be a queen. And your fame spread among the nations on account of your beauty, because the splendor I had given you made your beauty perfect, declares the Sovereign Lord (Ezek. 16:9-14).

And how did fair-maiden Israel respond? Was she grateful for the love that was shown her? No!

But you trusted in your beauty and used your fame to become a prostitute. You lavished your favors on anyone who passed by and your beauty became his. You took some of your garments to make gaudy high places, where you carried on your prostitution. Such things should not happen, nor should they ever occur.

You also took the fine jewelry I gave you, the jewelry made of My gold and silver, and you made for yourself male idols and engaged in prostitution with them. And you took your embroidered clothes to put on them, and you offered My oil and incense before them. Also the food I provided for you—the fine flour, olive oil and honey I gave you to eat—you offered as fragrant incense before them. That is what happened, declares the Sovereign Lord.

And you took your sons and daughters whom you bore to Me and sacrificed them as food to the idols. Was your prostitution not enough? You slaughtered My children and sacrificed them to the idols. In all your detestable practices and your prostitution you did not remember the days of your youth, when you were naked and bare, kicking about in your blood. Woe! Woe to you, declares the Sovereign Lord (Ezek. 16:15-23).

How this should stop us from sin! Even as I read this familiar passage, I have to stop and cry. Don't you feel God's pain? Sin hurts your Father! Transgression smites your Savior! Your disobedience causes Him grief (see Gen. 6:6; Luke 19:41-44). He takes your sin quite personally: "You adulterous wife! You prefer strangers to your own husband!" (Ezek. 16:32). (Look also at the graphic, intimate language used in Ezekiel 23.) Let's not commit adultery against our heavenly Groom!

It was Luke who gave us a unique detail about Peter's betrayal of Jesus that is not found in the other Gospels. Peter had followed Jesus from a distance when the Lord was taken into the house of the high priest, and he sat outside, warming himself at the fire. After Peter betrayed Jesus for the third time, Luke tells us that, "The Lord turned and *looked straight at Peter*. Then Peter remembered the word the Lord had spoken to him: 'Before the rooster crows today, you will disown Me three times.' And he went outside and wept bitterly" (Luke 22:61,62). Could it be that when we sin, rather than turning His gaze away from us, Jesus turns and looks straight at us? The very thought of it is agonizing.

#11
Sin Hurts the Sinner

The fact that sin hurts the Lord might help you to resist temptation when you're feeling spiritual. But that's probably the easy time for you. What about when you're feeling "natural"? What about when you hardly feel like overcoming or being a soldier in the army of the Lord? What about those times when lofty, spiritual thoughts don't seem to motivate you in the least? That's when you need to remember something simple and sure: Sin hurts *you*, too!

It messes everything up. It messes up your day, messes up your family, messes up your health, messes up your finances, messes up your job, messes up your mind . . . it makes a mess of everything. Why let sin mess with you?

Here's a graphic example you can probably relate to: You're cleaning the bathroom sink and you have a wad of paper towels in your hand, but you're too busy (or lazy) to walk to the other room and get rid of them properly, so you try to flush them down the toilet. The next thing you know, the toilet has overflowed. But you didn't catch it in time, so the bedroom carpet got stained, and you slipped on the wet bathroom floor when you came racing back, tearing your new shirt and re-injuring your fractured thumb . . . and on top of all this, by the time you've finished cleaning up the mess, two hours have gone by. And it all happened because you were too busy (or lazy!) to spend thirty seconds throwing something out in the proper receptacle. That's the way sin is. It messes everything up—first and foremost, you.

SIN WILL HAUNT YOU AND HUNT YOU UNTIL IT HURTS YOU.

What's really scary is that you never know where the mess might be. A car with a flat tire might end up hitting a truck carrying gas, and the fiery explosion might kill a pedestrian walking down the street. That's how it is with sin. That bold-faced lie to your boss today might cost you your engagement to your fiancée tomorrow. How so? It could simply be a matter of the blessing of God departing. It could be that you lose your job, fouling up your marriage plans. It could be that your sweetheart hates lies more than anything in this world. It could be that you start acting weird because you can't live with the conviction. It could be that you become calloused and insensitive, plunging you into worse, uglier sins that destroy your relationship. There doesn't have to be a logical connection for the negative outworkings of sin. The fact is, if you keep on sinning, it will haunt you and hunt you until it hurts you.

#12
Sin Hurts the Sinner's Family and Friends

Of course, sin never stops with the sinner alone. There are always wider consequences. With sadness I have followed the family histories of pastors who committed adultery and refused to truly repent and submit to biblical restoration. I have watched their wives, their children, their parishioners and their colleagues suffer. How tragic it is that whole families and entire congregations are deeply injured by one man's sin. As Thomas Brooks exclaimed, "Ah, how doth the father's sin infect the child, the husband's infect the wife, the master's the servant! The sin that is in one man's heart is able to infect a whole world, it is of such a spreading and infectious nature."[5]

This is something I often hold before my eyes: If I sin freely, I will hurt my precious wife—perhaps wounding her in ways that will scar her for life—and I will injure my priceless daughters (and soon enough, *their* spouses and children). What a sobering thought!

Fathers and mothers, you can literally make or break your kids by your lifestyle and conduct. You can put them through despair and grief, consigning them to years of futility and pain. Or you can plant their feet on a solid rock, pointing them to abundant life in Him. What kind of influence will you have?

Teenagers who love Jesus, you can show your peers that there really is a living God and that they don't need to do drugs and sleep around. Or you can preach one thing and live another, telling them that their sin is more real than your God. Which will it be?

No one is an island when it comes to sin, especially if you are in leadership. Your sin can affect a whole community, denomination, or movement. Doesn't that bring holy restraint to your soul? I have sometimes spurred myself to deeper godliness by asking, What would happen if I blew it? How would it impact people who have been challenged by my books or encouraged by my example? How much discouragement would it bring, how much backsliding? (Fellow leaders, whether you influence ten lives or ten million, ask yourself these same questions. They apply to all of us.) Will I ultimately be remembered for those I helped or those I hurt? What about you?

#13
Sin Brings Reproach—to the Sinner, to the Church, to the Name of the Lord

It's obvious that our sin brings reproach on our own lives. Ask Solomon about this, or see if you can get an interview with a famous personality now serving prison time because of tax evasion. But the reproach goes beyond the sinner himself (or herself): "Righteousness exalts a nation, but sin is a disgrace to any people" (Prov. 14:34). The disgrace falls on others too.

Just think of what it must have been like to have lived in Germany after World War II and to have had the last name Hitler. Even innocent, distant relatives must have been tainted by Adolf Hitler's atrocities. It's the same with the Church of Jesus. We are totally interrelated for better or for worse, as Paul explained to the Corinthians:

If one part suffers, every part suffers with it; if one part is honored, every part rejoices with it. Now you are the body of Christ, and each one of you is a part of it (1 Cor. 12:26,27).

This is why Paul warned them, "Your boasting is not good. Don't you know that a little yeast works through the whole batch of dough? Get rid of the old yeast that you may be a new batch without yeast—as you really are" (1 Cor. 5:6,7). Our sin is highly infectious!

When a Christian sins in public, it makes the Church as a whole look bad, just like when a fanatical Muslim blows himself up, killing and maiming infants and children, he makes Islam as a whole look monstrous.[6] How is the reputation of the community of the redeemed affected by your behavior? (Leaders in particular should chew on this, especially after considering verses like 1 Timothy 3:7 and Titus 2:3-5. Even slaves can make an impact for good or for bad, as the Word so clearly states in Titus 2:9,10: "Teach slaves to be subject to their masters in everything, to try to please them, not to talk back to them, and not to steal from them, but to show that they can be fully trusted, so that in every way they will make the teaching about God our Savior attractive.")

Our foolishness, our compromise, our hypocrisy, our worldliness, and our sin make the Church look bad. Our withered branches producing rotten fruit make the whole "Christian tree" seem suspect. In fact, it may only look like you're touching a few people through your quiet, godly life, but I assure you, if you give into sin, you'll touch a *lot* of people—driving them away from the Church.

Worse yet, you'll drive people away from Jesus Himself. Our sin makes *Him* look bad too. After all, we're His followers, the proof of His power and the fruit of His suffering. But now, because of some of us, He's associated with a sex scandal or a bloody divorce or a prima-donna, self-serving "faith." He gets blamed for our folly!

This is what happened when God scattered the Israelites because of their sin. His name was blasphemed and mocked:

And wherever they went among the nations they profaned My holy name, for it was said of them, "These are the Lord's people, and yet they had to leave His land" (Ezek. 36:20).

"And now what do I have here?" declares the Lord. "For My people have been taken away for nothing, and those who rule them mock," declares the Lord. "And all day long My name is constantly blasphemed" (Isa. 52:5).

This is quite a searing truth!

Jesus shed His blood for this world, but we can make it more difficult for sinners to come to Him by discrediting His holy name. Jesus lived a sin-free life on this earth, but we can sully His perfect reputation by our misdeeds. A stupid, petty, unrewarding sin can taint the very image of Jesus. Our godlessness can bring God reproach.

So put the sin down, my friend, and lift up Jesus instead. And rather than burdening Him with your disobedience, bless Him with a consecrated heart. He certainly deserves nothing less.

CHAPTER THREE

TWENTY REASONS
NOT TO SIN, PART III

If Christians were afraid of worldliness as much as they are of holiness, they would set the world on fire for Christ.

ANONYMOUS

The principal fight of the Christian is with the world, the flesh and the devil. These are his never-dying foes. These are the three chief enemies against whom he must wage war. Unless he gets the victory over these three, all other victories are useless and vain. If he had a nature like an angel, and were not a fallen creature, the warfare would not be so essential. . . . But let none of these things move you. Greater is He that is for you than all they that be against you. Everlasting liberty or everlasting captivity are the alternatives before you. Choose liberty, and fight to the last.

BISHOP J. C. RYLE

Once a person has committed a sin a single time and then a second time, it appears to him that it is permitted.

A SAYING FROM
THE BABYLONIAN TALMUD

Do you ever talk to yourself about life? Do you ever exhort yourself, rebuke yourself, encourage yourself, or give yourself a pep talk? When you're exercising, do you urge yourself on? "Come on, one more lap! It will be worth it. Don't be a wimp!" Or do you have a serious talk with yourself when you're dieting and that oh-so-delicious snack calls to you between meals? "Don't give in! You'll feel so good about it tomorrow when you get on that scale. And just think: You can almost fit into that outfit again. Do the right thing! Be proud of yourself. Your stomach is not your god."

You should do the same kind of thing when it comes to sin. Have a down-to-earth, no-nonsense talk with your soul when the tempter comes knocking at your door. Tell yourself, "It's not worth it! Just think of the guilt you'll feel afterwards. Come on! You're a child of God, a servant of the Lord, a sold-out, blood-washed overcomer. Remember what Jesus did for you and don't blow it now. Get a grip on yourself. Don't sin."

Talking to yourself in this way is actually scriptural (read Psalm 103:1,2, for example)—and it works. Quote the Word. Rebuke the enemy. Confess with your mouth who you really are through the Cross. The Holy Spirit lives in you! You're not some flesh-driven slave, a captive to lust and uncleanness. No way! You died to the ways of the world. Now you live for God. Give yourself a good reason not to sin.

You can also utilize some of the truths you have learned in the last two chapters. Refresh your mind with them. Remember that sin simply won't satisfy. Instead, it will lead to more sin and to worse sin. As Thomas Brooks pointed out, "The giving way to a less sin makes way for the committing of a greater."[1]

Sin will enslave you and degrade you, humiliating you and stealing your joy and confidence before God. It will only bring you death—and maybe even divine judgment. And it will hurt Jesus your Lord, not to mention injuring you, your family, and your friends, also bringing reproach on the Church and the reputation of our Savior. In the words of Pastor Carey Robertson, "There are three things sin will always do. It will keep you longer than you intended to stay, take you further than you intended to go, and cost you more than you intended to spend."[2] Sin is treacherous!

And since we know we're in a daily battle, let's arm ourselves with all the ammunition we can to help us submit to God and say no to the flesh, the devil, and the world. Here are a few more reasons not to sin, further incentives to holy living.

#14
Sin Makes Light of the Blood of Jesus

When you give in to sin, you willfully engage in the very things that cost Jesus His life. To quote the Puritan Thomas Brooks again, "Even those very sins that Satan paints, and puts new names and colours upon, cost the best blood, the noblest blood, the life-blood, the heart-blood of the Lord Jesus."[3] In view of that priceless blood, Peter calls us to holiness:

> Since you call on a Father who judges each man's work impartially, live your lives as strangers here in reverent fear. For you know that it was not with perishable things such as silver or gold that you were redeemed from the empty way of life handed down to you from your forefathers, but with the precious blood of Christ, a lamb without blemish or defect (1 Pet. 1:17-19).

Do you feel the impact of Peter's words? What if you were guilty of extortion and the judge handed down the sentence: Twenty years in prison or five years probation and a one-million-dollar payment to those from whom you extorted. You don't have a penny to your name, having squandered all the money you stole through your schemes. Yet your elderly parents, who have been carefully putting away money all their lives and who own a beautiful estate, sell their home and their property, cash in all their retirement funds, and pay the million-dollar fine, setting you free. That would be an incredible demonstration of love, and it would be the height of ingratitude—actually, it would be totally shocking—if you turned around and went back to your sinful ways, violating your parole and breaking the law again. What a betrayal of your parents!

But Peter tells us that silver and gold—really, all the money in the world—cannot possibly compare with one drop of the blood of Jesus. And that's the price the Father paid for our souls. How can we betray that blood with our folly?

There was no sacrifice more precious in the sight of God, none more costly, none more dear, none more priceless than the sacrifice of His Son Jesus on our behalf. The fact of it is almost too much to believe. It would have been amazing enough if God simply continued to love us after we rebelled against Him and just left us to go our own way. It would have been an extraordinary example of longsuffering if He simply allowed us to live, sustaining us with health and breath. But it is almost incomprehensible to think that He actually sent *His Son* into this world, and that His Son actually *died for us*. Yet it's true!

While we were yet sinners, the Messiah died for us (see Rom. 5:6-10). While we were ungodly rebels, the spotless Savior spilled His lifeblood on our behalf. What love! And He purchased us from the pit, cleansing us and washing us, making us His own, and bringing us into His Father's family. Yes, the blood He shed was indescribably valuable. *Nothing else* could have taken away our sins or repaid our debt of guilt before God. Oh, the blood of Jesus! Just listen to the Word and give thanks:

Since we have now been justified *by His blood*, how much more shall we be saved from God's wrath through Him! (Rom. 5:9).

In Him we have redemption *through His blood*, the forgiveness of sins, in accordance with the riches of God's grace that He lavished on us with all wisdom and understanding (Eph. 1:7,8).

But now in Christ Jesus you who once were far away have been brought near *through the blood* of Christ (Eph. 2:13).

How wonderful that blood is! Yet when we continue to sin, we spit on that very blood, despising it and degrading it. What an unspeakable insult! What a slap in God's face! How ugly our sin becomes when we see it in this light. That's why pastors and leaders are called to be extremely careful with the Church, because it was purchased with the blood of God's own Son (see Acts 20:28). Shepherds, handle your precious flock with care! It cost the Lord a lot to bring them into His fold. And Hebrews tells us that Jesus' blood did what no other sacrificial blood could do. It brought us into a right relationship with God, cleansing our conscience once and for all (see Heb. 9:13,14). Therefore Hebrews 10:28,29 also warns us strongly:

Anyone who rejected the law of Moses died without mercy on the testimony of two or three witnesses. How much more severely do you think a man deserves to be punished who has trampled the Son of God under foot, who has treated as an unholy thing the blood of the covenant that sanctified him, and who has insulted the Spirit of grace?

Those are hard words, trampling the Son of God underfoot,[4] treating the very blood that sanctified us as an unholy thing, insulting the Spirit of grace.[5] Again, I can relate to this warning firsthand.

On December 17, 1971, my eyes were dramatically opened. The month before, for the first time in my life, I began to believe that

Jesus died for my sins and rose from the dead. As a Jewish teenager who never believed in Jesus and who had no interest in God, that was quite a step. Yet I wasn't ready to repent yet, and for five weeks I struggled, shooting heroin or tripping on LSD one day and going to church the next. Then, during a simple Friday night service, singing some old-fashioned hymns and choruses, I was deeply moved by the love and joy of God. (This was really miraculous, too, when you think of it. For someone who used to listen daily to Jimi Hendrix and Led Zeppelin, it was a big jump to enjoy singing "In My Heart There Rings a Melody," "Softly and Tenderly," and "Make Me a Blessing"!)

But this indescribable, unmerited, totally pure joy brought me to the point of decision. I felt that night as if God had just washed me clean and clothed me in beautiful white robes; but instead of being grateful, I was going back into my filth and playing in the mud. How could I do such a thing? I couldn't! So at that very moment, broken by the love of God, I said to the Lord, "I will never put a needle in my arm again"—and it was done from that very hour. The blood that cleansed me from sin also empowered me to live above sin. And it will be the same for you. Don't *you* go and play in the mud after the blood of Jesus has washed you clean. Don't trample His crucified body under your feet. Instead, present your own body as a living sacrifice to Him.

#15
Sin Puts the Sinner on the Side of the Devil, Demons, and the World

There is a terrible war raging every single hour of every day. The forces of darkness assault all that is good in this universe, seeking to steal, kill, and destroy. If the devil and his demons can cause pain, they are glad. They delight in hearing the screams of a terrified child being abused and take pleasure in seeing the tears and broken hearts at the funeral of a young boy accidentally killed in a drive-by shooting. At this very moment, demon spirits are urging on a prison guard who is mercilessly torturing one of our own brothers or sisters in Jesus. At this very moment, the devil is birthing another false religion, designed to take more humans souls to hell. At this very moment, satanic agents are seeking to afflict a mother of four with a terminal illness. *And when we sin, we join forces with hell and become accomplices of the devil.* What a gruesome thought!

This world system is hostile to God (see John 15:19; 2 Cor. 4:4), yet when we sin, we side with the world. It's almost as if we become part of the crowd that yelled, "Crucify Him!" Every day, this world throbs with seductive power, using every possible means to turn people's attention away from the Lord. Yet when we sin, we become part of the world's team, helping to fuel the godless fires that it sets.

We yield to the pull of that lustful image, we bow down to that idol of carnal success, we worship that god of entertainment, and, at least for that period when we sin, *we side with demons.* They called to us and we heeded their call. They invited us to their party and we accepted their invitation. And when we party with the devil (sorry, but that's what sinning means) and become friends with the world, we become enemies of God (see Jas. 4:4).

#16
Sin Sets the Sinner Against God, the Church, Holiness, Life, Blessing, and Victory

There is no neutrality when it comes to spiritual things. Jesus said it plainly: "He who is not with Me is against Me, and he who does not gather with Me scatters" (Matt. 12:30). Every time I disobey, I not only *sin* against God (see Ps. 51:4), but I actually *set myself against* Him. And when I set myself against Him, I set myself against everything He stands for—and that includes His people (the Church, my own spiritual family!) and His principles (goodness, purity, blessing, life, peace, joy). I am working against the Holy Spirit, opposing the ministering angels, making life harder for my fellow believers. Sin is an active, aggressive force!

Paul wrote that a little leaven leavens the whole lump (see 1 Cor. 5:6; Gal. 5:9), and the Word tells us that one man's sin—Achan in Joshua 7—caused thirty-six Israelites to die, since his transgression stopped the Lord from going out to battle with His people. There was an enemy in God's own camp! Yet he sinned *secretly*, and none of the leaders knew anything about it—meaning that our secret sins can have public consequences too. This is a deep spiritual matter, my friend.

The next time you are tempted to gossip, or lust, or criticize, or lie, or deny the Lord, consider that at that very moment, there may be someone praying for you, holding your name up before the throne of God, asking your Father to bless you and strengthen you, petitioning Him to pour out His grace on you. Do you want to stand against that saint who intercedes for your soul and pit yourself against your Lord, who is ready to bless and strengthen you? Certainly not!

WE ARE ONE BODY. WHEN YOU SIN, YOU WORK AGAINST YOUR BROTHERS AND SISTERS IN CHRIST.

Right now, God's people around the world are giving themselves sacrificially for the lost, laying down their lives that others might be saved, saying "No" to all kinds of pressures and temptations. But because we are one Body, when you sin, you work against them! Surely you and I can do better than that. Surely, we can "go and sin no more" (John 8:11, *NKJV*).

#17
Sin Saps the Anointing

The anointing of God is a precious commodity. Through it, the sick are healed and captives are set free (see Luke 4:14-21; Acts 10:38). Through it, we are empowered to action and service. Through it, God's kingdom is advanced. Yet sin can render the anointing ineffective. It is literally poison to our whole spiritual system.

There are tragic stories, stories that we know too well, of men and women who were mightily used by God until sin drained them dry.[6] And there is no figure more tragic than Samson, once supernaturally empowered to lead all Israel, but worn down by the persistent pleadings of an unfaithful woman. With his hair cut off, not knowing that *the Lord had left him* (see Judg. 16:20), he was taken captive by his enemies, powerless. No sinful pleasure, however special it may be, can possibly be worth losing the anointing.

Think of a godly woman mightily used to heal the sick. How much suffering is relieved through her ministry, how much torment lifted, how much hope breathed into hopeless situations. But she gets caught up in greed, mishandling the ministry funds and lying to her constituents. Before you know it, the anointing is gone! For a while it appeared as if she could mess up and minister at the same time. But no, the pollution gradually drove the pure Holy Spirit away. Sin saps the anointing, be it the anointing to preach or teach, the anointing to heal or deliver, the anointing to counsel or lead—sin will steal it and leave nothing in return. Worst of all, by destroying the anointing on one person's life, hundreds, thousands, even millions of others who could have been blessed through that vessel will have to turn elsewhere.

This is particularly sobering for ministers: If God has seen fit to pour out His Spirit on you and richly gift you—as a result of His sovereign choice or in response to your prayer and fasting—you have a sacred duty not to squander that divine enabling. *Many lives* are dependent on your faithfulness. So don't let sin put out the embers that burn in your heart; rather, fan them into flame (see 2 Tim. 1:6).

#18
Sin Steals Time

There are very few things that frustrate me more than wasting time. I can never get it back! Stolen goods can be recovered or replaced with new ones. Broken relationships can be restored, even after decades. But lost time can never be regained, even in eternity. That's why the Word exhorts us to live wisely, "making the most of every opportunity" (Eph. 5:16), or "redeeming the time" (*NKJV*), and that means staying away from sin. Just think of the many different ways sin steals our time.

First, there is the time it takes to sin. How much time did you lose watching an inappropriate sitcom or movie, or finding and downloading trash from the Internet? Was it thirty minutes? An hour? More? You could have spent that time in prayer or reading the Word, or doing something constructive or fun with your family, or working on one of those projects you never seem to have time to complete. Instead, you were busy sinning! (That certainly sharpens the picture, doesn't it?) How much time was forfeited when you failed to control your temper, choosing instead to scream at a driver who cut you off the road, leading to a major confrontation at the next traffic light, leading to a near fistfight, leading to a talk with a police officer, leading to long explanations and a really red face (especially in light of your very visible Christian bumper stickers)? And all the while your friends were having a super choir practice, wondering where you were. Sin is so impractical!

It is one thing to give hours to the lost, to the sick, to those in need, to your spiritual and natural family, to your vocation. That time can be productive and well spent. But time spent sinning is time utterly wasted. *Any* other use of our time would have been better! And sometimes the loss comes to a lot more than minutes or hours. Believers who have pursued wrong relationships—especially with the unsaved—have sometimes wasted months and even years. They have no reward for their foolish actions, only regret. So much time was lost, so much emotion was expended, and all for nothing!

But that's just one way sin steals our time. Often, if you really blow it, you need some time to get your heart right with God—and that means more than a short, five-second prayer breathed between bites of a candy bar. Sometimes you are really conscience-smitten, and you need to get alone with God and repent and grieve and pray through the whole mess, trying to figure out how in the world you could have fallen so low. More time is wasted, even though it's time spent with the Lord, since all you are doing is regaining lost ground and trying to get back to square one. (This is like the time lost after you realize that you've made a wrong turn on the highway and headed fifty miles out of the way. Even though you have turned around and are headed back in the right direction, you're still spending time unnecessarily.)

Then there is the time lost battling that same sin in the future, since sin is highly addictive and dangerously habit-forming. Instead of walking through life victoriously, you're now bogged down with temptations that you used to shake off like a duck shakes water off its back. Now you're buffeted and pulled, and instead of flying high you find yourself drained, almost running in slow motion. And rather than concentrating on the things of the Lord, you're fighting off sinful voices. Worse still, you can fall into a mind-set of "I'm unclean! God will never accept me," losing hours and hours as you wallow in guilt. The vision has faded, the motivation is lost, the burden has vanished, the inspiration has waned—and precious, irretrievable time is gone too. Was it worth it?

#19
Sin Has Eternal Consequences

I don't want to get hyperspiritual about this, nor do I want to give the impression that if a Christian thinks one bad thought for a split second, it will result in a hundred souls being damned to hell. There's no need to exaggerate or get melodramatic. The consequences of sin are bad enough without us overstating the case.

But let's consider a thoroughly realistic picture: The very popular coach of the ladies' basketball team at a Christian college is caught in a lesbian relationship with one of her star players. What will that do to the other students who admired her and looked to her as a role model? How will that affect their relationship with Jesus? It is very possible that some of them will be damaged for years, while one or two might lose their trust for Christian leaders as a whole, even falling away from the faith. And so this woman's sin could help to destroy someone's life or cause them to get off track for years, bringing eternal consequences in its wake.

Paul tells us that we can destroy weaker saints by something as small as being insensitive to their consciences.

> Do not by your eating destroy your brother for whom Christ died. Do not destroy the work of God for the sake of food (Rom. 14:15,20).

> So this weak brother, for whom Christ died, is destroyed by your knowledge (1 Cor. 8:11).

How much more can we destroy lives when our careless example leads others into sin or damages their confidence in Jesus and His Church. The effects of that can last forever!

James warned his readers, "Not many of you should presume to be teachers, my brothers, because you know that we who teach will be judged more strictly" (Jas. 3:1). This is because of the influence they have and because they are called to interpret and expound the sacred Word. Teachers of the Scriptures can build people up or tear them down, instilling confidence in the Lord or stealing it away. If I sin against my hearers by misrepresenting God, think of the havoc I could work in their lives!

A story recounted to me by a caring pastor is still fresh in my ears. When revival broke out in his church, a young man was gloriously saved, getting delivered from a sinful, abusive life. Since he was about to enter college, the pastor sent him to a school run by his own denomination, but after a few months, the boy dropped out and completely fell away from the Lord. When the pastor reached out to him and asked what happened, he was given a tragic report. One of his professors had convinced him that the revival was not real and that the church was following some strange, Eastern type of mysticism, and this young man's faith was destroyed. The consequences of that professor's sin—his pride and his judgmental, critical attitude—could prove eternal.

Parents, remember the influence you have on the children the Lord has committed to you. If you molest your little one—physically or emotionally—you could scar that precious life for decades or even forever. If you set a lethargic, complacent example of Christianity in front of your kids, they might well follow in your footsteps. Or when they get old enough to think things through for themselves, they might not even be complacent or lukewarm. Instead, they might conclude that this whole "church thing" is a farce: "After all, *you* went to church every week, and all that preaching and praying didn't seem to affect you. It's probably not even real!" (Parents, it's so important for you to remember that, even when your child is disrespectful or in rebellion, he or she is still watching you, taking silent mental notes. Your consistent devotion to Jesus— or your lack of it—will make a lasting impression on them, even if they don't realize it at the time.)

Evangelists, remember that you represent Jesus to a hostile, lost world. If you take a fall, you may take lots of others with you. Believers in every walk of life—blue-collar workers, computer programmers, athletes, students, senior citizens, whoever you are— you will either take other souls to heaven with you (through your witness) or else leave them to die in their sins (through your failure to witness). Eternity makes things so weighty!

I once saw some pictures of babies and young children born to alcoholic mothers. The deformities and handicaps were almost indescribable. Yet the children were suffering because of the mother's sin! That's an earthly picture of what we give birth to in eternity when we disobey our Maker.

#20
Your Sin Will Always Find You Out

This was Moses' guarantee to some of the tribes of Israel with whom a special arrangement had been made. Keep your promises, men, and all will be well. "But if you fail to do this, you will be sinning against the Lord; and you may be sure that your sin will find you out" (Num. 32:23). Yes, it will!

When our older daughter, Jennifer, graduated from Christian high school and got her yearbook, we noticed that she had no Scripture verse under her picture. She explained that she was at work when the yearbook forms were given out, and so she didn't get to fill in some of the information. I asked her, "Jen, what verse do you think you would have used? What scripture has special meaning to you?"

She replied, "Your sin will find you out!" She had learned this lesson well!

When she first got her driving license, Jennifer was not allowed to go out in the car on her own. She had to have our permission. One night my wife and I were at the house of some of our friends, while Jen and our second daughter, Megan, were home with our other car. I began to feel uneasy and said to my wife, Nancy, "I'm going to call home. Something's funny. I think the girls may have gone out driving."

"Do you really think so?" Nancy replied with surprise. (By the way, this is not the normal pattern for us. I'm usually the trusting one and my wife the suspicious one. Parents, does this sound familiar?)

So I called home and—what do you know?!—there was no answer. I called a friend who lived about five minutes away and asked him, "Would you please go over to our house? If no one answers the door, here's the garage door code. Go inside and see if the car is there." He did—and it wasn't!

When we got home, we sat down with our daughters and asked them what they had been doing. "We called home," I told them, "and there was no answer."

"We were outside, sitting in front of the house," Jen replied, "and we didn't take the phone with us." (Right! Two teenage girls without a phone.) Then we took them into separate rooms so that they could have the opportunity to confess, and we questioned them individually. (I'm sorry if you're scandalized, but our teenagers sinned a few times and lied a few times too. I wish they were as perfect as your kids!)

What a shock it was for them when I told them that our friend had actually been in the empty garage. The secret was out. Their sin caught up with them in a matter of hours. (In case you're wondering what they did that night, I'll tell you the whole, sordid story: They went to McDonald's, less than two miles from our home, and ate a meal!)

But there was one part of this whole episode that did not shock them, and that was the fact that Dad (at other times, Mom) knew they had sinned because the Lord let them know. Sometimes He spoke to our hearts about it or simply allowed us to stumble onto their little plans, while other times they left some "evidence"—like a candy wrapper—behind. The fact is, they quickly learned that their sins would find them out. They expected it! And so, Numbers 32:23 took on a special meaning for Jen, who seemed to be the chief instigator, as opposed to younger Megan, who tended to follow her sister's lead. But both had no question that God was real and that He didn't like sin.

And this leads to an obvious question: Why sin if you know that sooner or later, you're going to get caught? Why do something in secret that eventually will be known in public? Why defile yourself under the covering of darkness if your unclean act will eventually be brought to the light? This may not be the most sublime, lofty motivation for holiness, but it certainly hits home. This is where the rubber meets the road!

You see, in God's universe, nobody really "gets away" with anything. "The sins of some men are obvious, reaching the place of judgment ahead of them; the sins of others trail behind them" (1 Tim. 5:24). One way or another, what we do will catch up with us, either in this world or in the world to come. "In the same way, good deeds are obvious, and even those that are not cannot be hidden" (1 Tim. 5:25).

Sometimes our sins leave a trail behind—like drops of the killer's blood at a violent murder scene where the victim was able to fight back—and in this way find us out. Sometimes it is the fruit of our sin that brings us down in the end—like a chronic, serious overeater, dropping dead of a heart attack while playing ball with his pals. Sometimes it is God Himself saying, "What you have done displeases Me, and I'm going to deal with it now"—like David's sin with Bathsheba (see 2 Sam. 11,12). But as surely as Jesus is Lord, our sin will eventually find us out.

Jesus taught, "What you have said in the dark will be heard in the daylight, and what you have whispered in the ear in the inner rooms will be proclaimed from the roofs" (Luke 12:3). Would you say the things you say about other people if one day those people would hear the tape? (Trust me, God has tapes of everything.) "For God will bring every deed into judgment, including every hidden thing, whether it is good or evil" (Eccles. 12:14).

Of course, if you truly repent and turn from your sins, the Lord will wipe them away, sometimes even softening the blow of the negative consequences of those wrongful acts. But if you are just playing games, or if you somehow think you can sin with impunity, or if you only ask the Lord for forgiveness so that you can go and sin again, or if you imagine that God in His mercy would never allow you to be exposed, or even worse, if you think you are too valuable for the Lord to allow you to fall, or if you deceive yourself into believing that your sin is not so bad, then write it down, dear reader, and bank on it: YOUR SIN WILL FIND YOU OUT. Wherever you go, however far you run, whatever efforts you make to cover it up, it will chase you and bring you down. Your nightmare will come true.

So I ask you, my brother, my sister: Does it make any sense to sin? Twenty strong reasons say, "No!" What do you say?

⌒

You have been given twenty reasons not to sin. But just in case you waver, here is reason number twenty-one: *Your sin could cost you your salvation.*

Listen to the saints rejoicing in heaven, free from pain and suffering, never to sorrow again, eating of the tree of life and drinking of the water of life, gazing on the face of their Savior. And then listen to the cries of the damned, weeping and gnashing their teeth, tormented in the flames, separated from God forever. What made the difference between heaven and hell? Sin. Don't let it rob your soul! Instead, give heed to the Master's words:

> If your right eye causes you to sin, gouge it out and throw it away. It is better for you to lose one part of your body than for your whole body to be thrown into hell. And if your right hand causes you to sin, cut it off and throw it away. It is better for you to lose one part of your body than for your whole body to go into hell (Matt. 5:29,30).

Jesus knew what He was talking about. If I were you, I'd take Him at His word.[7]

CHAPTER FOUR

THE FATEFUL END

Remorse is so bitter. I would give everything
just to turn the clock back.

CARMELA BOUCHBOUT

(Following her release from an Israeli prison, January 3, 1996. She had
killed her husband after years of being physically abused.)

For the last three chapters, we have been hammering home helps to holiness, carefully considering biblical incentives to keep us from sin. But there is one simple truth that ties them all together, and it is this truth that has burned in my heart for more than twenty years. I have preached about it around the world, and it has never failed to make a deep and lasting impact on the hearers. In fact, I honestly believe that this one, simple truth can change your life forever.

It is based on one Hebrew word, and that word is *'aḥarît* (pronounced ah-kha-REET).[1] Clear your throat and repeat after me: ah-kha-REET. That's it! Say it again slowly: ah-kha-REET.

"But how can one Hebrew word change my life?" you ask. Stay with me and you'll find out.

In the Hebrew language, just as in Arabic, Aramaic, and the other Semitic languages, many prepositions or words having to do with direction or orientation are derived from parts of the body. For example, in Hebrew, the words for "first" or "beginning" come from the word for "head," since in the human body, it is the head that comes first. And just as we can speak about being at the "head of the class" in English, so also in Hebrew you can speak about being at the "head" (= "top") of the mountain. Or, to give you other examples based on other parts of the body, when I am standing next to someone, in Hebrew I am literally "at the hand" of that person; if I am standing "before" him, I am literally "to the face of" that person. Are you getting the picture?

Now, the word *'aḥarît* is related to the Hebrew word for "back," and it literally means "that which comes after; after-effects; final consequences; end."[2] The principle is simple: From our normal vantage point, we cannot see someone's back. We don't see what comes after. And so, if I were to tear the back of my suit jacket, leaving an ugly hole, you would never know it if you only saw me from the front. From that angle, I would look fine. But as soon as I walked past you, you would gasp. Moments ago, everything seemed great; from behind, it was embarrassing. When you saw my back, the whole picture changed. Instead of looking sharp, I looked sloppy. And that's the biblical principle:

> From our ordinary, human vantage point, we cannot see that which comes after, the final consequences of a matter, the *'aḥarît*.

But God always sees the whole picture. In His eyes, the *'aḥarît* is always in full view.[3] And if we are to live holy lives, it is crucial that we gain His perspective. In a moment this will all become clear.

This word *'aḥarît* occurs sixty-five times in the Old Testament, but thirteen of those times—i.e., 20 percent of the time—it is found in the book of Proverbs. There is a lesson here! In fact, the whole purpose of Proverbs can be summed up in one verse:

> Listen to counsel and receive instruction, that you may be wise in your latter days (Prov. 19:20, *NKJV*).

Translated literally, this verse says, "Listen to counsel and receive discipline/instruction so that you will be wise in your final end," in your *'aḥarît*.[4] That's what really counts. When all is said and done, you will have acted and lived wisely. Your *'aḥarît* will be blessed.

The problem is that Satan never shows us the *'aḥarît*. Instead, his whole focus in on the here and now, on the pleasure of the moment, on the need of the hour. And so he does his best to get our eyes off the *'aḥarît*, the "end" of the story. Just think of Esau, who sold his lifelong birthright for one meal, just because he was hungry at that moment.

> Once when Jacob was cooking a stew, Esau came in from the open, famished. And Esau said to Jacob, "Give me some of that red stuff to gulp down, for I am famished"—which is why he was named Edom. Jacob said, "First sell me your

birthright." And Esau said, "I am at the point of death, so of what use is my birthright to me?" But Jacob said, "Swear to me first." So he swore to him, and sold his birthright to Jacob. Jacob then gave Esau bread and lentil stew; he ate and drank, and he rose and went away. Thus did Esau spurn the birthright (Gen. 25:29-34, *NJPSV*).[5]

Hebrews exhorts us *not* to be like this "godless" man, "who for a single meal sold his inheritance rights as the oldest son. Afterward, as you know, when he wanted to inherit this blessing, he was rejected. He could bring about no change of mind, though he sought the blessing with tears" (Heb. 12:16,17). Esau's *'aḥarît* was miserable.

One time, after disobeying the Lord in a relatively minor way, I felt grieved and said to myself, "*Before* I yield to sin next time, I need to remember how I felt *after* I sinned this time." That would be the antidote. But everything in our fallen nature works against that *'aḥarît* vision. It says, *Forget about the consequences. Just think about now.*

God says, "Focus on the *'aḥarît*." Let's take a look at the wisdom of the Word.

You may remember some of the verses from Proverbs we looked at earlier. Let's go back to Proverbs 5, one of the many passages in that book warning about the dangers of sexual immorality:

My son, pay attention to my wisdom, listen well to my words of insight, that you may maintain discretion and your lips may preserve knowledge. For the lips of an adulteress drip honey, and her speech is smoother than oil; but in the end she is bitter as gall [literally, her *'aḥarît* is bitter as gall], sharp as a double-edged sword. Her feet go down to death; her steps lead straight to the grave. She gives no thought to the way of life; her paths are crooked, but she knows it not (Prov. 5:1-6).

No matter how good the seductive woman looks, the final consequences of associating with her will be disastrous. Completely and utterly disastrous.

⌒

There is a story I read in a New York newspaper around 1984 that had my stomach in knots for almost two days. A wealthy Long Island businessman under investigation by the IRS had been kidnapped. According to the gruesome story, he met an attractive young lady who offered him sex, making arrangements with him to meet her at a specific location another day. But when he met her and went inside the house, he was ambushed by several other men and women, then bound and gagged and brought to an abandoned apartment building in the city. There he was held captive in a room that had been specially prepared for this moment, with extra boards over the windows to muffle the noise of his cries.

What the newspaper then described is still vivid in my mind: They began to torture and abuse this man, burning him with cigarettes over his whole body, sodomizing him with such force that some of his internal organs were severely damaged. They made him relieve himself in a diaper, and for the last five days of his life, they starved him as well. And, even though his wife agreed to pay a ransom for him, they beat him to death before the money could arrive. My stomach is in knots again even as I write!

If only he could have seen his 'aḥarît! If only he could have seen himself screaming in agony, pleading for mercy, tortured and molested, beaten and humiliated, starved and bound—then lying motionless, a bloody corpse. If he could have only seen the final consequences of his adulterous lust, he would have never gone near that young lady, no matter how good-looking she was, no matter what physical pleasures she offered him. He would have sworn off sex for the rest of his life rather than meet such a terrible fate. But he didn't see his 'aḥarît!

That's why the warnings in Proverbs are so urgent. There is no hyperbole here!

Now then, my sons, listen to me; do not turn aside from what I say. Keep to a path far from her, do not go near the door of her house, lest you give your best strength to others and your years to one who is cruel, lest strangers feast on your wealth and your toil enrich another man's house. At the end of your life [literally, in your *'aḥarît!*] you will groan [the *NJPSV* says "roar"], when your flesh and body are spent. You will say, "How I hated discipline! How my heart spurned correction! I would not obey my teachers or listen to my instructors. I have come to the brink of utter ruin in the midst of the whole assembly" (Prov. 5:7-14).

I have sat with friends of mine who destroyed their ministries through adultery, their faces twisted with shame, tears of sorrow streaming down their cheeks, their consciences racked with despair and disbelief. And I have prayed silently as I wept with them, *God, don't let me ever forget the expression on his face! Don't let me forget that look of anguish and pain! Let that vivid image stay with me for life.* It's not worth it, it's not worth it, it's not worth it! No amount of sexual satisfaction, no amount of romantic excitement, no amount of fulfillment and release is worth forfeiting the ministry. As George Hutcheson warned several centuries ago, "Take heed an hour produce not that which may shame us for ever."[6] Remember the *'aḥarît!*

There was a pastor and church planter who became very discouraged and as a result completely backslid one night. He ended up getting drunk and going to a party where people were exchanging sexual partners freely. And somehow, he fell so low that he had sex with another man. The next day reality set in: He agonized and grieved, repenting deeply, and gradually getting to a place of restoration. And then his ministry continued, as if everything were back to normal. But it wasn't. In that one night of terrible disobedience, he had contracted AIDS, and by the time he found out, he had infected his wife and the last child she bore him. When I met the family, he had just been buried. By now, the wife and boy are probably gone too. What a shame!

If only he could have seen his *'aharît!* If he could have seen his family and friends grieving at his funeral as the coffin housing his emaciated body was lowered into the ground.... If he could have seen his wife and son gradually withering under the onslaught of that same dread disease .... If only he had seen the final end! He would have never have gone near that bar where he got drunk, no matter how depressed he was. He would have said to his wife, "Tie me to the bedpost and lock the door!"—anything to keep him from that disastrous end. Instead, his life echoed those miserable words from Proverbs: "How I hated discipline! How my heart spurned correction! I would not obey my teachers or listen to my instructors. I have come to the brink of utter ruin in the midst of the whole assembly." One sin. One time. One fateful end.

It is for reasons such as these that I never cease to warn fellow ministers (along with all believers) about the dangers of sexual sin. And every time I preach this message on the *'aharît,* I preach it to myself. None of us are exempt from temptation here. Our society is totally oversexed, with a constant, lust-driven assault on our senses at every turn: Scantily clad men and women on magazine covers wink at us from the check-out counters of supermarkets; bikini-clad beauties smile at us on car and beer commercials on TV; thousands of pornographic sites wait for us on the Internet. Is it any wonder that the great majority of our teenagers are sexually active? There is a bombardment! And the Word knows our nature, too, warning us over and over again to keep ourselves sexually pure. In fact, if you read through Proverbs, you'll find that outside of several lengthy passages dealing with the themes of wisdom and folly in general, the lengthiest sections in the book deal with sexual sin (including virtually all of chapter five, some of chapter six, and every line of chapter seven).

In most of the passages, the seductive woman is described, reminiscent of the cover photos we see today of the "perfect" girl or guy. And that's the only image Satan wants us to see. He doesn't want us to realize that the picture has been airbrushed to remove a few of the flaws, or that the inviting smile is completely artificial, or that the almost-naked person posing there is someone's daughter or son. Satan doesn't show us that! Nor does he show us the emptiness of that sex symbol's life or the family problems that arise when a husband or wife becomes addicted to that porn star's flicks. No, he doesn't want us to consider the *'aharît*.

And there's another side to all these depictions in Proverbs of the sinful woman's seductive beauty: They remind us of the great pressure that is on women in our society to have knock-'em-dead, ideal bodies, to be visual objects of sexual stimulation to men, to be stylish to the point of being seductive. Ladies, be careful not to give in here! It is beneath you as a child of God to stoop so low, and you

FLIRTING HAS NO PLACE AMONG GOD'S PEOPLE. WHOSE SIDE ARE WE ON, ANYWAY?

dare not cause your brothers to sin. You know what those outfits do to men. You know the effect of those low-cut blouses, or those skin-tight jeans, or that really short skirt, or that revealing swimsuit. And isn't one of the reasons you dress like that—if you do—to look appealing to men? (If it's just for "comfort," then sacrifice your comfort for the sake of modesty and godliness.)

> Jesus said to His disciples: "Things that cause people to sin are bound to come, but woe to that person through whom they come. It would be better for him to be thrown into the sea with a millstone tied around his neck than for him to cause one of these little ones to sin" (Luke 17:1,2).

That is not a warning to ignore!

Blood-bought saints of God, *never* dress or carry yourself in such a way so as to be an object of sexual appeal to other men or women. *Never* allow yourself to be a stumbling block to the saved or to the unsaved. *Never* try to get someone to look lustfully after you. It's one thing for a married couple in the privacy of their homes to enjoy their physical relationship before the Lord. It's another thing to be a seducer or a seductress. Flirting has no place among God's people, nor does dress that draws special attention to the attractive curves or physical endowments of one's body. It's hard enough to keep oneself pure in this world when the people in church are living right. But it's really tough when *believers* dress and act in sexually suggestive ways. Whose side are we on anyway?

So Proverbs warns us again of the sinful pleasures that call out to us, describing them vividly. The wayward wife says to her lover:

I have fellowship offerings at home; today I fulfilled my vows. So I came out to meet you; I looked for you and have found you! I have covered my bed with colored linens from Egypt. I have perfumed my bed with myrrh, aloes and cinnamon. Come, let's drink deep of love till morning; let's enjoy ourselves with love! My husband is not at home; he has gone on a long journey. He took his purse filled with money and will not be home till full moon (Prov. 7:14-20).

How can he possibly resist? He remembers how it felt that last, special time. And she's a good "church girl" too, ritually clean with fellowship offerings at home. She's certainly not a tramp! (Tell me if this is not the height of religious hypocrisy.) And it's so safe tonight with her husband out of town, and it will be so sweet. How quickly it will turn sour!

With persuasive words she led him astray; she seduced him with her smooth talk. All at once he followed her like an ox going to the slaughter, like a deer stepping into a noose till an arrow pierces his liver, like a bird darting into a snare, little knowing it will cost him his life (Prov. 7:21-23).

The pleasure has passed, and he has been pierced. His little love affair cost him his life. So don't *you* follow him in his folly. Remember the *'aḥarît*, and don't be "like an ox going to the slaughter, like a deer stepping into a noose . . . like a bird darting into a snare." God shows us the traps in advance. Satan only shows us the bait.

In the mid-1980s, a mature-looking, attractive fifteen-year-old girl from Long Island fell into rebellion against her parents, upset with the constant conflicts in the home. She left New York and hitch-hiked out of state. Along the way, a trucker picked her up and paid her to commit a sexual act. Afterwards she wept in shame. But the guilt quickly disappeared, and within a few months of her arrival in Texas she had fallen into prostitution, working in a restaurant that showed pornographic movies on a big screen on the wall, as the men sat around at tables and picked the girl of their choice for the hour. But when she wrote to her family, she told them that all was well and that she was working as a waitress.

Soon she became so popular and made so much money that the other prostitutes began to turn on her. She decided to flee while she had the chance, but she was caught by the pimp and his wife—and they abused her in the most unspeakable ways, finally killing her and tossing her into the river. When her naked corpse was recovered, a police chief said that it was the most brutally tortured body he had ever seen. She had cigarette burns from head to toe, her jaw was broken, and she was shot through the mouth. If only she could have seen her *'aḥarît!* The devil is playing for keeps.

Remember Proverbs 23, warning us about the destructive effects of alcohol?

Do not gaze at wine when it is red, when it sparkles in the cup, when it goes down smoothly! In the end it bites like a snake [literally, its *'aḥarît* bites like a snake] and poisons like a viper" (Prov. 23:31,32).

Once again, sin's end result is the total opposite of what was promised, only this time it was not sex but alcohol. Drinking offered delight but in the end brought death. It guaranteed a high, but instead brought hell. It failed to warn you about the aftereffects of sin.[7]

Today, on the streets of some of our major cities in America, there are winos and crack addicts laying in their own waste, their faces bloodied from a fall on the concrete, their lives totally destroyed—but five years ago they were successful doctors, or prominent lawyers, or happily married athletes. What happened? Well, they were under a lot of pressure, or some tragic event took place, or one of their friends turned them on for the first time. And after a while, that shot of bourbon (or snort of cocaine) became a daily affair, and then it began to dominate them, until they ended up losing their jobs, losing their families, losing their homes, and then living on the street. If only they could have seen a picture of their *'aḥarît* in advance, nothing could have possibly driven them to drinking or drugs. Nothing!

But Satan is really clever. Did you ever see a liquor ad with a couple sitting at a table in some exotic location, the moon glistening in the background and a reflection of the champagne's sparkle dancing in the couple's eyes, as they gaze at one another with desire and affection? What a scene, what a couple, what a message. Yes, if *you* would drink that champagne, you too would become part of that picture. *You* would find yourself with the perfect date—even if you're a hundred pounds overweight and missing your two front teeth! *You* would be there on that wondrous island, waiters and servants catering to your every whim and desire—even if you don't have a dime in your pocket. Yes, one bottle of champagne will do it all for you!

What a stupid lie. Yet millions of people believe it—be it consciously or unconsciously. This wine will make your party great.

After the big sporting event, beer is a must. Jack Daniels will light up your life! Cirrhosis of the liver? Killed in a car wreck? The final consequences of alcohol? Don't think about any of that. It's party time!

When I was a boy, my father, who was a lawyer, explained to me that it was illegal for beer and wine commercials on TV to actually show anyone *drinking* the stuff. That's why you would see close-ups of that golden beer being poured into an ice cold mug, its white foam overflowing the sides—just like Proverbs described. ("Do not gaze at wine when it is red, when it sparkles in the cup. . . .") After seeing these ads for a few years, my best friend and I decided we just had to try a beer. So one night, when my parents were out, we went outside and exercised and played until we were sweaty and thirsty. (If I recall, we rode my parents' tandem bicycle around our neighborhood, even though the ground was covered with snow!) Then, we got out some of those big hard pretzels, along with a can of beer that my dad had in the refrigerator for some of his friends.

Then the big moment came: We poured the beer into our glasses (it looked just like the TV commercials!), ate a pretzel or two, lifted our glasses, took our first sip—and spit it out immediately! Yuck! It was nothing like we expected. What a gross, unsatisfying taste! But it wasn't long afterwards that we decided to try *again*. After all, it seemed so appealing on TV!

It's the same with cigarette advertising. Do you remember the Marlboro commercials of the 1960s? A handsome, strong cowboy, sitting on his majestic horse with an endless panorama of spacious green fields in the background. Yes, this is "Marlboro Country." You can live there, too! Just inhale that poison into your lungs, breathe that white smoke out through your pursed lips, and you'll be like the Marlboro Man, sitting on top of the world, the vast wilderness your playground and the cloudless sky the roof over your home. Breathe deep and enjoy the clean air. You're living in Marlboro Country—even as you sit on your torn couch in your roach-infested, stifling, one-room apartment in the Bronx, even as you cough and hack and choke. Ahhh, this is Marlboro Country!

Or maybe you should look again. The real Marlboro Country is the lung cancer ward in the local hospital, where a little girl watches her daddy breathe his last—still smoking through a hole cut in his throat. And what became of the statuesque Marlboro Man? He also died of lung cancer, a faithful witness to tobacco's *'aḥarît*.[8] I hope you understand!

⌒

It is the final end that counts, the final score that matters. How many sports teams have started fast and racked up a big lead, only to fail miserably at the end of the game or season. A good start made their poor finish all the more disappointing. Paul could say of himself, "I have fought the good fight, I have finished the race, I have kept the faith" (2 Tim. 4:7). His *'aḥarît* was glorious, the course of his life consistent. That's how it must be for us!

The Word assures us that the *'aḥarît* of the wicked is destruction (see Prov. 14:12) and that their hope is cut off (see Pss. 37:38; 109:13). In fact, Proverbs says the wicked don't even have a real *'aḥarît*, since all they will inherit is darkness and destruction (see Prov. 24:20). But the righteous have a wonderful *'aḥarît*. We have something to look forward to!

> Do not let your heart envy sinners, but always be zealous for the fear of the Lord. There is surely a future hope [*'aḥarît!*] for you, and your hope will not be cut off (Prov. 23:17,18; see also Prov. 24:14).

> Consider the blameless, observe the upright; there is a future [*'aḥarît!*] for the man of peace (Ps. 37:37).

> "For I know the plans I have for you," declares the Lord, "plans to prosper you and not to harm you, plans to give you hope and a future [*'aḥarît!*]" (Jer. 29:11).

The *'aḥarît* of believers will be blessed![9]

One day, we will stand before the throne of God, overflowing with His glory and beauty, radiant beyond description. I can almost imagine seeing my wife there, but she will be so transformed, so bright and luminous, so beaming and resplendent that I will hardly recognize her. "Is that really you? You look angelic!" Yes, that will be the *'aḥarît* of the righteous.

Even Balaam understood this truth: "Who can count the dust of Jacob or number the fourth part of Israel? Let me die the death of the righteous, and may my end [*'aḥarît*] be like theirs!" (Num. 23:10). Unfortunately for this mercenary prophet, he died the death of the godless, having "loved the wages of wickedness" (2 Pet. 2:15). His *'aḥarît* was cursed. What will your *'aḥarît* be?

Don't be like Esau who exchanged his birthright for a single meal.

Don't be like that rich businessman, tortured and beaten to death because his lust opened the door to destruction.

Don't be like that rebellious teenage girl, degraded, abused, and violently murdered because she just couldn't stay at home with her parents.

Don't be like that gifted pastor whose yielding to discouragement caused him to slide headlong into depravity, finally becoming both a receiver and transmitter of AIDS.

Don't be like that wino on the street, who fell from the pinnacle of success after cracking under the pressures of life, first mesmerized by alcohol's peace and then victimized by its poison.

Don't be like the Marlboro Man, a symbol of life, strength, and freedom, but really a slave to a three-inch nicotine master, ultimately a needless casualty to cancer.

No! Listen to counsel, submit to discipline, and your final end will be glorious.

You've been warned. Now be wise. Remember the *'aḥarît*.

CHAPTER FIVE

"GO AND SIN NO MORE": WHAT DOES THE BIBLE SAY?

Lord, who may dwell in Your sanctuary? Who may live on Your holy hill? He whose walk is blameless and who does what is righteous, who speaks the truth from his heart and has no slander on his tongue, who does his neighbor no wrong and casts no slur on his fellowman, who despises a vile man but honors those who fear the Lord, who keeps his oath even when it hurts, who lends his money without usury and does not accept a bribe against the innocent. He who does these things will never be shaken.

PSALM 15:1-5

Professing Christians must be brought to realize that the preeminent desire and demand of God for us is that of the continual pursuit of holiness of life, and the reflection of His own holiness. "Be ye holy, for I am holy."

HERBERT LOCKYER, SR.

Say not that thou hast royal blood in thy veins, and art born of God, except thou canst prove thy pedigree by daring to be holy.

WILLIAM GURNALL

All of us are familiar with the story in John 8 of the woman caught in adultery. This dramatic account is alive with vivid images. It's early in the morning and Jesus is teaching at the Temple, surrounded by a crowd of listeners who hang on His every word. Suddenly, a group of religious leaders appears, dragging along with them a woman caught in the very act of adultery. It's the opportunity these men have been waiting for, their chance to catch Jesus in a perfect trap: "Teacher," they ask, "this woman was caught in the act of adultery. In the Law Moses commanded us to stone such women. Now what do you say?" (John 8:4,5).

Would Jesus dare contradict the Law of Moses by taking pity on this woman? Or would He contradict His pattern of showing mercy to sinners, upholding the written Word? Either way, they win and He loses.

But Jesus bent down and started to write on the ground with His finger. When they kept on questioning Him, He straightened up and said to them, "If any one of you is without sin, let him be the first to throw a stone at her." Again He stooped down and wrote on the ground (John 8:6-8).

What an amazing response! The Lord turned things around in a moment. He was no longer the one on the hot seat. His opponents were.

They really thought they had Him this time. They knew there were only two possible answers Jesus could have given, and either one of them spelled disaster for His ministry. And He couldn't simply ignore their question. It was a public confrontation, and Jesus had to act. So what did He do? He found a *third* response to their challenge, and this one spelled disaster for Jesus' foes: "If any one of you is without sin, let him be the first to throw a stone at her." How suddenly everything shifted![1]

And what was it that Jesus wrote on the ground? I wish we knew! It would make for some fascinating reading. Obviously, we have no way of knowing, and apparently God didn't see fit to let us in on the secret. Still, most of us can't resist offering our opinions here. Some of the more interesting guesses I've heard include: He was writing down the Ten Commandments; He wrote down the names of the different women *the religious leaders* had slept with; He wrote the question, "Where is the man?"[2] Whatever He wrote, the effect was dramatic: "At this, those who heard began to go away one at a time, the older ones first, until only Jesus was left, with the woman still standing there" (v. 9). They were smitten in conscience, wanting to condemn this lady for her sin while they themselves were sinners.

And so Jesus was left alone with this terrified woman who moments before was barely an inch from death. Straightening up, Jesus asked her, " 'Woman, where are those accusers of yours? Has no one condemned you?' She said, 'No one, Lord.' And Jesus said to her, 'Neither do I condemn you; go and sin no more.' " (John 8:10,11, *NKJV*).

What extraordinary words!

Here is a sinner standing guilty before God, and yet she is not condemned. A woman is caught in a blatant violation of her marital covenant committing an act hated by the Lord, yet she is forgiven on the spot. What an example of mercy triumphing over judgment (see Jas. 2:13).

But the story doesn't end there. Jesus also gave this woman a solemn charge: "Go and sin no more." In other words, "Leave your adulterous ways behind and live in purity the rest of your days. I forgive your disobedience, but from here on you must be obedient. The time for sinning is over." Yes, God's mercy comes with a mandate. His compassion is coupled with a stern command. As expressed by John Wesley, "Let this deliverance lead thee to repentance."[3]

⌒

But what would have happened if the very next morning the religious leaders brought this same woman back to Jesus after catching her in the act of adultery *again*?

The fifth chapter of John's Gospel gives us a hint. There we find the familiar account of the healing of a man who had been crippled for 38 years. Every day, he was brought to the pool of Bethesda, waiting for the angelic moving of the waters. Whenever that sacred and supernatural moment came, the first sick person to get into the pool would be healed. Unfortunately for this lame man, he had no one to help him when the water was stirred, and while he was trying to get in, someone else would go down ahead of him (see John 5:7).

For this poor cripple, there was little hope of ever being healed—until the Son of God appeared on the scene. Visiting this pool one Sabbath, Jesus shocked the man with these words: "Get up! Pick up your mat and walk." The result was instantaneous and total: "At once the man was cured; he picked up his mat and walked" (John 5:8,9). Later that day Jesus found the man at the Temple and gave him another shocking word: "See, you have been made well. Sin no more, lest a worse thing come upon you" (John 5:14, NKJV). Or, as translated in the NIV, "Stop sinning or something worse may happen to you."

Sin no more? Stop sinning? What in the world did Jesus mean? How can it be possible for a human being to stop sinning? How can the Lord tell us to sin no more? In the case of the woman caught in adultery, it's clear that the Lord was telling her to turn from her adultery, once and for all. In the case of the healed cripple, it's possible that there was one specific sin that had led to his condition, and Jesus was simply telling him to give up that particular sin if he wanted to stay well.[4] Still, the words "sin no more" are pretty strong. How far does it go?

Let's take the woman caught in adultery. Would the Lord have been pleased if she repented of her adultery only to replace it with another serious sin? What if she turned away from sexual sin but went out and killed one of the men who exposed her in the first place? Do you think this would have qualified as fulfilling the Lord's command to "Go and sin no more"?[5] According to Charles Spurgeon, "Jesus will not walk with His people unless they drive out every known sin."[6] But how is this possible? How can human beings—even born-again, Spirit-filled human beings—drive out every known sin?

Before trying to answer this question, let's look at the testimony of the Word. If you're like me, you really want to please the Lord with all your heart and you're not looking for an excuse to sin. You love Jesus, you hate the devil, and you want your life to shine. You really want to know two things: (1) How high are God's standards? What does He require of me? and (2) How can I attain to those standards?

Let's answer the first question first. What does God require of His people? Does He really expect us to stop sinning? What does the Bible say?

Peter describes the false teachers of his day as men "with eyes full of adultery" who *"never stop sinning"* (2 Pet. 2:14)—a vivid description of godless living. The psalmist wrote that, even after God smote the Israelites for disobedience, "In spite of all this, *they kept on sinning*" (Ps. 78:32)—the epitome of rebellion and defiance. In fact, Moses told the terrified people of Israel who stood at the foot of Mount Sinai that the reason God had come down there in awesome, fiery glory was so "that the fear of God will be with you to keep you from sinning" (Exod. 20:20). The purpose of God's holy fear is to keep us from committing sin.

Paul was emphatic with the Romans about this. After teaching that where sin had abounded, God's grace abounded all the more (see Rom. 5:20), he asked, "What shall we say, then? Shall we go on sinning so that grace may increase? By no means! *We died to sin*; how can we live in it any longer?" (Rom. 6:1,2). That's the gospel message in a nutshell: Jesus came to save us *from* our sins, not *in* our sins.

Jesus came to take away the sin of the world (see John 1:29)—freely, by His grace, mercy, and goodness—so that we might serve Him with all our hearts, free from the dominion of sin (see Gal. 1:4; 1 Pet. 1:14-18). His blood not only cleanses us from sin (see 1 John 1:7), but it frees us from sin as well (see Rev. 1:5).[7] It liberates us from the tyranny of sin, enabling us to say no to temptation and to resist the pull of the flesh, consecrating our bodies and minds to the Lord. That's the power of the blood of Jesus!

Being born again signals a definite break with a lifestyle dominated by sin. And so Paul asks how we, who are new creatures in Jesus, can continue to live in sin. Paul says that we can't! "For if you live according to the sinful nature, you will die; but if by the Spirit you put to death the misdeeds of the body, you will live" (Rom. 8:13). This is violent language, without question or doubt. We are to treat sin ruthlessly by mortifying—killing, destroying, slaughtering—its power in our lives. As expressed by the Puritan theologian John Owen:

> To kill a man, or any other living thing, is to take away the principle of all his strength, vigour, and power, so that he cannot act or exert, or put forth any proper actings of his own; so it is in this case. Indwelling sin is compared to a person, a living person, called "the old man," with his faculties, and properties, his wisdom, craft, subtlety, strength; this, says the apostle, must be killed, put to death, mortified—that is, have its power, life, vigour, and strength to produce its effects taken away by the Spirit.[8]

The Word is calling us to declare war on sin in our lives. Truce is not an option!

～

When worldliness crept in among the Corinthians because of their denial of the future Resurrection, Paul rebuked them sternly: "Do not be misled: 'Bad company corrupts good character.' Come back to your senses as you ought, and *stop sinning*; for there are some who are ignorant of God—I say this to your shame" (1 Cor. 15:33,34). The warning to the Hebrews is stronger still:

> If we *deliberately keep on sinning* after we have received the knowledge of the truth, no sacrifice for sins is left, but only

a fearful expectation of judgment and of raging fire that will consume the enemies of God (Heb. 10:26,27).

It is one thing to struggle; all of us do. It is another thing to be a deliberate, willful sinner. It is one thing to slip and fall; who doesn't? It is another thing to habitually and consciously say yes to the flesh and no to the Spirit. Those who live like that—as purposeful, willful, deliberate, continual sinners—behave like God's enemies, not His friends—or His servants. How can they truly call Him "Lord"? (See Luke 6:46; Matt. 7:21-23.)

Even the apostle John, famous for his emphasis on the love of God, has some strong words to say about walking in sin:

No one who lives in Him keeps on sinning. No one who continues to sin has either seen Him or known Him. . . . He who does what is sinful is of the devil, because the devil has been sinning from the beginning. . . . No one who is born of God will continue to sin, because God's seed remains in him; *he cannot go on sinning,* because he has been born of God. This is how we know who the children of God are and who the children of the devil are: Anyone who does not do what is right is not a child of God; nor is anyone who does not love his brother (1 John 3:6,8-10).9

Now, it's obvious that John was not saying that anyone who claims to be a believer and sins even one time is not truly saved. Of course not! After all, John was the one who wrote these famous words, too:

If we claim to be without sin, we deceive ourselves and the truth is not in us. If we confess our sins, he is faithful and just and will forgive us our sins and purify us from all unrighteousness. If we claim we have not sinned, we make him out to be a liar and his word has no place in our lives.

My dear children, I write this to you so that you will not sin. But if anybody does sin, we have one who speaks to the Father in our defense—Jesus Christ, the Righteous One. He is the atoning sacrifice for our sins, and not only for ours but also for the sins of the whole world (1 John 1:8—2:2).

Thank God, there is provision for our sin—before we are saved and after we are saved. If we claim to be sinless, we are deceived and we deny the testimony of God. So we must confess our sins to Him, and He will be faithful to wash us clean. And even though God's will is for us *not* to sin, if we do sin (and we will) Jesus pleads our case with the Father. He is our Advocate!

Certainly these are glorious truths, and they bring me comfort and encouragement every day of my life. But I'm afraid many of us put the emphasis where it doesn't belong. You see, John was not making excuses for our sins, nor was he giving us a license to sin, nor was he treating sin lightly. It was sin that nailed John's dear Savior to the cross. Remember, John was an eyewitness. There was nothing John hated more than sin. The whole purpose of his first epistle was to call his readers to reach higher in their walks with the Lord. And so, he encouraged them to holiness as a father would lovingly exhort his children, challenging them to put one foot ahead of the other, to grow and mature and develop, yet encouraging them when they fall short.[10]

But make no mistake about it. John's emphasis was on growing, not on falling short. And no honest reader of 1 John would think for a moment that he was telling his readers it was fine to sin freely, as long they just confessed their sins along the way. Hardly! Instead, 1 John 1:9 affirms the words of Proverbs 28:13: "He who conceals his sins does not prosper, but whoever confesses and renounces [or, forsakes] them finds mercy."

The rest of John's first Epistle makes this perfectly clear: He emphasizes and repeats that believers must live radically differently from unbelievers. The former live in light; the latter live in darkness.

The former walk in truth; the latter walk in lies. The righteous do what is right. They are children of God, full of love, and they overcome the wicked one. The unrighteous do what is wrong. They are children of the devil, full of hate, and they are under the power of the wicked one (see 1 John 5:19).

In fact, immediately after we learn that Jesus Christ pleads our case with the Father when we *do* sin, John goes on to say:

> We know that we have come to know Him if we obey His commands. The man who says, "I know Him," but does not do what He commands is a liar, and the truth is not in him. But if anyone obeys His word, God's love is truly made complete in Him. This is how we know we are in Him: Whoever claims to live in Him must walk as Jesus did (1 John 2:3-6).

Now, it is true that John is not telling us *how* we can live like this, but he is telling us that this is how we *are* to live. After all, he was only reinforcing standards that God had already laid out in the Old Testament centuries before—spiritual standards that Jesus and His followers took even deeper. (See the Sermon on the Mount for the best example of this.)

Through the prophet Isaiah the Lord said, "Wash and make yourselves clean. Take your evil deeds out of my sight! Stop doing wrong, learn to do right!" (Isa. 1:16,17). The psalmist asked, "Who may ascend the hill of the Lord? Who may stand in His holy place?" (Ps. 24:3). His answer was direct and clear: "He who has *clean hands* and a *pure heart*, who does not lift up his soul to an idol or swear by what is false" (Ps. 24:4). That's the one who can live in God's presence.

In fact, all the prophets, with one voice, brought the same message from the Lord to His chosen people: "Turn from your evil ways. Observe my commands and decrees, in accordance with the entire Law that I commanded your fathers to obey and that I delivered to you through my servants the prophets" (2 Kings 17:13).

Now, by the Spirit, we can fulfill the Law's demands (see Rom. 8:1-4; 6:12-14). Now, holiness is written on our hearts (see Heb. 8:10; 10:16; Ezek. 36:26,27).

HOLINESS IS NOT AN OPTION.
WE ARE CALLED TO LIVE HOLY LIVES.
ANYTHING ELSE IS DISOBEDIENCE.

But holiness is not an option. We are *called* to live holy lives, and that means it is a divine requirement. Anything else is disobedience. That's why the Word is so strong on this subject: "Make every effort to live in peace with all men and to be holy; *without holiness no one will see the Lord.* See to it that no one misses the grace of God and that no bitter root grows up to cause trouble and defile many" (Heb. 12:14,15). Our very lives depend on it.

The question again is, How do we do it? Actually, that's one of the primary purposes of this book. It is designed to help you to be holy, to show you the way to freedom from bondage to the flesh, to give you a battle plan for life. This much is perfectly clear: According to the Word, whereas sin used to be the rule of our lives—most of us did whatever we wanted to do, with little or no thought of God— now sinning should be the exception to the rule. Now, we live to please our Master.

So, having been transferred from death to life and from the power of Satan to the rule of God (see Col. 1:13; Acts 26:18), we grow in the grace and knowledge of the Lord Jesus (see 2 Pet. 3:18), perfecting holiness in the fear of God (see 2 Cor. 7:1).[11] It is true that we are engaged in an ongoing, daily battle with sin. But we are no longer slaves to sin! We are now slaves to righteousness, and sin must not dominate us any longer.[12]

The great problem in the Church today is that we make light of our disobedience and freely excuse our sins. We live as if God actually *expects* us to continually scorn His commandments and disregard His standards, as if chronic disobedience was the anticipated norm for born-again believers. Jesus said, "I tell you the truth, everyone who sins is a slave to sin. Now a slave has no permanent place in the family, but a son belongs to it forever. So if the Son sets you free, you will be free indeed" (John 8:34-36). I'm convinced this is true!

The good news is that the Lord understands our frame, and He is not calling us to do anything we cannot do. He is not telling us to fly like birds or swim like fish when in fact we are not birds or fish. He is not telling us to live like the angels in heaven when in fact we are mortals living here on the earth. But if Jesus says we can be free from sin, if Paul tells us we have died to sin, if John tells us to live above sin, then somehow, some way, by God's enabling grace, we can do it.

It is fully possible to live a life characterized by obedience rather than disobedience, a life dominated by the Spirit and not the flesh, a life ruled by the Lord and not the devil. Deep down, you know it's true, don't you? Even if you find yourself in a terrible struggle right now, something inside you bears witness to this scriptural truth, and something tells you that you *can* be free. Let's go back to the Word.

Paul reminded the Colossians of their true spiritual state: "For you died, and your life is now hidden with Christ in God" (Col. 3:3). What does this require in practical terms? The answer is simple and clear:

> Put to death, therefore, whatever belongs to your earthly nature: sexual immorality, impurity, lust, evil desires and greed, which is idolatry. Because of these, the wrath of God is coming. *You used to walk in these ways, in the life you once lived.* But now you must rid yourselves of all such things as these: anger, rage, malice, slander, and filthy language from your lips. Do not lie to each other, since you have taken off

your old self with its practices and have put on the new self, which is being renewed in knowledge in the image of its Creator (Col. 3:5-10).

Because we have died to our old life and now live a new life in Jesus, we must put to death—there's that violent language again!—everything that pertains to the old, earthly life, putting on the new self. And notice that this is a command, not an option. It is a requirement for all believers, not a suggested goal for super saints. This is our calling in God, our spiritual and moral vocation, our reasonable conduct. We strip off the garb of the flesh and the world and dress ourselves in the garments of grace:

> Therefore, as God's chosen people, holy and dearly loved, clothe yourselves with compassion, kindness, humility, gentleness and patience. Bear with each other and forgive whatever grievances you may have against one another. Forgive as the Lord forgave you. And over all these virtues put on love, which binds them all together in perfect unity (Col. 3:12-14).

The life we are called to is beautiful, pure, clean, righteous, and holy. The life we leave behind is ugly, impure, filthy, unrighteous, and unholy. That's what God means when He calls us to stop sinning: Make a break with the old and walk in the new, offering our bodies as living sacrifices holy and pleasing to God, not conforming any longer to the pattern of this world, but being transformed by the renewing of our minds (see Rom. 12:1,2). There is no acceptable middle ground.

When John Wesley realized this early in his life, he came to an inescapable conclusion:

> Instantly, I resolved to dedicate all my life to God, all my thoughts, and words, and actions; being thoroughly convinced, there was no medium; but that every part of my life (not some only) must either be a sacrifice to God, or myself,

that is, in effect, to the devil. Can any serious person doubt of this, or find a medium between serving God and serving the devil?[13]

The two are as incompatible as light and darkness, the division between them infinite and eternal (see Matt. 6:24). That's why the Lord calls us to strict separation from sin:

> It is God's will [not suggestion!] that you should be sanctified: that you should avoid sexual immorality. . . . For God did not call us to be impure, but to live a holy life. Therefore, he who rejects this instruction does not reject man but God, who gives you His Holy Spirit (1 Thess. 4:3,7,8).[14]

> Do not love the world or anything in the world. If anyone loves the world, the love of the Father is not in him. For everything in the world—the cravings of sinful man, the lust of his eyes and the boasting of what he has and does—comes not from the Father but from the world (1 John 2:15,16).

> But among you there must not be even a hint of sexual immorality, or of any kind of impurity, or of greed, because these are improper for God's holy people. Nor should there be obscenity, foolish talk or coarse joking, which are out of place, but rather thanksgiving. For of this you can be sure: No immoral, impure or greedy person—such a man is an idolater—has any inheritance in the kingdom of Christ and of God (Eph. 5:3-5).

We must live in this world as worthy citizens of the kingdom of God if we want to inherit that kingdom in the world to come. Being "saved" is more than a ticket to heaven; it is a passport to a brand-new life here on this earth. In fact, without the passport, the ticket will do us little good! Once again, John Owen has expressed this clearly:

> There is no imagination wherewith man is besotted, more foolish, none so pernicious, as this—that persons not purified, not sanctified, not made holy in their life, should afterwards be taken into that state of blessedness which consists in the enjoyment of God. . . . Neither can such persons enjoy God, nor would God be a reward to them. . . . Holiness indeed is perfected in heaven: but the beginning of it is invariably confined to this world. . . . He leads none to heaven but whom He sanctifies on the earth. This living Head will not admit of dead members.[15]

Heaven is the home of the holy. The end of the Book makes it plain. (Really, these verses from Revelation are just too clear for fleshly comfort. Read them carefully, deliberately, and prayerfully.)

> He who overcomes will inherit all this, and I will be his God and he will be My son. But the cowardly, the unbelieving, the vile, the murderers, the sexually immoral, those who practice magic arts, the idolaters and all liars—their place will be in the fiery lake of burning sulfur. This is the second death. . . . Nothing impure will ever enter [the New Jerusalem], nor will anyone who does what is shameful or deceitful, but only those whose names are written in the Lamb's book of life (Rev. 21:7,8,27).

Those whose names are written in that book have been radically changed by His blood. They are not found among the vile and the sinful. That is an essential theme of the penultimate chapter of the Word, and it is repeated once more in the final chapter too:

Blessed are those who wash their robes, that they may have the right [yes, it is a right!] to the tree of life and may go through the gates into the city. Outside are the dogs, those who practice magic arts, the sexually immoral, the murderers, the idolaters and everyone who loves and practices falsehood (Rev. 22:14,15).

The separation will be eternal. Therefore the exhortation is given: "Let him who does wrong continue to do wrong; let him who is vile continue to be vile; let him who does right continue to do right; and let him who is holy continue to be holy" (Rev. 22:11). Jesus will reward us according to what we have done (see 2 Cor. 5:10; Rom. 14:11,12; 1 Cor. 4:5; Matt. 25:14-30).

It is absolutely essential that we recognize there is a complete contrast between the works of the flesh and the fruit of the Spirit. We should have nothing to do with the former and everything to do with the latter, our lives being *characterized* by Spirit-led, flesh-crucifying conduct and attitude.

Yes, there *is* a conflict between the flesh and the Spirit, but life in Jesus is marked by the *conquest* of the Spirit over the flesh. That is one of the glories of the new covenant. Our very nature is changed:

The acts of the sinful nature are obvious: sexual immorality, impurity and debauchery; idolatry and witchcraft; hatred, discord, jealousy, fits of rage, selfish ambition, dissensions, factions and envy; drunkenness, orgies, and the like. I warn you, as I did before, that those who live like this will not inherit the kingdom of God. But the fruit of the Spirit is love, joy, peace, patience, kindness, goodness, faithfulness, gentleness and self-control. Against such things there is no law. *Those who belong to Christ Jesus have crucified the sinful nature with its passions and desires* (Gal. 5:19-24).

True, we used to be "enslaved by all kinds of passions and pleasures... gratifying the cravings of our sinful nature and following its desires and thoughts" (Titus 3:3; Eph. 2:3). But now we have been washed and renewed (see Titus 3:5), sanctified and justified (see 1 Cor. 6:11), rescued from the dominion of darkness (see Col. 1:13), raised up with Christ and seated with Him in the heavenly realms (see Eph. 2:6). Therefore sin shall not have dominion over us, because we are empowered to holiness by the grace of God (see Rom. 6:14; Titus 2:11,12). We *are* new creatures in Christ!

> For we know that our old self was crucified with Him so that the body of sin might be done away with, that we should no longer be slaves to sin—because anyone who has died has been freed from sin. Now if we died with Christ, we believe that we will also live with Him. For we know that since Christ was raised from the dead, He cannot die again; death no longer has mastery over Him. The death He died, He died to sin once for all; but the life He lives, He lives to God. In the same way, count yourselves dead to sin but alive to God in Christ Jesus (Rom. 6:6-11).

We are no longer slaves to sin but slaves to righteousness (see Rom. 6:18). We have been set free from the tyranny of the flesh and the devil and are now under the holy yoke of our loving Lord. It is our awesome privilege to give ourselves to Him without reserve—spirit, soul, and body.

So, rather than making excuses for sin or looking for escape clauses to justify habitual compromise, we should be looking for God's solutions to overcome sinful living and to His divine ways of escape from bondage to the flesh. And rather than being discouraged and beaten down by the devil because we always seem to be falling short, we should be looking up to heaven, knowing that it is God's will to lift us above the powers of the flesh and the world. We *can* live holy lives that are acceptable and pleasing to our Lord!

So, when He says to us, "Go and sin no more," we should say with excitement, "Yes, Lord! You lead and I will follow. That's my desire too." We were created for holiness (that's our past), we have been redeemed for holiness (that's our present), and we are destined for holiness (that's our future)—all of which means that sin has *no place* in us. Say goodbye to it in Jesus' name! You'll be so glad you did.

CHAPTER SIX

LITTLE FOXES
SPOIL THE VINES

There is great danger, yea, many times most danger in the smallest sins. . . . Greater sins do sooner startle the soul, and awaken and rouse up the soul to repentance than lesser sins do. Little sins often slide into the soul, and breed, and work secretly and undiscernibly in the soul, till they come to be so strong, as to trample upon the soul, and to cut the throat of the soul. There is oftentimes greatest danger to our bodies in the least diseases that hang upon us, because we are apt to make light of them, and to neglect the timely use of means for removing of them, till they are grown so strong that they prove mortal to us.

THOMAS BROOKS

If thou wouldst live with Christ, and walk with Christ, and see Christ, and have fellowship with Christ, take heed of "the little foxes that spoil the vines, for our vines have tender grapes."

CHARLES SPURGEON

*Catch us the foxes,
The little foxes
That ruin the vineyards;
For our vineyard is in blossom.*

SONG OF SOLOMON 2:15
NJPSV

D rug addiction. Pornography. Child molestation. Adultery. Murder. Alcoholism. Sexual perversion. Violence. For some of you reading this book, these sins (hopefully not all of them!) are painfully relevant. Perhaps you've picked up this book with the hope of finding freedom and lasting victory over one of these strongholds in your life.

But if you're like most Christians, none of these sins present big problems. You either dealt with these issues when you were born again or never struggled with them before you were saved. One way or the other, you're free. You're a committed believer, serving God in purity and living above the ensnarement of gross sin, and you really can't relate to these kinds of vices at all. You're not bound by fleshly lusts, and as far as you can tell, you're not addicted to anything the Bible forbids.

But something is definitely missing from your life and you know it. You're dull, lacking in fervor, bearing very little fruit, and hardly growing at all in your walk with the Lord. You are absolutely *not* on fire and you're consistently falling short of the biblical norm to love God with all your heart and soul. In fact, Paul's exhortation to the Romans to remain fervent—literally, "boiling, seething"—in spirit seems unattainable (see Rom. 12:11).[1]

What is it that's dragging you down? Could it be that little foxes are spoiling your vines? These can be deadly too!

Think of it like this: If the essence of holiness can be described as loving and serving God with an undivided heart, then anything that divides your heart—even if it is "neutral" in and of itself—is sin. The same can be said for anything that dulls or distracts your heart. It's sin, even if it's commendable in the eyes of man, even if it's clean in the eyes of man, even if it's correct in the eyes of man. If it takes you away from devotion to the Lord or blunts your spiritual sharpness, it's sin.

Does anyone or anything other than the Lord completely dominate your thinking and your dreams or pull at you to the point of distraction? Does anyone or anything other than the Lord ultimately direct your thoughts or order your steps?

It's one thing to be devoted to your family, or education, or job, or career. It's another thing to put any of these before your relationship with the Lord. (In other words, the other things come first; Jesus comes second—if at all.) It's one thing to enjoy the things of this world—like nature, or music, or sports. It's another thing to be consumed with them. What about you? Does anything have your heart?

Let's say that you really enjoy baseball, and one night each week (or every few weeks, according to your schedule) you sit down with your son and watch a game. It's a relaxing time, a time to chat with your boy about the ins and outs of the sport, and an opportunity to watch some talented players doing what they do best. It all seems perfectly fine, and for the moment, it may well be. But there could be a little fox lurking in the background, looking for a chance to steal your time and divide your heart, first by creating a greater and greater desire in you to follow your team's schedule, then by playing with your emotions and consuming your thoughts.

How does it happen? Well, maybe your team has always come in last, but this year, it's different. They're going to make the playoffs! Now, you find yourself watching two or three games a week. You even miss a church service because a big game's on! Now, you read the newspaper every day, checking the standings and the latest statistics.

When your team wins, you're flying high, full of joy and excitement. When they lose—especially a tough, close game— you're down and dejected, even grumpy and lacking motivation. Baseball has your heart! A little fox has damaged your vine. When you pray, you think of baseball. When you talk with people, you talk sports and not the gospel. When you make plans, you plan them around the game. *Your holiness has been compromised.* Your heart has become divided. You are loving the things of this world, and your love for God has cooled off. This is how it happens to millions of believers every day, especially in our entertainment-inebriated, sports-saturated, carnality-crazed society. Even the "neutral" things can destroy.

Little foxes come in all shapes and sizes, and, all too often, they go unnoticed. Why? Because they are so little! They might even seem cute! You see, if you engaged in Internet pornography, that would get your attention. If you struck your spouse, that would get your attention. If you lied on your job, that would get your attention. If you found yourself attracted to another person's husband or wife, that would get your attention. If you went out and got drunk or high, that would get your attention. But watching several games of baseball every week might not get your attention. Spending two hours a day reading the newspaper might not get your attention. Using every spare minute of your time to pursue a hobby, or work on the house, or perfect your golf swing might not get your attention. But I assure you: It will get God's attention. Another "god" is vying for His spot in your life. Another "master" is calling you by name. From whom are you taking orders? Who (or what) really rules you? Who (or what) do you really worship?

Look out for the little foxes! Charles Spurgeon gives us some needed warnings:

> Christian, beware how thou thinkest lightly of sin. Take heed lest thou fall by little and little. Sin, a little thing? Is it not a poison? Who knows its deadliness? Sin, a little thing? Do not the little foxes spoil the grapes? Doth not the tiny coral insect build a rock which wrecks a navy? Do not little strokes fell lofty oaks? Will not continual droppings wear away stones? Sin, a little thing? It girded the Redeemer's head with thorns, and pierced His heart! It made Him suffer anguish, bitterness, and woe. Could you weigh the least sin in the scales of eternity, you would fly from it as from a serpent, and abhor the least appearance of evil. Look upon all sin as that which crucified the Saviour, and you will see it to be "exceeding sinful."[2]

This certainly puts things into perspective, doesn't it?

It's not that we are *driven* to holiness, as if God were some old-fashioned killjoy who gets jealous and upset every time we have fun. Absolutely not! In fact, when Paul was writing Timothy about the dangers of the love of money, he was careful to speak about our Father as the One "who richly provides us with everything for our enjoyment" (1 Tim. 6:17). That's our God! He's the One who handcrafted every bird that flies in the sky and designed every fish that swims in the ocean, the One who created the surging seas and loosed the raging rapids, the One who molded the mighty mountains and painted them white with snow. He's the builder of the butterfly and the architect of the antelope, the One who fashioned every flower and shaped every sparrow.

He's a God of vitality, of energy, of life. He's no joy killer; He's a joy filler. He's not dreary; He's delightful. He's not morbid; He's marvelous. Our God is wonderful in every way, and nothing about Him is negative—which is why it's so foolish to get caught up with *things* instead of with Him and so crazy to serve another master in place of the Lord. It makes no sense whatsoever to allow our hearts to become divided.

The Lord should be our all in all, and whatever we do—even eating and drinking—we should do with Him in mind, to His glory (see 1 Cor. 10:31; Col. 3:17). Weddings, birthdays, and holidays should be celebrated with Him. Vacations and family activities should be enjoyed with Him. Sports and music should be played before Him. Business and education should be pursued with Him. Relationships should be developed with His guidance and blessing and involvement.

Through all my years in the Lord, whenever my heart is ablaze, all that I have done or that I do—working a sales job, eating out with the family, studying, playing drums or sports, preaching, teaching, praying, worshiping—all of it has been done with zeal and a real sense of divine nearness. The Lord and I are in everything together!

But that's not how all of us always live. Those little foxes can be so subtle. Are any of them spoiling your vineyard? Are any of them running loose and destroying your vines? You need to be on guard against all fetishes and fixations. Be on the lookout for all addictions and distractions. First they divide your heart, challenging the Lord for the number one place in your life. Then they dull your heart, making you insensitive to your gradual backslidings. Then they dominate your heart, pushing you, prodding you, ruling you. They are deadly, they are destructive, and they must be driven out. Are they wreaking havoc in your vineyard? It's time to take inventory.

Here is a sampling of some of society's shrewdest little foxes. Are any of them gnawing at your vines? Take a careful look:

- Sports. Is there is really a good reason to get so excited about someone throwing or kicking or catching a ball, and is it really that big a deal—seemingly something of cosmic, almost eternal importance!—if someone breaks another record?
- Stocks. Many hearts literally rise and fall with the stock market.
- Computers and gadgets. This is one fox I deal with all too often!
- Cars. You may be either lusting after the latest car or polishing and caressing your current car.
- News. How many times do you need to hear the same headlines in a day?
- Books. You read everything *but* the Bible.
- Gardening. You spend hours on your knees planting and working, but minutes on your knees praying and worshiping.
- Cleaning. Must everything in the house shine?
- Food addictions. Lack of discipline is contagious, and if you can't discipline your belly, you'll find it hard to discipline your brain.
- Technology. Do you *really* need to be current on everything?

- Antiques. You can't take them to heaven anyway!
- Fashion. Vanity, vanity, vanity!
- Decorating. Your "mansion" down here will never be perfect anyway, so why not moderate your taste a little?
- Documentaries or nature shows. (Yes, these can become fetishes too!)
- Puzzles. How in the world can you give more time daily to crossword puzzles or 1,500-piece puzzles than to the Word and prayer?
- Information. Internet overload—surfing the Net until you drown.
- Talk radio. What would happen if God had your ear as much as the talk show host?
- Chat rooms. So many hours, so little content.
- Video games. They're only going to get better, more exciting, and more addictive, so you better get control over them *now*.
- Leisure and vacations. Life does not consist of the amount of free time we can find.
- Movies. If you can find any good ones to watch!
- Weather. I'm sure someone reading this book has a Weather Channel habit!
- Success. Whatever form it takes—in business, in the arts, in education—it can be a harsh taskmaster, always calling you one step higher, always needing one more minute of your time, never releasing you to spiritual pursuits. "Do *those* things tomorrow," it always says.

Look out for the little foxes!

Chart how you spend your time—every hour of every day—for one week. How much time is wasted? You might be in for a shock! Forget about all the hours you normally spend watching TV and videos; you'll probably cut back on those activities because you're monitoring yourself this week. (If you don't cut back, you might be in for an even greater shock.)

The fact is that just plain "busyness" is a terrible time robber. Leaders can get bogged down with administrative matters and buried under a paperwork avalanche, even though most of it is really petty and unessential. Look out!

And then there is the "silly stuff" that assaults us all, like filling out sweepstakes coupons (did I hit your weak spot here?) or reading every piece of mail (or e-mail!) that comes in, no matter how irrelevant it may be. (Really now, you don't *have* to read it all. No one is going to test you!)

Talking can also be a dangerous little fox. So much useless talk, so much idle talk, so much unedifying talk, so much stupid talk. This is a hindrance to holiness! What do you think Jesus meant when He said, "Men will have to give account on the day of judgment for every careless word they have spoken" (Matt. 12:36)?[3] If we followed the counsel of Ephesians 4:29, the amount of our speech would probably be cut down by 50 to 75 percent! "Do not let any unwholesome talk come out of your mouths, but only what is helpful for building others up according to their needs, that it may benefit those who listen."

It's not just a matter of gossip or grumbling or criticizing or complaining; such sins are hardly *little* foxes. It's the careless, fruitless use of our words that can be such a problem. That's why Proverbs has so much to say about the tongue. The tongue can literally kill or give life (see Prov. 18:21):

When words are many, sin is not absent, but he who holds his tongue is wise (Prov. 10:19).

He who guards his lips guards his life, but he who speaks rashly will come to ruin (Prov. 13:3).

Reckless words pierce like a sword, but the tongue of the wise brings healing (Prov. 12:18).[4]

A man of knowledge uses words with restraint, and a man of understanding is even-tempered. Even a fool is thought wise if he keeps silent, and discerning if he holds his tongue (Prov. 17:27,28).

Do you see a man who speaks in haste? There is more hope for a fool than for him (Prov. 29:20).

The use (or misuse) of the tongue is certainly something to chew on (pardon the pun). If we don't bridle it, it will bridle us.

It's the same with every area of our lives. We must ask ourselves if the things we are doing are serving us (and, in that sense, serving God's purposes for our lives) or if we are serving them. Are they tools or are they idols?

At one time in my life (from the late 1970s into the early 1980s), scholarship became an idol for me. I *had* to be the number one person in my field. That was my long-term goal. I *had* to learn more languages. I *had* to memorize more material. I *had* to be recognized as a scholar. I *had* to get my work published. But for what purpose? Ultimately, it was the pride of knowledge, the god of learning, and the

IF WE'RE NOT CAREFUL, THE LITTLE FOXES— OUR "LITTLE SINS"—WILL GET THE BETTER OF US.

standards of this world that had my heart.[5] How foolish! I will never learn one-thousandth of everything there is to know—even in "my field." (In fact, the best any of us can hope for is to be *less ignorant* than someone else!) I will never be accepted or recognized by everyone. (Who are they, anyway?) All knowledge that is not consecrated to God will be of no eternal value in the end. Thankfully, since 1982, scholarship and knowledge have been nothing more than tools in my life.

Let our learning be subservient to His purposes, and then it makes sense. Let our talents—our musical virtuosity, our athletic prowess, our academic brilliance, our physical strength and endurance, our business acumen, our creative skills, our parenting abilities—be given over to the Master, and then everything we have and everything we are can glorify Him. Otherwise, of what use is it?

You see, this world *does* pull at us, the flesh *does* influence us, the devil *does* distract us, and we really *are* in a battle for spirituality and devotion. If we're not careful, little foxes—"little sins"—will get the better of us. And it is wrong for us to think that because we got rid of the "big sins" the little ones won't wear us down and eventually conquer us. (Remember the Lilliputians, the little people in *Gulliver's Travels*.) In fact,

Little sins can become big sins.
Little sins slow us and distract us.
Little sins dull us and desensitize us.
Little sins sap our strength and steal our time.
Little sins can more easily be justified and excused
    than "big" sins.
Little sins multiply more quickly than "big" sins.

Look out for little sins!

Actually, it is one of Satan's most effective tactics for bringing us to a place of vulnerability to larger sins—sins we normally wouldn't even think about committing—by getting us to yield to smaller sins. So, for example, the man who has been free from drinking for a year and can easily resist the temptation to go and sin "with the boys" might just yield to that temptation—or even pursue it—if he just had a terrible blowout with his wife, or if he just lost his job and became discouraged, or if sudden tragedy hit and he lost faith. Watch out for little chinks in the armor! Patch up the holes in the wall before the crack spreads.

As Spurgeon exhorted:

Ask, then, the question, what has driven Christ from thee? He hides His face behind the wall of thy sins. That wall may be built up of little pebbles, as easily as of great stones. The sea is made of drops; the rocks are made of grains: and the sea which divides thee from Christ may be filled with the drops of thy little sins; and the rock which has well nigh wrecked thy barque, may have been made by the daily working of the coral insects of thy little sins.[6]

Beware of holes in your spiritual shield, be they areas of fleshly laziness or attitudes that are undisciplined. And beware of anything—even if it is not sinful in and of itself—that slows you down spiritually.

Hebrews 12 calls on us to "throw off everything that hinders and the sin that so easily entangles" so that we can "run with perseverance the race marked out for us" (Heb. 12:1). It is not only sin that slows us down and entangles us. There are other things that hinder us from running (and winning) our race, and we must cast off each and every one of them.

At the end of 1982, when I began to fast more frequently than I ever had before, a pattern started to emerge. After a few days of fasting, I would have such a bad headache and would feel so weak that I became completely ineffective. The problem was that, even after I would break the fast with a meal, I still found no relief until I ate something sweet—specifically chocolate. You see, I have never had a cup of coffee in my life, I have never smoked a cigarette, and I have never had a Big Mac. (The Big Mac is irrelevant to my point here, but most people find it interesting.) When I gave up drugs—remember, I was shooting heroin at the age of 15—I thought I was free from addictions. After all, I had never had to deal with giving up cigarettes or *needing* a cup of coffee. Instead, I discovered that I was a "chocoholic," having had something sweet virtually every day of my life for as long as I could remember. I had to kick this habit too.

Once I got myself free from the need for sweets, I began to discipline myself, first allowing myself sweets one day a week, and then, with the encouragement of my dear wife, Nancy (bless her!), allowing myself sweets only one day a *month*. I kept this up, with some variation, for a number of years, and then I would get a little slack, always having to watch myself lest chocolate became a habit again. (Bear in mind that nutrition was not the big issue for me here, although it certainly is an important one. I'm one of those who gagged the only time I tried to eat brussel sprouts, so healthy eating is something else I'm working on. For me, the first battle was one of discipline.)

Through the years, I have been amazed to watch how the Lord has "exposed" me in my chocolate sins—in other words, the times I would devour some peanut M&Ms or consume a Hershey's chocolate bar with almonds after I had told Nancy that I wouldn't be having anything sweet for a while. Sometimes, I would *wear* my sin. (That elusive M&M that got lost in my car actually ended up melting on my lap.) Other times, it would be supernaturally exposed. I say this tongue-in-cheek—but only partially!

For example, one night I ran an errand for Nancy to the local grocery store, picking up some items we needed in the house. While shopping, I noticed a display with chocolate fudge (this is "hardcore" stuff for a former chocoholic) and decided I really needed a chunk of it. The only problem was this was supposed to be a no-sweets time for me. Well, as I was checking out of the store, the cashier picked up the fudge and said to me, "Mmmm, good!" and then—to my shock—she looked at me and said, "Sinful!"

The Lord doesn't allow me to get away with much, does He?! (I'm sorry to tell you that I ate the fudge anyway, although I couldn't really enjoy it. Still, it was only a "little" piece, less than $1.50 worth to be exact, so my sin wasn't that serious, right?) Seriously now, aside from the issue of nutrition, I don't believe that my eating sweets has as much to do with "sinning" as it has to do with discipline, with keeping the flesh under control, with not being enslaved to worldly habits of any kind.

Listen to Paul's words to the Corinthians:

Do you not know that in a race all the runners run, but only one gets the prize? Run in such a way as to get the prize. Everyone who competes in the games goes into strict training. They do it to get a crown that will not last; but we do it to get a crown that will last forever. Therefore I do not run like a man running aimlessly; I do not fight like a man beating the air. No, I beat my body and make it my slave so that after I have preached to others, I myself will not be disqualified for the prize (1 Cor. 9:24-27).

Do you see what Paul is saying? First, he is telling us that we are in a spiritual race (Are you?), and that we are to be running our race (If you're in the race, are you running?), and that we are to be running as fast as we can, so as to get the prize (If you're running, are you running so as to win?). This speaks of discipline, of purpose, of focus. There's no laziness or lethargy or sleepiness or slothfulness here! Second, he tells us that athletes who compete in the Olympic games go into strict training—the training has only intensified through the years—in order to get a crown (today, a medal) that will not last.

Athletes will put themselves through rigorous and demanding exercise routines, working out six or eight hours a day, subsisting on a harsh diet for months just to win a race, or set a new record, or defeat an opponent. They will torture their bodies and deny themselves the ordinary pleasures of life just to come out on top. They will jog for miles in pouring rain or under a beating sun. They will work on the same move for weeks at a time, until they can perform it flawlessly. Some athletes—like boxers—will even abstain from sexual relations for a month or more before their event, believing that any kind of sexual release will deplete them of needed energy. Yes, such are the lengths to which athletes will go.

But look at what Paul says: "*They* do it to get a crown that will not last; but *we* do it to get a crown that will last forever."[7] Yes, *we do it*—we discipline ourselves, we deny ourselves, we put the flesh under, we take up our cross, we persevere, we say no to the world, we resist the devil—we do it too. But in our case, the motivation is far higher. We do what we do to get a crown that will last forever!

Is this how you live? Are you as devoted to the Lord as a professional athlete is to his sport or a professional musician is to her music or a driven businessman is to his money? Maybe the biggest problem in your life is simply lack of discipline, lack of control, lack of focus. Maybe you need to get ruthless with your schedule and get yourself in shape. God only knows how many times I have preached this same message to myself!

Once again, it's the little foxes—the "neutral things" or the "little sins"—that hurt us more than we know. And it's the increase of those little foxes that often alert us that something is really wrong. Don't let them make their den in your vineyard, no matter how "small" they are. Take a good, hard look at your life and rout out those little foxes and "minor" sins.

Maybe the "big sin" of pornography is out of your life, but do your eyes wander after other people in church? Maybe the "big sin" of lying is out of your life, but do you find it necessary to exaggerate and inflate your stories? Maybe the "big sin" of irresponsible slothfulness is out of your life, but do you have a terrible time spending even thirty minutes alone with the Lord on your knees? Maybe the "big sin" of violence is out of your life, but are you still prone to temper tantrums and childish anger? Charles Bridges had this to say about being out of control:

A former proverb declared "him that had rule over his spirit" to be a mighty conqueror (Prov. 16:32). And certainly the noblest conquests are gained or lost over ourselves. He that hath no rule over his own spirit is an easy prey to the invader. Any one may irritate and torment him (see Esther 3:5,6,13). He yields himself to the first assault of his ungoverned passions, offering no resistance; like a city broken down and without walls, the object of contempt (see Neh. 1:3; 2:17). Having no discipline over himself, temptation becomes the occasion of sin, and hurries him on to fearful lengths that he had not contemplated. The first outbreak of anger tends to murder. Unwatchfulness over lust plunges into adultery. The mightiest natural strength is utter feebleness in the great conflict. How should such an object excite our tenderest compassion!

But there are many cases of this moral weakness, less shameful, and yet scarcely less injurious to the soul. Every outbreaking of irritation, every spark of pride kindling in the heart, before it ever shews itself in the countenance or on the tongue, must be attacked, and determinately resisted.[8]

Yes, every outbreaking of sin in our lives, every spark of the flesh rising in our souls, every little fox in our vineyards must be utterly purged and relentlessly pursued. Those bushy-tailed, bright-eyed creatures may seem cute and harmless, but they are gnawing nuisances and miserable marauders. They must be caught, they must be captured, and they must be killed. After all, the branches they chew on and the tendrils they tear apart are attached to the chief Vine, Jesus Himself. That's why Spurgeon urged us to go with Jesus to the hunting.[9]

So animal activists, out of my way. This fox hunt is for me. Are you coming along?

CHAPTER SEVEN

NO CONDEMNATION!

And can it be, that I should gain
  An interest in the Saviour's blood?
Died He for me?—who caused His pain!
  For me?—who Him to death pursued.
Amazing love! How can it be
  That Thou, my God, shouldst die for me?

Long my imprison'd spirit lay,
  Fast bound in sin and nature's night:
Thine eye diffused a quickening ray;
  I woke; the dungeon flamed with light;
My chains fell off, my heart was free,
  I rose, went forth, and follow'd Thee.

No condemnation now I dread.
  Jesus, and all in Him, is mine:
Alive in Him, my living Head,
  And clothed in righteousness Divine,
Bold I approach th' eternal throne,
  And claim the crown, through Christ, my
  own.

CHARLES WESLEY
SELECTED FROM THE HYMN,
"AND CAN IT BE?"

Justification deals with our actual sins. When we go to Him and repent, God washes all the guilt and pollution out of our hearts, and we stand justified like a new babe that never committed sin. We have no condemnation. We can walk with Jesus and live a holy life before the Lord, if we walk in the Spirit.

WILLIAM SEYMOUR

Do you frequently feel spiritually condemned? Do you often feel as if you are a second-class citizen in the kingdom of God, tolerated, but hardly loved by the Lord? Is it common for you to feel guilty and unclean no matter how "right" your life seems to be? And do you find yourself identifying with the sinner-under-judgment passages in the Word, always carrying around a "Woe is me" attitude, while you find it difficult to relate to the positive, "I've-been-made-righteous" portions of the Bible?

Of course, you know that the New Testament teaches that "there is now no condemnation for those who are in Christ Jesus" (Rom. 8:1),[1] but knowing what is written and experiencing the reality of what is written are two separate things. Plus, you may not be entirely sure that you know exactly what Paul meant when he wrote those famous words. Did he mean that as born-again believers we need never again feel condemned regardless of how we live, or did he mean that we have no reason to feel condemned as long as we live consistent, godly lives?

Or is Romans 8:1 unrelated to feelings? Does it teach that no amount of sin and disobedience can affect our status as heaven-bound children of God, or does it teach that believers in right relationship with God are not condemned to hell? And whatever it teaches, how we can get it off the written page and into our hearts and minds?

We know that one of Satan's favorite tricks is to drag God's people down with discouragement and hopelessness, making them feel alienated from their heavenly Father. He frequently uses this tactic with believers who have sensitive consciences or who lack security in their relationship with the Lord. And this sense of despair, of never measuring up, can actually lead to more sin. What's the use of trying anyway?

As for believers who are confident and secure, the devil uses the exact opposite approach, trying to lull them to sleep with false assurances, telling them that all is well even when nothing is well (see Jer. 6:14; 8:11),[2] encouraging them to believe that there is no amount of sin they can commit that could ever change God's attitude toward them.³ It doesn't take a rocket scientist to figure out how this kind of thinking can lead to a lifestyle of casual, premeditated sinning.

Of course, these are deceptions of the devil, but before we can unmask Satan's lies and renew our minds to the truth, we must *understand* the truth. In what sense are we "not condemned" in Jesus? And how can this biblical fact help us to overcome sin as well as rid ourselves of guilt?

For the moment, let's put aside the question of "once saved, always saved," because it is *not* a central issue in Romans 8:1.⁴ The question we need to ask is this: What does the word "condemnation" (Greek: *katakrima*) actually mean in its New Testament context? It is Paul himself who supplies us with a definitive answer, since he is the *only author* who uses this Greek noun in the entire New Testament, and he uses it *only three times*, all in Romans 5 and 8.⁵ This makes it relatively easy to figure out exactly what he was talking about.

Of course, the great theme of Romans 8, especially through the first seventeen verses, is the law (or principle) of life in the Spirit. Through this principle, we put to death the misdeeds of the body and enter into a glorious walk with God. And since this chapter shows us how to crucify the flesh and live in the Spirit—and so fulfill the law's demands—it is perfectly clear that Romans 8:1 was *not* written to give us a license to sin.⁶ What then does Paul mean when he speaks of "no condemnation"?

We'll let him speak for himself. He has just explained that Adam's sin brought death to all, whereas the grace of the Lord Jesus overflowed to all:

The judgment followed one sin and brought *condemnation*, but the gift followed many trespasses and brought justification. For if, by the trespass of the one man, death reigned through that one man, how much more will those who receive God's abundant provision of grace and of the gift of righteousness reign in life through the one man, Jesus Christ. Consequently, just as the result of one trespass was *condemnation* for all men, so also the result of one act of righteousness was justification that brings life for all men (Rom. 5:16-18).

Therefore, there is now no *condemnation* for those who are in Christ Jesus, because through Christ Jesus the law of the Spirit of life set me free from the law of sin and death (Rom. 8:1,2).

Adam's sin condemned us to hell, as each of us followed in his footsteps. His fall was our fall, and so all of us were separated from God and lost. The guilty verdict was passed, and we were doomed. But through Jesus we have been justified and declared righteous. In Him we are no longer condemned! As James Moffat translated Romans 8:1, "Thus there is no doom now for those who are in Christ Jesus." Yes, the fleshly nature is damnable and through it we are damned, but there is a new power at work in us, a power called life in the Spirit, and through the Spirit we put to death the sinful deeds of the flesh. "Therefore, there is now *no condemnation* for those who are in Christ Jesus." This is glorious news!

If you are a born-again believer, a blood-washed child of God, you are not damned and doomed. God is not saying, "To hell with you! Depart from Me, you wicked one." Absolutely not! He is saying, "You are Mine! I accept you fully through My Son."

And what if you turn your back on God and give yourself to sin? Do you still have this assurance? Study the Word carefully on this. Search the Scriptures from beginning to end: You will not find a single verse that gives godless rebels any kind of assurance of salvation or blessing at all. Not one! Rather, as we have already seen, Paul states plainly, "For if you live according to the sinful nature, you will die; but if by the Spirit you put to death the misdeeds of the body, you will live" (Rom. 8:13).[7] Even those who are "five-point Calvinists" agree with this: There is no assurance of divine favor for those who willfully forsake God.[8]

The Arminian would say you can lose your salvation by completely and ultimately turning away from the Lord. The Calvinist would say that if you completely and ultimately turn away from the Lord, you were never truly saved. But that means that both Arminians and Calvinists agree on this: If you die in your sins, unrepentant and hostile to God, you are hell bound.[9]

I would strongly urge you *not* to listen to anyone who tells you that you can live in your sin, freely and flagrantly, and one day enjoy heaven too. As Thomas Brooks wisely warned, "Men must not think to dance and dine with the devil, and then to sup with Abraham, Isaac, and Jacob in the kingdom of heaven," explaining that, "Many eat that on earth that they digest in hell."[10]

But there is no need for any kind of rhetoric here. You're reading this book because you *want* to be holy—even if you're getting a stiffer challenge than you expected, and even if the standard of the Word is a little higher and more inflexible than you realized. The fact is, you're a believer, and you're not looking for a way to go back to the world. (If you are, the warnings in the previous chapters have certainly given you something to think about!)

Paul writes Romans 8 to believers who want to follow the Lord, and I also write to believers who want to follow the Lord—and that does not mean perfect people, but rather earnest Christians who know the reality of temptation and the daily battle with the flesh. It is to such people that I bring a word of encouragement: There is no condemnation for you! Let me unfold this wonderful biblical truth.

First, it is essential that you understand God's posture toward you: He *wants* to bless you, He *wants* to fellowship with you forever, He *wants* to do good to you. He's the one who took all the initiative in the relationship. He chose to send His Son into the world to seek and save you—even when God was the last thing on your mind—and He's the one who continues to draw you to Himself. The more miserable a sinner you were, the more He saw you as an ideal candidate for salvation. And the more you struggle with accepting His love as His child, the more He reaches out to you.

Jesus came looking for people just like you. That is no light matter! It's an incredible thing for a young man when he learns that the girl of his dreams is also interested in him. Wow! And when that young lady gets word about that very special guy who is now convinced that she is the one for him, she can hardly believe it's true. How then should we feel when we realize that Jesus, the perfect, spotless, righteous Son of God, Jesus the very image of His Father, Jesus the holy Word made flesh, JESUS set His love on us, gave His life for us, and continues to intercede for us every day? What can we say in response? What love! As Charles Wesley wrote, "Amazing love! How can it be that Thou my God shouldst die for me?"[11]

The Lord actually loves to love us. He *delights* in showing mercy (see Mic. 7:17-19; also Ezek. 18:23,30-32; 33:11). He takes pleasure in forgiving. If you sin, the Lord wants you to come to Him in repentance. That's what He desires! He is *not* sick and tired of hearing your voice. He does *not* wish that you would just go away.

"And what if I keep blowing it?" you ask. I tell you again: He would rather hear your voice in sincere repentance—even if the repentance needs to go much deeper than it has so far—than not hear your voice at all. He would rather that you come back to Him in brokenness than grovel in your shame. That's why He kept saying to His people through the prophets, "Turn back to Me!"[12] He is not looking for an excuse to get rid of you, nor does He have some run-down shack waiting for you at the far side of heaven—far enough from His throne where He won't have to see you and you will never bother Him again. Nonsense! *All* of God's people are beloved in His sight. He will welcome *all* of His children into their heavenly homes. I know that this may upset someone's pity party, but the Word is clear.[13]

"But I don't understand," you say. "In fact, I'm really confused. If what you're saying is true, I shouldn't feel condemned all the time. And yet I do! Something is not adding up."

Well, it could be that you need to renew your mind with the Word. Forget how you feel in your heart; ignore what your mind tries to tell you. Just believe the Word. (Would it be too blunt to say, "Get it through your thick skull"?) Renewing our minds with Scripture is like reprogramming our systems. In time, it always works. Keep the Word before you, reading it, meditating on it, repeating it, declaring it, believing it, receiving it. As Smith Wigglesworth exhorted, "Read it through; write it down; pray it in; work it out; pass it on. The Word of God changes a man until he becomes an Epistle of God."[14]

The problem for many of us is that we read the Word faithfully, but we don't read it in faith. In other words, we don't really believe and receive what it says. For example, we read the account of the prodigal son as he comes to a place of repentance, realizing that he has messed up his life and squandered his inheritance. He is determined to say to his father, "I have sinned against heaven and against you. I am no longer worthy to be called your son; make me like one of your hired men" (Luke 15:18,19). Some of you read that and say, "That's me! That's how I always feel. I'll be content if God will simply let me work near His house again, even if I never have a personal relationship with Him."

But that is not the will of the Father. No! Instead, while the prodigal was "still a long way off, his father saw him and was filled with compassion for him; he ran to his son, threw his arms around him and kissed him" (Luke 15:20).

That's how our Father treats each of us when we return in true repentance. In fact, as we humble ourselves before Him and confess our sins and tell Him that we're not worthy, He almost ignores us, just as the prodigal's father ignored his once-wayward son's pleas to be made like one of his hired men. He was already planning a party!

But the father said to his servants, "Quick! Bring the best robe and put it on him. Put a ring on his finger and sandals on his feet. Bring the fattened calf and kill it. Let's have a feast and celebrate. For this son of mine was dead and is alive again; he was lost and is found." So they began to celebrate (Luke 15:22-24).

God is ready to celebrate over *you* when you truly turn back from your sin. That's what the Scriptures teach, and that's what we are called to believe.

It's so important that we identify with *those* passages in the Word, too, not just with the portions that tell us how ugly our sin is and our much the Lord detests it. We must believe Him when He tells us how gladly He receives backsliders and penitent sinners into His home. We must take hold of His Word and conform our thinking to its truth. You see, we are made holy by the Word (see Ps. 119:9; John 8:31,32; 17:17), and part of the sanctification process includes getting our hearts and minds in agreement with what God says, both *about* us and *for* us. Sometimes our feelings are totally misleading. In fact, few things are more unstable than human emotions.

So, the reason you feel "condemned" all the time could simply be your failure to accept and embrace what is written in the Scriptures. On the other hand, there could be a very different reason for the uncomfortable feelings you are experiencing.

Could it be that the Spirit is dealing with you because of unconfessed, unforsaken sin in your life, but you are mistaking conviction for condemnation? This confusion can be fatal, since conviction is something we must have if we become insensitive to sin. Conviction is good, not bad; it's something sent from heaven, not manufactured in hell.

If we can continue in sin without conviction, that is a real danger sign. Either our hearts have become so hard that we no longer sense the prodding and reproof of the Spirit, or worse than that, the Spirit has simply left us alone—an absolutely dreadful prospect. You should thank God when His conviction breaks your heart, causing you to fully yield to the Spirit, since heeding His rebuke always brings life.

Maybe there's something wrong in your life and you know it. That's why there is that gnawing pain deep within. Unfortunately, many believers who confuse conviction with condemnation are driven away from the Lord, always feeling rejected and therefore dejected. Other believers, also mistaking conviction for condemnation, react in the opposite way, saying, "That feeling is not from God. I rebuke you, Satan![15] That's just legalism at its worst." And so rather than repent, they run.

What then is the difference between conviction and condemnation? Conviction is like the work of the prosecuting attorney, proving his case against the defendant and exposing his crime.[16] Condemnation is like the judge's gavel coming down with a final, irreversible verdict of "Guilty!"[17]

Conviction says, "You have sinned. Come back to Me!" Condemnation says, "You are guilty. Get away from Me!"

CONVICTION OR CONDEMNATION, THE SOLUTION IS THE SAME: BELIEVE THE WORD AND DO WHAT IT SAYS. THERE IS MORE THAN SUFFICIENT GRACE FOR YOU.

When God convicts the unsaved, He does it to bring them to conversion. As long as they are being convicted, they are not yet hopelessly condemned. When God convicts the saved, He does it to bring His straying saints back to Himself. Conviction for us means that we are still part of the family because, "If you are not disciplined (and everyone undergoes discipline), then you are illegitimate children and not true sons" (Heb. 12:8).

When we are convicted and even chastised by our Father, that is the time to come to Him and confess our sins, finding mercy through the blood of Jesus and receiving grace to turn from sin. But condemnation is an entirely different story. There is no mercy there! It is a place where judgment rules and damnation reigns. It has nothing to do with us!

So, to say it once more, if you are truly in Jesus, you are not condemned and therefore you should never *feel* condemned.[18] Either your mind is refusing to accept what the Word says, or there is a pattern of disobedience in your life and conviction is gnawing at you. Either way, the solution is the same: Believe the Word and do what it says. There is more than sufficient grace for you.

There is something else you must understand if you are to fully appreciate the truth of Romans 8:1. Although many believers do not know this, if you are saved, you are no longer a "sinner," nor should you think of yourself merely as a "saved sinner." According to the Scriptures, "sinners" are the enemies of God whereas His people are called "saints."[19]

It is one thing to sin and repent, even as a believer; it is another thing to *be* a sinner. It is one thing to do something bad and then correct it; it is another thing to *be* bad. It is one thing to think an adulterous thought and turn from it immediately; it is another thing to *be* an adulterer. I *was* a heavy drug user, I *was* a rebellious snob, I *was* a filthy sinner. Now I'm a saint—imperfect, but nonetheless radically transformed and wonderfully changed. Sin is no longer the rule of my life, it's the exception to the rule. My habit now is to live for God, whereas before I knew Him, my habit was to sin.

Does this challenge some of your church traditions, traditions which have taught you to think of yourself as a "sinner"? Then those traditions need to be challenged![20] Consider this representative sampling of what the Word of God says on the subject, then decide for yourself. You can check your English concordance under the word "sinner(s)." Or you can check a Hebrew concordance under the word *hote'* (from the root *hata'*, *chata'*, meaning to sin) or a Greek concordance under the word *hamartalos*. You'll be surprised at what you find. First, let's look at the Psalms:

> Blessed is the man who does not walk in the counsel of the *wicked* or stand in the way of *sinners* or sit in the seat of *mockers*. . . . Therefore the *wicked* will not stand in the judgment, nor *sinners* in the assembly of the *righteous* (Ps. 1:1,5).

> Do not take away my soul along with *sinners*, my life with *bloodthirsty men*, in whose hands are wicked schemes, whose right hands are full of bribes. But I lead a *blameless life*; redeem me and be merciful to me (Ps. 26:9-11).

> Consider the *blameless*, observe the *upright*; there is a future for the *man of peace*. But all *sinners* will be destroyed; the future of the *wicked* will be cut off (Ps. 37:37,38).

> Restore to me the joy of Your salvation and grant me a willing spirit, to sustain me. Then I will teach *transgressors* Your ways, and *sinners* will turn back to You (Ps. 51:12,13).

> May my meditation be pleasing to Him, as I rejoice in the Lord. But may *sinners* vanish from the earth and the *wicked* be no more (Ps. 104:34,35).

It is quite clear from these verses that the sinners are the "bad guys" while the righteous are the "good guys." Believers reading these verses immediately know whose side they are on and with whom they identify. Our place is with the godly, the redeemed, the blameless, the saved; not with the wicked, the mockers, the transgressors, the sinners.

Now let's hear the testimony of Proverbs:

My son, if *sinners* entice you, do not give in to them (Prov. 1:10).

If the *righteous* receive their due on earth, how much more the *ungodly* and the *sinner!* (Prov. 11:31; see also 1 Pet. 4:18).

Righteousness guards the *man of integrity*, but *wickedness* overthrows the *sinner* (Prov. 13:6).

Misfortune pursues the *sinner*, but prosperity is the reward of the *righteous*. A *good man* leaves an inheritance for his children's children, but a *sinner's* wealth is stored up for the *righteous* (Prov. 13:21,22).

Do not let your heart envy *sinners*, but always be zealous for the fear of the Lord (Prov. 23:17).

Any questions here? Obviously not. The meaning of the words is too clear for confusion. Praise God, we are not sinners, nor do we follow their ways. We are righteous—and in a book such as Proverbs, that means we conduct ourselves righteously. In other words, to be "righteous" speaks of our conduct and actions, not just our standing before God (i.e., acquitted by faith). Wickedness is not our lot; instead, we fear the Lord and shun evil (e.g., see Prov. 3:7).

Next, we turn to Ecclesiastes:

To the *man who pleases Him*, God gives wisdom, knowledge and happiness, but to the *sinner* He gives the task of gathering and storing up wealth to hand it over to the *one who pleases God* (Eccles. 2:26).

I find more bitter than death the woman who is a snare, whose heart is a trap and whose hands are chains. The *man who pleases God* will escape her, but the *sinner* she will ensnare (Eccles. 7:26).

All share a common destiny [i.e., death]—the *righteous* and the *wicked*, the *good* and the *bad*, the *clean* and the *unclean*, those who offer sacrifices and those who do not. As it is with the *good man*, so with the *sinner*, as it is with those who take oaths, so with those who are afraid to take them (Eccles. 9:2).

Notice the contrasts: The man who pleases God is in opposition to the sinner. The former is spared, the latter is judged. And the world is divided into two classes: the righteous, good, and clean people and the wicked, bad, and unclean people. The second class consists of "sinners."

Are you beginning to see how inappropriate it is for justified, redeemed children of God to call themselves sinners? The prophets were equally clear:

Zion will be redeemed with justice, her *penitent ones* with righteousness. But *rebels* and *sinners* will both be broken, and *those who forsake the Lord* will perish (Isa. 1:27,28).

See, the day of the Lord is coming—a cruel day, with wrath and fierce anger—to make the land desolate and destroy the *sinners* within it (Isa. 13:9).

The *sinners* in Zion are terrified; trembling grips the *godless*: "Who of us can dwell with the consuming fire? Who of us can dwell with everlasting burning?" (Isa. 33:14).

All the *sinners* among My people will die by the sword, all those who say, "Disaster will not overtake or meet us" (Amos 9:10).

Friend, if you are saved, you are not a sinner! If you belong to the Lord, you are not a godless rebel. God is not out to destroy and devastate you. He's out to deliver you!

In the New Testament, Jesus received sinners and called them to repent (see Matt. 9:10-13; 11:19), and so sinners who turn from their sin are commended. (This theme is especially prominent in Luke's Gospel. See 7:37-50; 15:7,10; 18:9-14; 19:1-10.) But it is clearly understood that God's people are no longer "sinners." Instead, the term "sinners" is reserved for those who are hostile to God—according to Matt 26:45, Jesus is "betrayed into the hands of sinners"—and the righteous are contrasted with them (see Luke 6:32-34;[21] 7:39; 13:2).

Jesus came to call sinners to Himself, not so they could continue in their sin (remember Zacchaeus?), but so they could be changed. He came to heal their spiritual diseases, not simply to surround Himself with the dead and dying.

When we turn to the Gospel of John, we see that because the word "sinner" was understood to mean a transgressor, a lawbreaker, or an enemy of God, Jesus was called a sinner by the religious leaders of the day (see John 9:16). This led to an enlightening interaction between those leaders and the blind man whom Jesus had just healed: "A second time they summoned the man who had been blind. 'Give glory to God,' they said. 'We know this man is a sinner.' He replied, 'Whether he is a sinner or not, I don't know. One thing I do know. I was blind but now I see!'" (John 9:24,25).

This reminds me of a saying I often heard from the lips of Leonard Ravenhill: "A man with an experience is never at the mercy of a man with an argument." There is no way the religious leaders could talk *this* man out of his experience, and the more they pressed him, the bolder he became:

Then they hurled insults at him and said, "You are this fellow's disciple! We are disciples of Moses! We know that God spoke to Moses, but as for this fellow, we don't even know where he comes from" (John 9:28,29).

Really? Well, the time had come for this uneducated, once-blind man to teach these leaders a lesson in theology:

The man answered, "Now that is remarkable! You don't know where He comes from, yet He opened my eyes. *We know that God does not listen to sinners. He listens to the godly man who does His will.* Nobody has ever heard of opening the eyes of a man born blind. If this man were not from God, He could do nothing" (John 9:30-33).

Yes, this man who had been miraculously healed knew that Jesus was not a sinner because God doesn't listen to such people! Read the verse again: "We know that God does not listen to sinners. He listens to the godly man who does His will." So I ask you, are *you* a sinner, or are you a godly man or woman who does God's will? If you can't say yes to the latter, I question your relationship with God. If you can say, "Yes, that's me!" then you have no reason to feel condemned. Condemnation is for sinners!

Look once again at Romans 5:

You see, at just the right time, when we were still powerless, Christ died for the *ungodly*. . . . God demonstrates His own love for us in this: While we *were still sinners*, Christ died for us (Rom. 5:6,8).

And now, being saved, we are no longer ungodly sinners! That is who we *were*.

Paul wrote, "For just as through the disobedience of the one man the many were made sinners, so also through the obedience of the one Man the many will be made righteous" (Rom. 5:19; see also 1 Tim. 2:14). Sin was not only imputed to us through Adam's fall; we actually became sinners. Now, righteousness is not only imputed to us through Jesus' death and resurrection, we actually become righteous.

Let's look at some more New Testament evidence. Writing to the Corinthians, Paul explained that a proper use of the gift of prophecy will convince the visiting *unbeliever* "that he is a sinner" (see 1 Cor. 14:24,25). In contrast with this, Paul vigorously disputes the notion that he and the other apostles were sinners, since that would mean Jesus promoted sin (Gal. 2:17).[22] Far be it! Rather, Jesus as the great, holy High Priest is totally set apart from sinners, but He always lives to make intercession for us, His family (see Heb. 7:25,26). Do you see the pattern here?

In James, we discover the one time in the New Testament when a group of believers are addressed as sinners.[23] But that's because *these* believers were backslidden, becoming friends with the world and committing spiritual adultery. They were fleshly and living in sin (see Jas. 4:1-4). And what does James say to them?

Come near to God and He will come near to you. Wash your hands, you *sinners*, and purify your hearts, you *double-minded*. Grieve, mourn and wail. Change your laughter to mourning and your joy to gloom. Humble yourselves before the Lord, and He will lift you up (Jas. 4:8-10).

These are strong words! James is saying that this is *not* the way things are supposed to be. No, God's people should be single-minded, holy, and clean. When they are not, it's time for searching repentance, time for wailing and grieving. It is a serious thing when believers are called sinners! Such a situation calls for mourning and gloom. It is hardly the expected norm (as in, "We're just a bunch of sinners, saved by grace"). It is a terrible reproach on the Body of Christ. And so James closes his Epistle with the following exhortation:

> My brothers, if one of you should wander from the truth and someone should bring him back, remember this: Whoever turns a sinner from the error of his way will save him from death and cover over a multitude of sins (Jas. 5:19,20).

Sinners are those who wander from the path and are on the road to death. It is our job to turn such people back to the Lord! God forbid that we think of *ourselves* as sinners, or live as sinners, or relate to our Father as sinners.[24] No! We are righteous by His grace, and by that grace we live righteous lives. For us, the sentence of condemnation is past (see John 5:24).

Of course, if you want to fully enjoy your relationship with God, you must walk in reverential fear, keeping yourself free from defilement and pollution. And in light of His great love for you, you should be careful to please Him, always being quick to respond to His voice and swift to repent. This way you can live with a conscience that is clean, free from mental torment. If there is a recurrence of old sinful habits, you must take it seriously, making every effort to purge the sin from your life. You must be *ruthless* with sin! This kind of action demonstrates your commitment to walk in harmony with the Lord. And, if you want to stay free from thoughts of condemnation, you must learn to take God at His Word. If He says, "I forgive and I forget," then accept it at face value.

Our Father cannot lie, and He emphatically tells us, "I cast your sins into the depth of the sea. I remove them as far as the East is from the West. I put them behind My back. I blot them out and I remember them no more. My people, I forgive you!" (see Pss. 51:1,9; 103:12; Isa. 38:17; 43:25; Jer. 31:34; Mic. 7:19).

The devil, on the other hand, will always lie to you, repeatedly saying, "God will never forgive *you*. And even if He said the words, He wouldn't really mean it. He'll never forget what you have done!

He will always look at you as a filthy, rotten sinner. So give up, you're doomed. You'll never amount to anything good."

So says Jesus the Lord, and so says Satan the liar. Whose voice will you believe?

CHAPTER EIGHT

"THE LETTER KILLS": THE PERIL OF LEGALISTIC RELIGION

I do not mean by holiness the mere performance of outward duties of religion, coldly acted over, as a task; not our habitual prayings, hearings, fastings, multiplied one upon another (though these be all good, as subservient to a higher end); but I mean an inward soul and principle of divine life (Romans 8:1-5), that spiriteth all these.

RALPH CUDWORTH

Make not laws upon the saints where Christ hath not made any.

WALTER CRADOCK

The preference of legal norms and rules above moral and spiritual values.

DEFINITION OF "LEGALISM"
ACCORDING TO
*THE ENCYCLOPEDIA OF
JEWISH RELIGION*

A central theme of this book is that God desires holiness for His people. No student of the Word can doubt this for a moment, and no honest child of God should *want* to doubt it for a moment. Holiness is beautiful!

The Puritans found some of the best ways to get this point across. George Swinnock said, "There is a beauty in holiness as well as a beauty of holiness,"[1] while Joseph Caryl observed that, "Perfect holiness is the aim of the saints on earth, and it is the reward of the saints in heaven."[2] According to John Whitlock, "The Christian's . . . way is holiness, his end happiness."[3] That's why Oswald Chambers could say, "God has one destined end for mankind—holiness! His one aim is the production of saints. God is not an eternal blessing-machine for men. He did not come to save men out of pity. He came to save men because He had created them to be holy."[4]

Holiness is our goal, our destiny, our portion. It expresses the very essence of the nature and character of God and describes the highest level of spirituality attainable by man.[5] Holiness is just plain wonderful. Certainly no genuine believer would ever argue with that, right?

Wrong! Many believers actually recoil at "holiness teaching," calling it unscriptural and contrary to the gospel. How can this be?

For some, it is a simple reaction of the flesh. They don't want to be challenged. They don't want to be shaken out of their comfort zones or called to take up their crosses and deny their own wills and desires. They don't want to be confronted with the high standards of God and would rather live in their snug (and smug) shelters of self-justification than to come out and hear the truth. They are like the rebellious Israelites of old who were unwilling to listen to the Lord's instruction.

They say to the seers, "See no more visions!" and to the prophets, "Give us no more visions of what is right! Tell us pleasant things, prophesy illusions. Leave this way, get off this path, and stop confronting us with the Holy One of Israel!" (Isa. 30:10,11).

For such people, the Holy One of Israel has a word: Repent—or else (see Isa. 30:12-17).

But for many believers who spurn "holiness teaching," rebellion, self-will, and love of the world are *not* the problems at all. The problem for them is that they equate holiness with *legalism*, finding it binding and not beautiful. In their minds, holiness is a system based on fear and characterized by joyless judgmentalism, producing futility instead of freedom. They perceive the "holiness message" to be a man-made brand of religion governed by law and not love, a mere following of rules without a relationship. That is not holiness! Holiness is being like Jesus in thought, word, and deed. As Samuel Lucas noted, "The essence of true holiness consists in conformity to the nature and will of God."[6]

Legalism grasps part of this truth, rightly understanding that holiness requires us to put away sin and uncleanness, calling for a change of conduct and attitude. But legalism is more wrong than right, failing miserably to understand the *essence* of holiness (it concentrates on outward forms and not inner realities) and the *process* of holiness (emphasizing human effort without the grace and power of the Holy Spirit). Legalism kills!

Perhaps no contemporary author has written against legalism with more passion than Chuck Swindoll in his book *The Grace Awakening*. Pulling no punches, he warns, "There are grace killers on the loose!" Their effect, according to Swindoll, is devastating, wreaking havoc on other believers:

> Bound and shackled by legalists' lists of do's and don'ts, intimidated and immobilized by others' demands and expectations, far too many in God's family merely exist in the tight radius of bondage dictated by those who have appointed themselves our judge and jury. Long enough

have we lived like frightened deer in a restrictive thicket of negative regulations. Long enough have we submitted to the do's and don'ts of religious kings of the mountain. Long enough have we been asleep while all around us the grace killers do their sinister nighttime work. No longer! It's time to awaken. The dawn is bright with grace.[7]

And that's just Pastor Swindoll's preface! He devotes a whole chapter to confronting and exposing a legalistic spirit, grieving over the fact that so many believers have fallen prey to this dangerous and deadly method of religion.[8]

What exactly *is* legalism? It has several different forms, but all of them flow from the same source, namely, religion without relationship, emphasizing standards more than the Savior. To an unsaved person the legalist preaches justification by works, saying, "You're a wicked sinner and you need to get rid of all your filthy habits if you want the Lord to accept you." There is no grace in this message, no exalting of the life-changing, sin-cleansing power of the blood of Jesus, no clear proclamation of mercy. The declaration of God's love expressed through the Cross is muffled—if it is even heard at all. Consequently, the proof of the new birth is seen almost entirely in what someone *no longer does*.

Let me illustrate this with the amusing story of two farmers who had a talk about Christianity. One of them said to his friend, "I hear that you're a Christian."

"That's right," the other replied.

"Well, what does it mean to be a Christian?" the curious farmer asked.

"Well, I don't drink, smoke, or run around with women."

"In that case," the friend responded, "my mule must be a Christian too, because my mule doesn't drink, smoke, or run around with women!"

That's legalism in a nutshell, and that's how it makes Christianity sound to many a sinner.

Within the church, legalism is also easy to spot. It judges almost entirely by externals—and boy does it judge!—quickly condemning those who don't immediately conform to the particular group's outward norm. And, generally speaking, the more legalistic a church group is, the more particular they will be about one or two specific aspects of behavior or dress, making those the standard by which everything else is measured.

For example, a legalistic "bonnet" church might completely overlook the Christlike character of a young, godly, modestly dressed woman, ignoring her compassionate work with the poor and paying no attention to her dynamic prayer life simply because she doesn't wear a bonnet to church. A "King James Only" church (i.e., a church that believes that the King James Version is the only English translation accepted by God) will actually condemn to hell other believers—including missionaries and even martyrs—because they read another English version of the Bible.[9] How narrow and exclusive legalism is!

Interestingly, as Max Lucado observed, legalists end up in "either despair or arrogance" with remarkable predictability. "They either give up or become stuck-up. They think they'll never make it, or they think they are the only ones who'll ever make it."[10] What an apt summary of the twofold perils of legalism!

"But doesn't the Bible hold us to high standards?" you may ask. "Isn't the whole purpose of your book to call believers to live up to the standards of God?"

Of course, God has high standards, and He calls us to live up to those standards. The problem with legalists is that: (1) they try to change a person from the outside in, whereas God deals with us from the inside out; (2) they fail to present a balanced picture of the Lord, putting too little stress on His mercy and too much emphasis on His wrath; (3) they do not point the struggling sinner (or believer) to the Lord's supernatural empowerment, making holiness a matter of human effort alone; and (4) they adds laws, standards, commandments, customs, and traditions that are not found in the

Word, making them even more important than the biblical commandments themselves.

The legalistic Christian can mockingly rail on those who don't live as he does, feeling that his lack of love is fine. Yet he will be quick to condemn a loving, gentle-hearted Christian who wears a wristwatch or wedding ring. The minors become major (even in cases where the minors are purely human issues that are of no concern to the Lord at all) and the majors (which are of great concern to the Lord) become minor.

More ominously, because the legalist is firmly convinced he is doing God's service, he is full of passion, often acting as a modern-day inquisitor. And because legalism is driven by the flesh and not the Spirit, it finds it necessary to enforce its religion on others. The legalist cannot prayerfully depend on God to change people; he must change them himself!

All this stands in stark contrast to the biblical message and method of holiness. Biblical holiness begins with the heart and flows from an encounter with God and His Word. It calls for repentance in response to the Lord's gracious offer of salvation, and it offers a way to be holy—the blood of Jesus and the Spirit of God. Biblical holiness is free, although it requires discipline and perseverance. For the legalist, nothing is free. Everything must be earned! Legalism leads to bondage; holiness leads to liberty.

What are the roots of legalism? It tends to arise when the inner core of true religion grows cold but the outward form of religion is maintained. Legalism is loveless.[11] It remembers what true spirituality produced in the previous generation of believers—including turning from sin and embracing a holy lifestyle—and then imposes those end-results on those who have not had that same experience. And inevitably, it tries to take those standards even further, attempting to please God by demonstrating an even greater zeal than that displayed by the previous generation (or trying to safeguard those standards by putting a protective hedge around them).[12]

Christian service that once arose out of a heart ablaze for God is now a requirement performed out of habit and motivated by fear. Acts of giving and sacrifice that once came as a natural expression of gratitude to the Lord are now forced on the believer and used as a measure of spirituality.

Dr. Kent Hughes put it like this:

> There is a universe of difference between the motivations behind legalism and discipline. Legalism says, "I will do this thing to gain merit with God," while discipline says, "I will do this because I love God and want to please him." Legalism is man-centered; discipline is God-centered.[13]

But legalism is not only man-centered in its orientation, it is man-centered in its efforts too, calling us to walk in the Spirit in the power of the flesh. Holiness, on the other hand, is God-centered in its efforts, calling us to walk in the Spirit in the power of the Spirit. As Oswald Chambers observed:

> A bird flies persistently and easily because the air is its domain and its world. A legal Christian is one who is trying to live in a rarer world than is natural to him. Our Lord said, "If the Son shall make you free, ye shall be free indeed," i.e., free from the inside, born from above, lifted into another world where there is no strenuous effort to live in a world not natural to us, but where we can soar continually higher and higher because we are in the natural domain of spiritual life.[14]

Unfortunately, many believers who flee from the clutches of legalism—especially when they never seemed to measure up to legalism's demands—fall right into the grasp of libertarianism. Now, almost anything goes! They have cast off all restrictive rules and oppressive regulations, and in the name of liberty, they have opened the door to license. Whatever comes naturally to this "liberated" believer is accepted as normal (and "understood," of course, by the Lord). Biblical commandments are brought down to the level of this Christian's own experience, and anything that brings any kind of spiritual pressure to bear on this previously discouraged believer is rejected as *not* being the easy yoke and light burden of Jesus.

LEGALISM IS DEADLY, BUT LICENSE IS DAMNABLE. WHILE LEGALISM SLAYS ITS THOUSANDS, LIBERTARIANISM SLAYS ITS TENS OF THOUSANDS.

Making things even worse is the fact that many preachers and teachers who glory in the grace of God often do so at the expense of the Bible's clear call to holy living, helping to push the libertarian Christian further and further away from discipline ("No one is going to tie me up again!"), conviction ("You're not going to condemn me anymore!"), and biblical standards ("Who are you to tell me what to do?").[15] And so, while legalism slays its thousands, libertarianism may even slay its tens of thousands.

How can I say that? It's simple. Just look at our American society today. It is saturated with sensuality and permeated with pleasure. Most Americans—in the Church and in the world—watch unclean videos or movies (containing nudity, sexual scenes, profanity, gratuitous violence or blatantly un-Christian themes); have various habits or addictions ranging from drugs and alcohol to sports, sex, or foods; are seriously in debt, largely due to the pull of materialism; waste countless hours every week watching TV or (needlessly) surfing the Net or playing video games; are overweight to the point of being considered obese (meaning 20 percent higher than our proper body weight—Ouch!). . . . Need I say more?[16]

Of course, legalism is *not* the answer to these serious problems—

absolutely, categorically, emphatically not! The best legalism can do for struggling sinners is put a Band-Aid on their deep heart problems, offering no real cure. And more often than not, it will condemn rather than convert, destroy rather than deliver. It will only make the self-righteous feel better about themselves while lost sinners and hurting believers are trampled under their feet. Plus, legalists are as likely as anyone to have their own secret addictions or hidden sins, since they have personally experienced very little of the transforming power of grace.

Obviously, I don't for a moment deny the widespread, destructive effects of legalism in America today, especially in the more "religious" parts of the country (e.g., the "Bible Belt"). But I am acutely aware of the fact that God is calling His people to come out of the world and be separate, to repent of our sinful compromise, to break free from the dominion of the flesh and to present ourselves as living sacrifices on the Lord's altar, set aside totally to the will of our Maker and Redeemer. It is imperative that we heed that call. Otherwise, our nation will fall and rise no more, and we will sail off into spiritual and moral oblivion.[17]

Yes, legalism is deadly, but license is damnable. Listen once more to Oswald Chambers:

The only liberty a saint has is the liberty not to use his liberty . . . Liberty means ability not to violate the law; licence means personal insistence on doing what I like . . . To be free from the law means that I am the living law of God, there is no independence of God in my makeup. Licence is rebellion against all law. If my heart does not become the center of Divine love, it may become the center of diabolical licence.[18]

Think of sin as a spiritual cancer, a destructive plague, a lethal virus. Jesus came to save us from sin. Sin is the problem, the pollutant, the poison. Sin is the whole reason that the human race experiences such horrific suffering on a daily basis. Sin is the reason that millions of people will go to a Christless hell. And all sin is sin against God. So why would genuine Christians want to embrace a message that supposedly gave them liberty to sin? Why would true lovers of the Lord look for a theology that justified disobedience of their Deliverer and mocking of their Master?

What an error it is to run from the lethal clutches of legalism and fall right into the quicksand of license! And so, I urge you: *If you are one of those who has been badly burned by a negative and condemning experience with legalism, do not cast off all discipline, restraint, and holy fear and give place to the flesh.* You will only be moving from the pressure cooker of man-made religion into the fire of demonic lust and evil desire. Beware!

☙

The fact is, there is no need to bounce from one extreme to the other. Spirit-empowered holiness, not sin-driven license, is the biblical option to legalism. The apostle Paul can help us with this too. He wrote the words "the letter kills" when explaining to the Corinthians that their very lives served as a letter of commendation for his ministry, written "not on tablets of stone but on tablets of human hearts" (2 Cor. 3:3). Paul then took up this image and expanded on it, explaining that: "[God] has made us competent as ministers of a new covenant—not of the letter but of the Spirit; for the letter kills, but the Spirit gives life" (2 Cor. 3:6).

What did Paul mean by this? He was referring to the effects that the Law of Moses, engraved on tables of stone, had upon the Israelites, calling it "the ministry that brought death" and "the ministry that condemns men" (2 Cor. 3:7,9). Yet Paul still called it a "glorious" ministry (v. 9)! This is in keeping with the fact Paul was always careful to state that the Law itself is good (see, for example, Rom. 7:12).[19] The problem is that the Law does not give us the power to live for God (see Rom. 8:1-4). It shows us the way without enabling us to go that way. As the anonymous poem states so well:

To run and work, the law commands
Yet gives us neither feet nor hands.
But better news the gospel brings;
It bids us fly and gives us wings.

Through the New Covenant, we can now fly![20] Listen again to Paul:

Now the Lord is the Spirit, and where the Spirit of the Lord is, there is freedom. And we, who with unveiled faces all reflect the Lord's glory, are being transformed into his likeness with ever-increasing glory, which comes from the Lord, who is the Spirit (2 Cor. 3:17,18).

Yes, where the Spirit of the Lord is, there is freedom, but it is freedom to become like Jesus, freedom to fulfill the Law's demands, freedom to be holy. There is no room for license here. Rather, through the power of the new covenant, we are presently being transformed into the Lord's likeness. How glorious this spiritual operation is!

Really, there is no mistaking the point. Paul's Epistles to the Corinthians are *strong* holiness letters. In 1 Corinthians, he instructed the believers that they "must not associate with anyone who calls himself a brother but is sexually immoral or greedy, an idolater or a slanderer, a drunkard or a swindler. With such a man do not even eat" (1 Cor. 5:11). Why such a severe exhortation? Paul answered that question in the clearest possible terms:

Do you not know that the wicked will not inherit the kingdom of God? Do not be deceived: Neither the sexually immoral nor idolaters nor adulterers nor male prostitutes nor homosexual offenders nor thieves nor the greedy nor drunkards nor slanderers nor swindlers will inherit the kingdom of God (1 Cor. 6:9,10).[21]

Those kinds of people will one day be put out of God's kingdom, so if such people—without repentance and change—claim to be believers, they must be put out of the Church *today*.

It was also in Paul's first letter to the Corinthians that he explained to them the harsh reality that some of their own friends or family were *sick* or had *died* because they partook of the Lord's Supper in an unworthy manner (see 1 Cor. 11:28-32). And this was immediately after he warned his readers to learn from the example of God's dealing with the Israelites, who perished in the wilderness because of their sin (1 Cor. 10:1-12).

But in his second letter to the Corinthians, Paul gave one of the most beautiful calls to holiness found anywhere in the Bible. That passage associates believers with righteousness, light, Christ, and the temple of the living God, telling us, in fact, that we *are* that temple! How then should we live? Read Paul's words carefully.

Do not be yoked together with unbelievers. For what do righteousness and wickedness have in common? Or what fellowship can light have with darkness? What harmony is there between Christ and Belial? What does a believer have in common with an unbeliever? What agreement is there between the temple of God and idols? For we are the temple of the living God. As God has said: "I will live with them and walk among them, and I will be their God, and they will be my people.

"Therefore come out from them and be separate, says the Lord. Touch no unclean thing, and I will receive you. I will be a Father to you, and you will be My sons and daughters, says the Lord Almighty."

Since we have these promises, dear friends, let us purify ourselves from everything that contaminates body and spirit, perfecting holiness out of reverence for God (2 Cor. 6:14—7:1).

And these verses appear just a few chapters after that famous phrase, "the letter kills." Obviously, Paul was not advocating license! Rather, he was calling us to make holiness perfect in the fear of the Lord, cleansing ourselves from *everything* that pollutes body or spirit. That's pretty holy!

So then, if it is clear that Paul was not coming against God's standards for holy living, what did he mean when he wrote that "the letter kills"? Simply that externally imposed religion brings death while internally birthed religion brings life. One is written on stone, a covenant that condemns men. The other is written on the heart, a covenant that transforms men.

Throughout the third chapter of 2 Corinthians, Paul made reference to the work of the Spirit, just as he did throughout Romans 8, where Paul taught that, through the Spirit's new covenant work, we have the supernatural ability to keep the Law's demands. Romans 8:4 says that Jesus died on the cross for us "in order that the righteous requirements of the law might be fully met in us, who do not live according to the sinful nature but according to the Spirit." That's not legalism, that's freedom! Sin enslaved us; the Spirit emancipated us. The flesh brought us into bondage; the Spirit set us free! A holy life is a liberated life.

Following God's Word means peace, joy, and blessing. Following God's Word means harmony with our Maker and intimacy with our Savior. Following God's Word is the only sane way to live. Unfortunately, as Robert D. Brimstead observed, "The idea of living strictly by what the Bible says has been branded as legalism."[22]

It's time, my friend, that we dispel that notion. It's time that we *preach* holiness (but not with legalistic judgments) and *live* holiness, but from the inside out. It's time we show the world the image of our Savior—instead of the image of the flesh. Let people see Christ, not carnality, in the Church.

But how can we strive for holiness with all of our hearts and yet stay clear of legalism? Here are a few helpful hints:

1. *Make every effort to keep your first love.* A heart aflame with love for Jesus will not quickly degenerate into legalism.
2. *Live a life of thanksgiving and praise.* Be a worshiper, not a murmurer or a complainer. This will help you to keep your focus in the right place, looking upward with gratitude as opposed to outward with grumbling. In fact, a liberated believer will be overflowing with thanksgiving; a legalist primarily thanks God that he is not like other people, sinful and unclean! (See Luke 18:9-14, where Jesus spoke a parable "to some who were confident of their own righteousness and looked down on everybody else." It is one thing to be holy; it is another thing to be a hypocrite.)
3. *Be very conscious of your own sins and shortcomings.* Always look to remove the beam from your own eye before you point out the speck in the eye of your brother or sister (see Matt. 7:1-5).
4. *Give yourself to private prayer for those with whom you differ—* and for those you don't particularly like! This will produce in you a genuine desire to see them blessed and lifted up, as opposed to a fleshly, immature desire to see them brought down or hurt. You won't become critical of others if you spend quality time interceding on their behalf.
5. *Learn to appreciate the beauty of holiness.* Recognize holiness as one of the most wonderful aspects of our eternal destiny and as something marked by the very character of Jesus. This way, you won't be able to reduce holiness to a mere system of laws and regulations. You will embrace holiness as a wonderful, pure way of life.
6. *Be quick to recognize narrow judgmentalism arising in any area of your life,* such as negatively judging other churches that don't worship exactly the way your church does, or becoming exclusive in what you are open to spiritually, taking in teaching material only from those within your own small

camp, as if the rest of the Body was somehow subpar and had nothing to offer you. Don't fall into this trap!

7. *Never use the Bible as a weapon against other believers.* Avoid bashing people with Scripture quotes, allegedly backing up your position in the name of "My Bible says . . . !" This is a common tactic of legalists, as the Bible for them is often more a textbook to be used for reference than a living Word to be imbibed and embraced.

And then stand firm for holiness! In fact, the next time someone tries to reject a strong, biblical call to holiness by telling you that "the letter kills," you can tell them what the verse really means (externally imposed religion kills!), remind them of the dangers and horrors of sin (sin kills even more than "the letter" kills!), and point them to the purpose of the Cross of our Savior (to save us from our sins).

Quote for them the rest of the passage: "The letter kills, but the Spirit gives life" (2 Cor. 3:6). Then read them the conclusion of Paul's thoughts on the matter: "And we, who with unveiled faces all reflect the Lord's glory, are being transformed into His likeness with ever-increasing glory, which comes from the Lord, who is the Spirit" (2 Cor. 3:18). Such lofty heights of holiness are foreign to the legalist and forbidden to the libertarian. But they are familiar to those of us who have been set free from sin and have become slaves of righteousness.

The bottom line is that Almighty God is at work in us to make us like His Son. *That* is not legalism.

CHAPTER NINE

GOD'S CURE FOR
DIRTY FEET

*He who is washed "who is justified through
the blood of the Lamb, needeth only to wash
his feet" to regulate all his affections and desires;
and to get, by faith, his conscience cleansed
from any fresh guilt, which he may have
contracted since his justification.*

ADAM CLARKE

*Just as the sweeper who cleans the courtyard
gets dirtied himself, so can one who seeks to repair
the world be contaminated by evil.*

ISRAEL "BAAL SHEM TOV"
AN 18TH-CENTURY
MYSTICAL RABBI

Have you ever studied 1 John 1:7? The verse itself seems simple enough, telling us, "If we walk in the light, as He is in the light, we have fellowship with one another, and the blood of Jesus, His Son, purifies us from all sin." But there is something many of us miss when we read this verse. In fact, even if you read it again several times, you still might not see anything unusual in it. So look at it once more. Does anything get your attention? Not yet?

Then maybe this question will help you: If we are walking in the light as God is in the light, why do we need to be purified from sin? After all, according to the previous verse, "If we claim to have fellowship with Him yet walk in the darkness, we lie and do not live by the truth." Therefore, if we *do* walk in the light, then we *do* live by the truth and we *do* have fellowship with God. So what need is there for the blood of Jesus to purify us from our sins? What sins are we committing if we are walking in the light?

There is only possible answer: As long we live in this world, even as born-again, Spirit-filled children of God, walking in the light doesn't mean living without any sin. We will never reach total perfection in this life. We will always need purification.

Of course, this does not give us a license to sin. To the contrary, rightly understanding 1 John 1:7 should actually spur us to deeper holiness and push us toward more serious consecration. How so? Well, if you think that walking in the light means never sinning a single time in thought, word, or deed, you may well conclude that you can never come close and that there's really no use even trying.

But when you realize that you *can* walk in the light—being ruled by the Spirit and not the flesh, living in harmony with the Word and not the world, saying yes to Jesus and no to the devil, walking in habitual obedience and not consistent disobedience—*even though you are not yet perfect*, you will come into a place of freedom, victory, and confidence. Yes, you can lead a blameless life, even though you still need to be purified by the blood of Jesus. Let's take a look at the thirteenth chapter of the Gospel of John for clarification and insight.

Jesus knew He was about to be betrayed and that He was about to return to His home with God. Before He left this world, He wanted to show His disciples "the full extent of His love" (John 13:1-3). So what did He do? "He got up from the meal, took off His outer clothing, and wrapped a towel around His waist. After that, He poured water into a basin and began to wash His disciples' feet, drying them with the towel that was wrapped around Him" (vv. 4,5).

This was too much for Simon Peter. "Lord," he exclaimed, "there's no way You're going to wash *my* feet!"

But Jesus insisted. "Unless I wash you, you have no part with Me."

This left impetuous Peter with only one response: "Then, Lord, not just my feet but my hands and my head as well!" (v. 9).

Amen, Peter! You're my kind of guy—all or nothing at all, both feet in or both feet out. Peter was saying, "If getting my feet washed is essential to staying in right relationship with You, then wash my whole body. Give me the whole package, Lord!"

Jesus answered Peter, saying, "A person who has had a bath needs only to wash his feet; his whole body is clean. And you are clean, though not every one of you" (v. 10). For He knew which of the disciples was about to betray Him, and that was why He said not every one was clean (see v. 11).

What did Jesus mean? Well, you need to remember the culture of the day. The houses back then didn't have running water or plumbing, and that meant homes had no private showers or baths. When you wanted to bathe, you would either go to the river or to a public bathhouse. There you would wash your whole body, cleaning yourself from head to toe. But then you had to walk back home, and that meant trekking down grimy, dusty roads. No matter what you did, your feet would get dirty. So, when you arrived at someone's house, it was a customary act of kindness for them to have a basin of water ready and a servant waiting to wash your feet. But that didn't mean that you needed another bath. You only needed to have your feet washed.

How did Jesus apply this custom spiritually? Well, all of His disciples (except Judas, who was about to betray Him) were in good standing with Him. He had received them as His own, forgiving their sins, and in His words, they were already "clean." (See also John 15:3, "You are already clean because of the word I have spoken to you.") Their heads, hands, and whole bodies were bathed. They needed only to have their feet washed.

"That's nice," you say, "but I still don't get it. What does this have to do with 1 John 1:7?" Simply this: When we get saved, we get bathed from head to toe. God cleans us up big time, scrubbing away the accumulated filth. And there is a lot of filth to wash away! For some of us, it amounted to thirty, forty, fifty years or more of sin and pollution—in other words, *decades* without a bath. Can you imagine how miserably we stunk (spiritually speaking) when we first asked God for mercy?

I think immediately of the roadside beggars we see each year on our ministry trips to India. It is difficult to describe the utter squalor in which these men live. Dressed in torn clothes (sometimes just soiled rags) that look as if they have been soaked in motor oil, their bodies are covered with dirt and sores, their long hair stiff and matted. (God only knows what kind of little creatures live in that hair.)

I once asked one of my Indian friends, "Why don't they shave their heads instead? Wouldn't they be more comfortable?"

He explained, "No, they leave their hair like that to get more money begging." Really, I cannot describe just how repulsive and tragic a sight it is.

Yet that's how we looked when we got saved! We were utterly repulsive, coated with grime, a mass of "wounds and welts and open sores, not cleansed or bandaged or soothed with oil" (Isa. 1:6). Yet in one moment of time, when we put our faith in the Lord Jesus and asked Him to save us from our sins, He healed our sick spirits and made us white as snow. He made us pure and holy. He made us clean!

This is what the Word says: "You were washed, you were sanctified, you were justified in the name of the Lord Jesus Christ and by the Spirit of our God" (1 Cor. 6:11).

Yes, Jesus cleansed us "by the washing with water through the word" (Eph. 5:26) and "saved us through the washing of rebirth and renewal by the Holy Spirit" (Titus 3:5). Now, we can "draw near to God with a sincere heart in full assurance of faith, having our hearts sprinkled to cleanse us from a guilty conscience and having our bodies washed with pure water" (Heb. 10:22).

There's just one problem: We still live in *this* world! We still have to walk along dusty, dirty roads, and sometimes our feet get dirty, even though we have been washed and bathed. There is simply no way to avoid all the dirt all the time. It's like walking into a room filled with cigarette smokers. Even though you don't smoke yourself, you come out smelling of smoke—and some of the fumes get into your lungs too. That's a picture of the polluting power of sin.

Sometimes we are enveloped by profanity on a job site, even though we ourselves never utter such words. Still, just hearing filth can make you feel unclean. Other times we find ourselves coming into contact with people whose dress and behavior is lewd and sensual, and we feel dragged down by their sinful ways, even though we have kept ourselves morally upright. We feel dirty. But that doesn't mean we need another bath! We just need to get our feet washed. "Father, cleanse me from this junk in Jesus' name!" Purification in the Bible was required for uncleanness as well as for sin.[1]

A Christian friend from Israel sent me an E-mail the other day, telling me how appalled he was by the decadent, immoral lifestyle of some Israelis. He was with his family on an isolated part of the beach recently when a woman drowned and died there. As her body was being removed by ambulance, he and his family—all of whom were shocked and distressed—began to drive away from the beach. And then something more distressing happened.

"When the ambulance had picked her up and we drove off in shock with our four wheel [vehicle]," my friend wrote, "three ladies without one single thread of clothing walked right into the water in front of everyone. I said, 'God, what have we come to?' This is like an inferno. We come [originally] from 'sinful Sweden' but I have never experienced anything like this."

Thank God for the purifying blood! This dear brother, who is walking in the light, got his feet washed on the spot. Sinful people paraded shamelessly right in front of his eyes, but he himself did not sin. He was immediately purified by the blood.

Yet there are times when we do sin. And that means getting our feet dirty, even though we are walking in the light and our lives are no longer dominated by disobedience and self-will. The fact is, every day all of us fall short to one extent or another. Perhaps we have a fleeting thought of envy or competition. Or maybe we speak a judgmental word about a fellow believer, or we fail to focus on the Lord during prayer. Perhaps the problem one day is our lack of compassion for a church member in need, or maybe we cast a fleeting, lustful glance at someone. Or we momentarily become swelled with pride because the Lord saw fit to use us.

One way or another, even as consecrated, dedicated, separated children of God, we still have momentary blemishes and temporary spots.[2] But that doesn't mean that we need to get saved all over again every time we fall short! Instead, we immediately turn to the Lord for cleansing, wiping the grime from our feet as soon as we recognize it and receiving mercy and grace from His hand.

One sign that we are living in fellowship with our Father is that we are quick to repent and careful to guard our hearts. If we are not, how can we claim to be walking in the light? In what sense then are we participating in communion with our God? If sin is our mainstay, if lust rules us, if pride dominates us, if hatred controls us, if materialism governs us, where is our fellowship and solidarity with the Holy Spirit, our intimacy and closeness with Jesus? How are we walking in the light?

The light is glorious, the light is pure, the light is full of life, and God always divides it from darkness. He separates those who walk in the light from those who dwell in the dusk of sin. If we are truly children of God, we *will* live in the brightness of His presence, abiding in Him and bearing much fruit (see Eph. 5:8; Phil. 2:15; John 15:7,8). Still, that does not mean that we live without any sin. It means that we live in purity to the point that sin is an aberration, an abnormality, an oddity—merely dust and dirt on our feet while our whole bodies are clean.

Walking in the light presupposes regular, daily repentance, since "it is light that makes everything visible" (Eph. 5:14), causing any sin to stand out. When we are washed and bathed in the righteousness of our God and Savior Jesus the Messiah, we spot impurity quickly and, just as quickly, we turn from it through the blood.

This is in total contrast with those who despise the grace of God and go back to their old ways. "Of them the proverbs are true: 'A dog returns to its vomit,' and, 'A sow that is washed goes back to her wallowing in the mud'" (2 Pet. 2:22). That does not describe us! Rather, we are those "who wash [our] robes, that [we] may have the right to the tree of life and may go through the gates into the city" (Rev. 22:14). We are careful to keep our garments clean, and total spiritual purity is always our goal.

As Paul exhorted the Corinthians in light of the Father's pledge to receive us as His own, "Since we have these promises, dear friends, let us purify ourselves from everything that contaminates body and spirit, perfecting holiness out of reverence for God" (2 Cor. 7:1).

We are called to stay free from contamination. In other words, God commands us to be blameless. Throughout the Word it is the blameless who are blessed. It was this quality that caught God's attention when He searched the earth for people to use:

Noah was a righteous man, blameless among the people of his time, and he walked with God (Gen. 6:9).

In the land of Uz there lived a man whose name was Job. This man was blameless and upright; he feared God and shunned evil (Job 1:1).

For I have kept the ways of the Lord; I have not done evil by turning from my God. All His laws are before me; I have not turned away from His decrees. I have been blameless before Him and have kept myself from sin (Ps. 18:21-23, written by David).[3]

You are witnesses, and so is God, of how holy, righteous and blameless we were among you who believed (1 Thess. 2:10, written by Paul).

When Abram was ninety-nine years old, the Lord appeared to him and said, "I am God Almighty; walk before Me and be blameless" (Gen. 17:1).

But it is not just the super saints who are called to be blameless. This calling applies to every one of us (especially leaders!—"An elder must be blameless . . . an overseer . . . must be blameless"—Titus 1:6,7). This is what the Lord *expects* from us.

You must be blameless before the Lord your God (Deut. 18:13).

Lord, who may dwell in Your sanctuary? Who may live on Your holy hill? He whose walk is blameless and who does what is righteous (Ps. 15:1,2).

And this is my prayer: that your love may abound more and more in knowledge and depth of insight, so that you may be able to discern what is best and may be pure and blameless until the day of Christ, filled with the fruit of righteousness that comes through Jesus Christ—to the glory and praise of God (Phil. 1:9-11).

So then, dear friends, since you are looking forward to this, make every effort to be found spotless, blameless and at peace with Him (2 Pet. 3:14).

Look at this last verse again. The key to being at peace with God is living a spotless, blameless life. In fact, there are wonderful promises given to the blameless—and only to the blameless:

To the faithful You show Yourself faithful, to the blameless You show Yourself blameless (2 Sam. 22:26).

For the Lord God is a sun and shield; the Lord bestows favor and honor; no good thing does He withhold from those whose walk is blameless (Ps. 84:11).

Blessed are they whose ways are blameless, who walk according to the law of the Lord (Ps. 119:1).

He holds victory in store for the upright, He is a shield to those whose walk is blameless (Prov. 2:7).

The Lord detests men of perverse heart but He delights in those whose ways are blameless (Prov. 11:20).

He whose walk is blameless is kept safe, but he whose ways are perverse will suddenly fall (Prov. 28:18).

Being blameless is our destiny:

He will keep you strong to the end, so that you will be blameless on the day of our Lord Jesus Christ (1 Cor. 1:8).

For He chose us in Him before the creation of the world to be holy and blameless in His sight (Eph. 1:4).

Christ loved the church and gave Himself up for her to make her holy, cleansing her by the washing with water through the word, and to present her to Himself as a radiant church, without stain or wrinkle or any other blemish, but holy and blameless (Eph. 5:25-27).

May God Himself, the God of peace, sanctify you through and through. May your whole spirit, soul and body be kept blameless at the coming of our Lord Jesus Christ (1 Thess. 5:23).

"But," you wonder, "how can I possibly lead a blameless life in this world?" Just remember the principle of 1 John 1:7! Being blameless does not mean being totally and completely sinless; it means living a consistent, committed, uncompromised, unwavering life in the Lord, so that you are complete in Him.[4] And we *can* live like this. We *can* offer our bodies "as living sacrifices, holy and pleasing to God" (Rom. 12:1). Our feet may get dirty, but we ourselves can stay clean. Are you ready for the challenge?

James describes the essence of true religion as this: "to look after orphans and widows in their distress and to keep oneself from being polluted by the world" (Jas. 1:27). We don't have to be polluted! We can walk with God, just like Enoch, who kept it up for 300 years (see Gen. 5:22). And if he could do it for 300 years, surely we can keep it up for the rest of our relatively short lives. We must recognize that our calling is that of the cleansed and our walk that of the washed. Filth and grime are not for us. It's time we get consistent. It's time we walk with the Lord.

The Hebrew verb used to described Enoch's walk with God (as well as that of Noah and Abraham)[5] speaks of ongoing, continuous activity, of enduring action. They walked and walked and walked with God. If you saw Enoch one year and then didn't see him again for 50 years, his life would still be the same.

"Enoch, what have you been up to?"

"I've been walking with God, back and forth, in and out, day after day, night after night, just walking and walking with the Lord."

Did he get his feet dirty? You bet! Did he *live* in sin? Impossible! Was he righteous and godly? Absolutely! Was he perfect? No way!

Was Enoch consistent? No doubt. The *pattern* of his life was unquestionable. He was godly and he walked with God, regardless of his emotions, regardless of the circumstances, regardless of his temptations. We can live like this too!

We've got to get over the "quick-fix" mentality and stop trying to follow spiritual "crash diets." It's the day-to-day discipline we need, the day-to-day repentance, the day-to-day commitment, the day-to-day cleansing.[6] (I'm reminded of a story I heard about the president of a well-known Bible college. One of his students came to him the day before her wedding. She was terribly over-weight and wanted special prayer: "Would you pray for me that I would lose this weight before the wedding tomorrow?" According to the story, he replied, "I'm sorry, but this kind only comes out with prayer and fasting!") The only way you will get somewhere with the Lord is one step at a time.

And what about those dirty feet? Unfortunately, some of us can't seem to get this right. Either we think that we're *always* going to sin, we're *always* going to blow it, we're *always* going to mess up—

and so we might as well sin! Or we think that if we sin one single time, we need to go the church altar, weep and wail and feel miserable, and pray the sinner's prayer all over again.

FOOT WASHING IS ONLY EFFECTIVE FOR THOSE WHO DO NOT RETURN TO THE MUD.

Those in the "I-might-as-well-sin" camp need to take careful notice of Paul's words:

> For of this you can be sure: No immoral, impure or greedy person—such a man is an idolater—has any inheritance in the kingdom of Christ and of God. Let no one deceive you with empty words, for because of such things God's wrath comes on those who are disobedient (Eph. 5:5-7).

Foot washing is only effective for those who do not return to the mud.

On the other hand, those in the "I-need-to-get-saved-again-every-week" camp need to embrace and believe the Lord's words: "A person who has had a bath needs only to wash his feet; his whole body is clean" (John 13:10). It is crucial that you learn to make this distinction.

To be around sinners may give you an unclean feeling. But if you didn't join with them in their sin, *you* are not unclean. Just wash off your feet! To be tempted with ungodly desires may make you feel polluted. But if you didn't yield to those thoughts, then you are *not* polluted. Just clean off the dust! And if you did yield for a moment (and who among us has never yielded?), then confess your sin, renounce your sin, and receive cleansing from your sin through the blood.[7] Prove that you are walking in the light by immediately leaving the darkness.

"And what if I *like* the darkness and begin to make it my habit to live there?" Danger! There is no such option for the people of God.

We are commanded to "put aside the deeds of darkness and put on the armor of light" (Rom. 13:12), since it is those whose deeds are evil who choose darkness rather than light (see John 3:19). The fact is that, "We do not belong to the night or to the darkness," because "those who sleep, sleep at night, and those who get drunk, get drunk at night. But since we belong to the day, let us be self-controlled, putting on faith and love as a breastplate, and the hope of salvation as a helmet" (1 Thess. 5:5,7,8).

Yes, it is true that we "were once darkness, but now"—glory and praise to God!—we are "light in the Lord." Therefore we must "live as children of light" (Eph. 5:8).

We're not who we used to be, and we must never forget how much God has done for us in the past and how much He does for us in the present. As Matthew Henry noted, "The provision made for our cleansing should not make us presumptuous, but the more cautious. *I have washed my feet, how shall I defile them?* (Song of Sol. 5:3, *NKJV*). From yesterday's pardon, we should fetch an argument against this day's temptation."[8]

In fact, Henry took the fact of our cleansing to be a very serious exhortation to continued holiness:

See what ought to be the daily care of those who through grace are in a justified state, and that is to wash their feet; to cleanse themselves from the guilt they contract daily through infirmity and inadvertence, by the renewed exercise of repentance, with a believing application of the virtue of Christ's blood. We must also wash our feet by constant watchfulness against every thing that is defiling, for we must cleanse our way, and cleanse our feet by taking heed thereto (see Ps. 119:9). The priests, when they were consecrated, were washed with water; and, though they did not need afterwards to be so washed all over, yet, whenever they went in to minister, they must wash their feet and hands at the laver, on pain of death (see Exod. 30:19,20).[9]

But if we walk in humble dependence on the Lord, keeping our hearts free from presumption and willful sin, we can rest in our once-and-for-all, lifetime cleansing and our "take-as-often-as-needed" daily cleansings. We don't need to get saved afresh several times a week. We don't need to be baptized over and over again. Once is enough! After that, it's a matter of keeping our feet clean.

When I came to the Lord in 1971, there was an older Italian man who came to the services periodically. Of course, being an Italian Pentecostal church, most of the people who went there were Italian, and since I was only sixteen, most of them seemed old! But there was one thing that stood out about this man: When he did come to church, he always responded to the altar call to get saved—and I mean always—and dutifully prayed the "sinner's prayer" with the pastor every single time. (We could never figure out why the pastor prayed with him every time either, but we assumed he knew what he was doing. After all, we were just a bunch of raw, inexperienced teenagers! Still, it struck us as odd.) This dear man must have gotten "saved" twenty-five times!

"How pathetic!" you might say. "It's obvious that this man didn't understand what it means to be justified through faith, and he probably never really met the Lord. It's obvious that something was missing somewhere." I couldn't agree with you more. Either he was not able to distinguish between being bathed and having his feet washed, or else he failed to grasp what it means to come into a personal relationship with the Lord, somehow thinking of "getting saved" as something you did in church every week, like Catholics participating in the Mass on Sundays. It really was sad to watch.

And yet some of us are just like that. We seem to think that our standing with God vacillates from moment to moment, that He can be smiling on us one second and frowning on us the next, blessing us one minute and casting us out of His presence the next.

Some of us actually think that our names get erased from the book of life, and then written down again, and then erased, and then rewritten several times a day.[10] It's not like that!

It's one thing to turn your back on God, to walk away from Him, to renounce and deny Him. If you die in that state, He will renounce and deny you too (see Matt. 10:33; Luke 12:9; 2 Tim. 2:12). It is quite another thing to walk in the light, to walk back and forth with the Lord, to live a blameless life, and to sometimes get stained or tainted with the filth of the world and the flesh.

Friend, you need to accept the fact that you have been received by Almighty God through the blood of His Son, and that same blood cleanses you daily as you walk in the light. So, get your feet washed several times a day and recognize how clean the Lord has made you. And don't mar those white, linen garments or spot that wedding gown (see Rev. 19:8,14). For you were once a soiled sinner. Now you're a sanctified saint. You used to be condemned and carnal. Now you're consecrated and clean. You've taken your bath and it's time to walk home to Father's house.

So, get up and get going, walking in the light as you walk in this world. There's a divine remedy for dirty feet.

CHAPTER TEN

THERE'S ALWAYS A WAY
OF ESCAPE!

For if God did not spare angels when they sinned,
but sent them to hell, putting them into gloomy
dungeons to be held for judgment; if He did not
spare the ancient world when He brought the flood
on its ungodly people, but protected Noah, a
preacher of righteousness, and seven others; if He
condemned the cities of Sodom and Gomorrah by
burning them to ashes, and made them an example
of what is going to happen to the ungodly; and if He
rescued Lot, a righteous man, who was distressed by
the filthy lives of lawless men (for that righteous
man, living among them day after day, was
tormented in his righteous soul by the lawless deeds
he saw and heard)—if this is so, then the Lord
knows how to rescue godly men from trials and to
hold the unrighteous for the day of judgment,
while continuing their punishment.

2 PETER 2:4-9

November 12, 1971, was the first time I responded to an altar call. It was only the second time I had been in a real church service, and I went forward only because I knew it would mean a lot to those sincere "Christian" people who had been praying for me. After all, I knew what they thought of me and how I looked in their eyes. I was the worst of sinners! In fact, when I first visited the church in August of 1971—with the express purpose of pulling my two best friends out of there—one of the young ladies wrote in her diary, "Antichrist comes to church tonight." My reputation preceded me!

But on this night in November something happened, and it was as big a surprise to me as anybody. You see, when I went forward, I had no intention of changing or really believing. I was actually thinking to myself, "These dear old folks will really be happy that I'm doing this, and it will mean a lot to the church." But as I prayed out loud with the pastor, faith began to rise in my Jewish heart, and I actually believed that Jesus died for me and rose from the dead. There was only one problem: I wasn't ready to give up my sin! Although I said the words, "God, I promise to live for You the rest of my life," I knew that I didn't really mean it.

So I had a talk with the Father. "God," I said silently, "You know that I believe Jesus died for me. But I'm not ready to give up my drugs." To this day, I believe it's good to be totally honest with the Lord in prayer. After all, He knows what's in your heart anyway!

Then I prayed a really stupid prayer. (Remember, I was just a stupid kid, so you need to give me some slack.) "God," I prayed, "You know when I go home I'm going to shoot cocaine." This was the new drug on the scene for me in 1971, and I had just purchased enough to use for a few weeks, as well as to sell to some friends. "So, if You don't want to me to shoot it into my veins when I go home, don't let anything happen when I try to get high. Don't let me feel a thing." (I told you it was a stupid prayer!)

As I was leaving the church, ready to go home and test out my prayer, there were two wonderful Christian brothers standing in my way, each about sixty years old. One was known as Brother Trixie, a nickname he got as a little boy because he used to round up alley cats and throw them into the local church building during services. The other was Brother Nick. He was in trouble with the Mafia before he was saved. He had also been arrested and worked on a chain gang. Both of them were incredibly zealous, saintly brothers.

These men were so excited that I had gone forward to receive the Lord that night, and they were overflowing with encouragement for me. I didn't have the heart to tell them I wasn't ready to repent of my sins just yet, and that I was about to go home and smoke some "angel dust" (a.k.a. PCP) and then shoot a large dose of cocaine. One of them said to me, "No matter how near the devil is, Jesus is always nearer." I had no idea what he meant. I would understand soon enough!

Anyway, I went home from church with my two friends, and we smoked angel dust together. My friends were gradually "getting serious" with God, so they wouldn't shoot cocaine with me. But they figured it couldn't hurt to just "taste" the angel dust—a psychedelic drug substantially stronger than marijuana or hashish—so they took a few tokes. What patience the Lord had with us in those days of ignorance!

Then came my moment. I was just getting used to cocaine, and my previous two times, I hardly got high when I used it. So this time, I smoked a pretty potent drug first and then shot a very ample dose of "coke" into my arm—all the while wondering what God would do. (Let me urge you *never* to do things the way I did. It's like putting a gun to your head and saying, "Lord, if You don't want me to kill myself, when I pull the trigger, don't let anything happen to me." I really didn't know any better back then. All of us certainly know better now.)

I remember experiencing great anticipation as I heated up the cocaine and prepared to mainline it. You see, I thrived on moments such as these, when I would pump hard drugs into my system. There was nothing like that initial "rush," and now it was time. I pumped the syringe once or twice, my heart began to pound as the drug started to take effect. . . . I waited for the expected sensations . . . but nothing happened! A few rapid beats of my heart and that was it. In a moment, everything was back to normal. I felt no different than I had before, and there was no evidence that I had just taken a big hit of cocaine or even smoked angel dust. None!

At that moment, I knew that God was real and that He didn't want me to continue using drugs anymore. Still, my will was weak and my resolve somewhat uncertain, and for six weeks I wavered, attending church one night and shooting heroin or smoking pot the next. I was completely double-minded.

But God was totally single-minded about bringing me to Himself, and that's when I began to see the reality of the words that were spoken to me the night I first believed: "No matter how near the devil is, Jesus is always nearer."

First He was there to counteract the effects of a powerful drug called cocaine. A few weeks later, He was there to deal with me about drinking, convicting me deeply the morning after I downed a ridiculous quantity of hard liquor. Then on the night of December 17, 1991, He was there to make His love so real to me at church that I cried out, "Lord, I will never put a needle into my arm again!" Immediately I was free! I went home, gathered all my needles and cocaine, and threw everything off a nearby bridge. Then and there, an enslaving habit that had seemed like a mountain too tall to climb was now completely under my feet. God's grace had triumphed over my stubbornness, and His ability to save triumphed over my propensity to stray. How faithful He is! From that day forward, I never put a needle in my arms again.

Over those six formative weeks from November 12 to December 17, I watched Him convict me of sin, leading me to repentance. I watched Him deliver me from my own foolishness, putting His fear within me. I watched Him send me a word of encouragement when I needed it, lifting me above the temptations. I watched Him make a way of escape!

Then, on December 19, 1971, two days after I had sworn off shooting drugs for life, I told the Lord I would never get high again in any way. Then the test came.

About two weeks later, I found myself in a jealous depression because a girl in the church that I liked a little started to like one of my best friends. (Remember the one who wrote, "Antichrist comes to church tonight"? That was her!) I got really angry and decided I couldn't take the pressure of living for God anymore. (As you can see, I was not totally sanctified yet, and in those days, I still had a terrible temper.)

So I called a junkie friend named Mike and asked him if he could help me score some heroin from another junkie "friend" named Richie. Richie had previously stolen money from me while claiming to work out a drug deal on my behalf, and I was never able to get the money back. Mike told me that this was the night I could get paid back—in the form of heroin.

I was really down and dejected, and I was bent on giving in to the flesh. Still, I couldn't believe what I was doing, and there was an inner cry within me to get me out of the mess. But Richie was loaded with heroin, and I heard through the grapevine that this batch was unbelievably potent.

"God, please help me," I prayed, even as I made my way to meet up with Mike. He did help me—but not in the way I expected.

Feeling *completely* miserable, I found Mike and then Richie, knowing that in a little while, I might well have a needle in my arm. What was I doing? This was crazy, and I knew it. Then God did something awesome. He let the bottom fall out!

As we went into a store to get some food, we met a young lady known as "Foxy." She had no morals whatsoever, and she was so base that most men did not even consider her attractive. Even in my most worldly days, I thought this poor gal was vulgar, a total lowlife. But now, I was in a taxi with her and two junkies headed for her apartment, and I was beginning to recoil from the ugliness of the situation. Immediately, she and the other two guys began to make plans for the night. I was getting completely grossed out. "God, this is not me! This is not who I am anymore!"

Soon we arrived at her apartment, and I can hardly describe the scene. There was another young lady there, along with two men and a number of little babies. Whose babies were they anyway? Were they white babies or black babies or mixed? Who were the parents? Were there a few infants and some toddlers? Or were there some twins or triplets? The whole scene was *very* weird, and minute by minute, everything was sinking lower and lower. Some marijuana was being passed around, but the moment I went to smoke it, I knew I had to stop.

My mind was racing: "God! What I am doing here? This place is a cesspool. These girls are shameless sluts, the men in the apartment seem like spineless slaves, the guys who brought me here are lawless junkies—I'm in a pit!" (I'm sure I didn't pray with such poetic alliteration, but I assure you, those were my very sentiments.)

I felt as if the walls were closing in and I had to get out in a hurry. There I saw sin for what it really was. I was in a den of iniquity, and it was as repulsive to my eyes as a puss-filled wound, as nauseating to my senses as a pool of vomit. (Forgive the graphic imagery, but that's how disgusting sin is.) Somehow, I managed to get out of the apartment without creating a stir.

By now, my pockets were filled with some pills I had just been given. I got to a phone booth, called a friend and asked him to pick me up in a hurry. When he arrived, I got rid of the pills, heaved a sigh of relief, and turned my back on that whole filthy world. From that moment on, I never looked back again. No more drugs or alcohol for life!

The Lord made a way of escape for me, and He has been making them for me ever since—although, thank God, they have been a whole lot less dramatic than the terribly debased scene in that apartment that night. The fact is, there's *always* a way of escape for God's people. None of us have to fall—ever. The Word is clear: "Cast your cares on the Lord and He will sustain you; He will never let the righteous fall" (Ps. 55:22). And never means *never*, as surely as God is God.

And what if we stagger a little when hit hard by temptation and trial? Even then, we have a promise:

If the Lord delights in a man's way, He makes his steps firm; though he stumble, he will not fall, for the Lord upholds him with His hand (Ps. 37:23,24).

We don't have to hit the deck, no matter how viciously the enemy attacks. If you "put on the full armor of God," then, "when the day of evil comes" you can "stand your ground, and after you have done everything," you *can* stand (Eph. 6:13). You may stumble. You may stagger. But you need never go down.[1]

In light of these assurances—and no doubt, based on personal experience too—Jude could speak of God as the one "who is able to keep you from falling and to present you before His glorious presence without fault and with great joy" (Jude 24). Rather than dreading the day when we will stand before God—as if it would be a time of abject terror causing us to hang our heads in great shame—we can look forward to that time with great joy. What glorious keeping power! God can finish what He starts (see 1 Cor. 1:8; Phil. 1:6; Heb. 12:1), and He can keep and deliver His own.

As Peter expressed it, "The Lord knows how to rescue godly men from trials" (2 Pet. 2:9). He's been doing it for quite a long time. Still, He will not do it without our active cooperation. He will not force us to flee.

Of course, if we put our confidence in ourselves, trusting in our own strength and abilities, we might be headed for a crash. Paul warned the Corinthians about this very danger, reminding them of Israel's history: "So, if you think you are standing firm, be careful that you don't fall!" (1 Cor. 10:12). Complacency and pride are twin sins that will slay any giant, no matter how big and strong. They are fatal to smug saints too! But if our trust is in the faithfulness of the Lord, we can be assured of this:

No temptation has seized you except what is common to man. And God is faithful; He will not let you be tempted beyond what you can bear. But when you are tempted, He will also provide a way out so that you can stand up under it (1 Cor. 10:13).[2]

Do you see what this verse is saying? Sometimes we don't really need a way of escape. We simply need to resist: "Submit yourselves, then, to God. Resist the devil, and he will flee from you" (Jas. 4:7). In such times of demonic testing, we place ourselves under the authority of God and say "No" to Satan. And he will run. He *will* get up and go. And we will stand firm—which means that we don't have to give in to temptation. We don't have to bite the bait. Falling is *not* a foregone conclusion. Yielding and messing up is *not* the expected course of events. We will not be tempted beyond what we can bear.

Of course, it doesn't always *feel* like that. Sometimes temptation assaults us with the fury of a driving storm, and the pull of sin buffets and batters us. At those moments, demonic forces feel so much closer to us than the Holy Spirit. Still, the Word is true: Having submitted ourselves to God, we *can* resist the enemy, and the strength of that trial can be broken. Before we know it, there is calm instead of storm and peace instead of torment. That's the power of the gospel!

⌒

When Moses and the Israelites were faced with the crisis of a lifetime— the Egyptian army was behind them, and the Red Sea was in front of them—the Lord told Moses to use the authority He had given him. After all, the rod of God was in his hand: "Moses, why are you crying out to Me? Pick up that rod, stretch out your hand and divide the sea. You do it, Moses! And get those Israelites to start marching forward. This is no time to stop and have a prayer meeting. This is time to move!"[3] (See Exod. 14:15,16.)

There's a lesson for us here too! Sometimes we cry out to God to help us when He has already given us all the help we need. Sometimes we want Him to fight for us when He has already given us all the weaponry necessary to defeat the foe. The fact is, in Jesus we do have authority to trample the enemy of our souls under our feet (see Luke 10:19).[4] We are called and equipped to overcome.

On the other hand, there are certain times when we do need a way of escape, and rather than resist, we need to cry out for help. "The righteous cry out, and the Lord hears them; He delivers them from all their troubles" (Ps. 34:17; those troubles include temptations too).[5] Sometimes our way of escape sounds something like, "JESUS! Help me . . . ! Now! Please!"

Have you ever prayed similar prayers—not necessarily beautiful, articulate, eloquent, or mellifluous prayers, but certainly effective prayers? Somehow these kinds of prayers are not found in any prayer book. They come from a desperate heart. They come during desperate times—and desperate times there will be.

Those are the times when pressures build up and we find ourselves in a squeeze, feeling "overmatched" for the moment. And even though we have at our disposal the authority of the Word of God, the authority of the name of Jesus, and the authority of the indwelling Spirit, Satan can be very clever, setting up a situation tailor-made for our demise. Suddenly, we find ourselves facing the "perfect" temptation. Relentlessly it stares us down and blocks out all thoughts of spiritual authority or victory. We can't remember a single scripture to quote, the very thought of rebuking the devil sounds like a joke, and all our wisdom and maturity seem to have vanished into thin air. What can we do? "Help me, Lord! Deliver me, God! Please get me out of this mess! Show me the way!"

He can! He has! He will!

GOD SPECIALIZES IN SUPERNATURAL DELIVERANCES. AFTER ALL, HE'S THE DELIVERER.

He will create an escape route if He has to, or He will help us get back to our senses, or He will cause our tempters to flee. One way or another, He will make a way even where there is no way. He specializes in supernatural deliverances. After all, He's the Deliverer.

Listen to this psalm of victory. David wrote it after he experienced a mighty deliverance from a life-and-death crisis:

> I call to the Lord, who is worthy of praise, and I am saved from my enemies. The cords of death entangled me; the torrents of destruction overwhelmed me. The cords of the grave coiled around me; the snares of death confronted me. In my distress I called to the Lord; I cried to my God for help. From His temple He heard my voice; my cry came before Him, into His ears (Ps. 18:3-6).

First David was in deep trouble. He called to the Lord—and then it was David's enemies who were in trouble! Almighty God had responded:

> The earth trembled and quaked, and the foundations of the mountains shook; they trembled because He was angry. Smoke rose from His nostrils; consuming fire came from His mouth, burning coals blazed out of it. He parted the heavens and came down; dark clouds were under His feet. He mounted the cherubim and flew; He soared on the wings of the wind (Ps. 18:7-10).

Help—and I mean *help*—is on the way!

> He shot his arrows and scattered the enemies, great bolts of lightning and routed them. . . . He reached down from on high and took hold of me; He drew me out of deep waters. He rescued me from my powerful enemy, from my foes, who were too strong for me. They confronted me in the day of my disaster, but the Lord was my support (Ps. 18:14,16-18).

That's good enough for us too: The Lord is our support! Let the forces of hell gang up against us, let circumstances overwhelm us, let godless people plot to bring us down. God will save us from disaster! He will keep our foundation secure.

Yes, the Lord invites our cries, saying to us, "Call upon Me in the day of trouble; I will deliver you, and you will honor Me" (Ps. 50:15). We should never be afraid to ask God for help in a pinch or to look to Him for grace in times of trouble. And if we're crying out when we should be fighting back, the worst the Lord could say to us is what He said to Moses: "Don't cry out to Me! *You* do something about it. You've got all the authority you need."

That kind of divine rebuke I can handle! That kind of exhortation builds me up. It makes me turn to the devil and his demons and say, "You lose, Satan! I refuse to yield to you. Leave now!" *And he will!*

⌒

"But," you say, "I know some people who need long-term help. The simple solutions don't seem to work for them. They rebuke. They pray. They resist. They cry out. What about them?" They have a way of escape too! God also specializes in long-term cures, not just deliverances from momentary crises. He knows how to make things last.

Jesus told His fellow Jews who believed, "If ye continue in My word, then are ye My disciples indeed; and ye shall know the truth, and the truth shall make you free" (John 8:31,32, *KJV*). This speaks of lasting relationship with the Lord and of enduring liberty in the Lord. It speaks of a process (continuing in the Word) and an end result (freedom). This can be God's way of escape from lifelong habits and bondages. This can be the divine way out.

How so? For some drug addicts, a scriptural, disciplined rehabilitation program like Teen Challenge may be the path to complete restoration.[6] This may be exactly what they need, and it is to meet that need that the Lord raised up this ministry (along with other, similar ministries). For other troubled individuals, a caring Christian family may be God's healing balm for the wounds in their soul, while for others, a solid, Bible-based church home may provide all the necessary ingredients for wholeness. One way or another, if we truly cry out, God will bring us out.

Early in 1998, a distressed mother living in Chicago sought the Lord on behalf of her teenage daughter. This girl had already fallen heavily into drugs, even supporting herself as a prostitute in England for a time. She was back in the States, but her mom, whom we'll call "Angie," had no idea where she was. Still, through prayer, she was convinced that God would bring her daughter back and save her soul. (We'll call the girl "Louise.") Angie called a local Teen Challenge and asked them to hold a bed for Louise, assuring them that soon her straying daughter would return—and she was right!

Several days later, Louise called home, telling her mom that she just had to get out of the place where she was living. She even said that she would give Teen Challenge a try, although she was not yet saved. When she got home, her mother and stepfather decided to take her down to Florida to see her grandparents before getting her into the rehab program. As they were driving, Angie felt the Lord say to her, "Go to Pensacola." So she told her husband what she heard God say, and they agreed to drive a little out of their way to stop by Pensacola. It turned out to be hundreds of miles across state!

But here is the fascinating part of the story. When they arrived at a hotel in the city, Angie asked the desk clerk, "Is there anything religious going on here?" She had no idea that the largest local-church revival in the history of America had been taking place in Pensacola for the previous two and a half years![7] Of course, the clerk told the family of the revival—the local hotels in Pensacola have maps to the revival at the front desk—and they attended the meetings. Louise was dramatically converted and baptized, and she checked into Teen Challenge a brand-new person. Through the prayers of her mother, God made a way of escape for her, bringing her back from England to the States, then from Illinois to Pensacola, then from the revival to a proven Christian rehabilitation ministry. He will do whatever it takes!

Yet we must always remain vigilant and alert. In other words, God expects us to do what we can do to stay free. He will not force us to stop sinning! We must make lifestyle choices. We must make our stand. Otherwise, if we knowingly walk into temptation, if we play games with sinful fire, if we violate our convictions and step right into a trap, we have no guarantee that a supernatural way of escape will be made available to us. The only way out may be to run for our lives. We can rebuke Satan as much as we want, but he's not going anywhere. We have walked right onto his turf and played right into his hands! We are the ones who have to get up and go. Or, to put it simply, it's not time to fight; it's time to flee.

Paul urged the Corinthians to *flee* from sexual immorality and idolatry (see 1 Cor. 6:18; 10:14), and he exhorted Timothy to *flee* from greed and evil, youthful desires (see 1 Tim. 6:10,11; 2 Tim. 2:22). "Hightail it out of there! If you stay around those things, you'll be in big trouble." Who can promise that God will deliver us then?

All of us must avoid known places and sources of temptation, by any means and at any cost. If we don't, if we walk right into spiritual quicksand, we have no right to expect God to throw us a vine as we sink. He may just let us reap what we sow! It was one thing for the Lord to graciously save me from my folly when I knowingly walked headlong into disaster as a newborn babe in the Lord. It would be another thing if I expected Him to do the same for me over the next fifty years.[8] One reason I was able to quickly get free from drugs was because I stayed away from the whole drug scene. No more drug-shooting and booze-drinking parties for me!

One of the catchy slogans used in the war against drunk driving is, "Stay alive. Don't drink and drive." As believers, we can adopt a similar slogan in our war against sin: "Stay strong. Keep away from wrong." As Proverbs says in concise and forceful Hebrew: "Do not set foot on the path of the wicked or walk in the way of evil men. Avoid it, do not travel on it; turn from it and go on your way" (Prov. 4:14,15). That is the formula for life: If you know that something is sinful, avoid it, don't get involved with it, turn away from it, and go the opposite way. Do what God has called you to do, and don't go near those things that pollute and destroy.

Some Christian men say, "I don't know what's the matter with me. I must be really weak. When I go to the beach and see all those bikini-clad women, I feel so unclean. And I can't seem to control my eyes and my thoughts. I'm so weak!"

My brother, I beg to differ. You're not weak, you're stupid! Why in the world are you putting yourself into such a sensual environment? (If you don't think it's sensual, I would strongly encourage you to ask the Lord if your heart has become hard and if you have been so influenced by this world that you don't even realize how far your standards have fallen—and I say this to both men and women. For the moment, chew on this: If the typical swimwear at our beaches is not sinful and seductive, then why wouldn't it be appropriate for a Christian sister to get up in front of the congregation in a slinky bathing suit and lead us in worship?) God's counsel to those who go to beaches and pools and find themselves filled with lust is simple: Flee for your life!

In the same way, if a former alcoholic were to say to me, "I'm so weak. Every time I go to the bar, I'm tempted to drink," I would reply again, "You're not weak, you're stupid! You have no business being at bars anymore. Get out of there and never go back. You can reach out to your lost friends in places other than cocktail lounges and pubs." We have no right blaming God for traps into which we willfully wander:

> When tempted, no one should say, "God is tempting me." For God cannot be tempted by evil, nor does He tempt anyone; but each one is tempted when, by his own evil desire, he is dragged away and enticed. Then, after desire has conceived, it gives birth to sin; and sin, when it is full-grown, gives birth to death. Don't be deceived, my dear brothers. Every good and perfect gift is from above, coming down from the Father of the heavenly lights, who does not change like shifting shadows (Jas. 1:13-17).

Often, we are tempted because we open the door to sin's knock, or even worse, we open the door without a knock and go *looking* for opportunities to sin. Again, the word for us is, "Flee! Run! Get those feet moving and don't look back." All the binding and loosing and rebuking and resisting and driving out and casting down will not be as effective as simply turning around and staying away. It's really not that complicated! Here we are, taking authority over the devil when we really need to be taking authority over our own flesh. Here we are, cursing the spiritual darkness over a particular location when we simply need to *leave* that location.

Yes, brother, it *is* very oppressive standing in line outside of a strip club. But the way to break the oppression is to get out of there. You'll be amazed at how quickly freedom will come when you simply get up and go. Often, the way of escape is as easy as saying "good-bye"—good-bye to partying with sinful friends, good-bye to old hangouts where you always got into trouble, good-bye to ingrained habits that opened the door to the devil (like flirting or dressing sensually or acting deceptively or being lazy and slothful), good-bye to anything that you know displeases the Lord.

You'll find that staying free is a whole lot easier than getting free, and that keeping the enemy out of your home is a whole lot easier than getting him to leave once you've let him in. And when temptations come and make their appeal, remember: God is not a liar, and He assures us that the temptations are "such as are common to man." In other words, they are nothing unusual or unique; plenty of others have already successfully overcome similar enticements. The temptations are not too much for you to handle, and there will always be a way of escape at just the right time.

So hold your ground, resist the devil, refuse to sin, cry out for help when you need it, and keep your distance from willful transgression. When the temptation has passed and you have not yielded or caved in, you'll be smiling from ear to ear. It feels so good to be clean. Doesn't it?

CHAPTER ELEVEN

CUT OFF YOUR HAND AND
GOUGE OUT YOUR EYE

*Cutting off or gouging out the offending part is a
way of saying that Jesus' disciples must deal
radically with sin. Imagination is a God-given gift;
but if it is fed dirt by the eye, it will be dirty.
All sin, not least sexual sin, begins with the
imagination. Therefore what feeds the imagination
is of maximum importance in the pursuit of
Kingdom righteousness . . . . Not everyone reacts
the same way to all objects.
But if . . . your eye is causing you to sin, gouge it
out; or at very least, don't look . . . . The alternative
is sin and hell, sin's reward. The point is so
fundamental that Jesus doubtless repeated it
on numerous occasions.*

D. A. CARSON

Every Friday afternoon in Saudi Arabia, in celebration of the Muslim Sabbath, a unique event occurs in a place commonly known as "Chop Square." A large crowd of interested onlookers gathers and before their eyes, convicted criminals are paraded one by one, some of them stripped naked, all of them humiliated.

A first-time offender who has committed minor crimes—like being caught drunk on the streets, or stealing a piece of fruit—is whipped. An adulterer or adulteress is beheaded. A man who has stolen repeatedly is brought forward, his right hand put on the block and—whack!—that hand is cut off at the wrist. Then, the maimed arm is treated by a doctor who works to stop the bleeding. (Eyewitnesses say that in the past, the arm was plunged into a vat of boiling oil to cauterize it.)

What a grotesque scene! How primitive! Cutting off the hand that committed a crime? Isn't that a little extreme? Jesus didn't think so—at least spiritually speaking. The Gospels give us these severe words of warning on three different occasions. And remember, they come from the lips of our wonderful Savior. This is what He said, and this is what the Scriptures record, not one time, not two times, but three times:

"If your right eye causes you to sin, gouge it out and throw it away. It is better for you to lose one part of your body than for your whole body to be thrown into hell. And if your right hand causes you to sin, cut it off and throw it away. It is better for you to lose one part of your body than for your whole body to go into hell" (Matt. 5:29,30).

"Woe to the world because of the things that cause people to sin! Such things must come, but woe to the man through whom they come! If your hand or your foot causes you to sin, cut it off and throw it away. It is better for you to enter life maimed or crippled than to have two hands or two feet and be thrown into eternal fire. And if your eye causes you to sin, gouge it out and throw it away. It is better for you to enter life with one eye than to have two eyes and be thrown into the fire of hell" (Matt. 18:7-9).

"If your hand causes you to sin, cut it off. It is better for you to enter life maimed than with two hands to go into hell, where the fire never goes out. And if your foot causes you to sin, cut it off. It is better for you to enter life crippled than to have two feet and be thrown into hell. And if your eye causes you to sin, pluck it out. It is better for you to enter the kingdom of God with one eye than to have two eyes and be thrown into hell, where 'their worm does not die, and the fire is not quenched' " (Mark 9:43,45,47,48).

There are few things more radical than amputation. Doctors only cut off hands, feet, or legs as a last resort when all else has failed. They do it because they have no choice. If they don't, the infection will spread, destroying the whole body. So it's either one limb that goes or the whole body that dies. And once the amputation is done, it can't be undone. Once the limb is severed it will never be used again. Yet Jesus tells us to amputate our hands or feet if they cause us to sin.

Of course, this is *spiritual* imagery that graphically explains the ruthless way in which we must deal with sinful tendencies and habits, so you can put the meat cleaver or hatchet away for now! But let's not weaken the force of Jesus' words. They are absolutely radical, totally extreme, completely final: "Cut off that hand and throw it away"—even if it's the hand that you rely on in your daily labor, the hand with which you write, your strong hand. Even that hand must go if it leads you into sin.

The same goes for our eyes. He said that if our eye causes us to sin, we should gouge it out and throw it away. Think of it! Military men in hand-to-hand combat only gouge out the enemy soldier's eye when there is no other way to subdue or stop him. Even if he survives, he's blind for life. But Jesus said it's better for people to be right with God—even if it means being blind or maimed—than to have two hands, two feet, and two eyes and go straight to hell, "where their worm does not die, and the fire is not quenched."

And notice that Jesus spoke about three parts of the body: our hands, signifying what we do; our feet, signifying where we go; and our eyes, signifying what we see and desire. What does it mean to have a hand, foot, or eye that causes us to sin? And what does it mean to cut them off or pluck them out or throw them away?

Let's say you're a computer whiz, spending ten hours a day developing new programs. Half of that time, you're doing research on the Internet, downloading information about technological advances in your field. But you also spend some time every week surfing the Net for pornographic sites, even entering sexually explicit chat rooms. For you, the Internet is like your right hand, connecting you to the outside world through E-mail and Web sites, serving as the mainstay of your life and the key to your livelihood. But it's also causing you to sin.

So what do you do? If you can't break your sinful habit, then you need to cut off the Internet, no matter how much it costs you to make the break and regardless of the inconvenience and loss. Tell your employer that you can still work on computers, but not if they have modems and Internet access. And if that's not possible, or if you still find yourself getting on the Net whenever you're around a computer, then you may have to sever your ties with computers entirely. Cut off the hand that causes you to sin, even if it's your right hand. It would be better for you to work as a janitor and earn tens of thousands of dollars less every year than to keep your high-paying, high-tech job and lose your soul. That's what Jesus meant.

Maybe it's your foot that causes you to sin. Let's say that you're a young woman on a path to "stardom" in Christian music. Your voice is lovely, you have a beautiful, wholesome smile, and there's something "charismatic" about you, something special. The problem is, the path that you're on is one of self-exaltation, one where you—and not Jesus—have become the center of attention, one where you're asked to make music to make money, one where outward performance becomes more important than inward purity. Little by little, you find yourself backsliding, losing your intimacy with the Lord, forfeiting the reality of the words that you now sing so professionally.

Perhaps you've tried to work with different Christian agents, but each time, regardless of their assurances, you keep falling into the same trap. And maybe it's not their fault at all. Maybe the problem is with you. Every time you go out in front of the crowds you realize that worship of God is no longer the goal. (Wasn't it as a worship leader that you were "discovered"?) A wonderful concert is now the goal. True, the money is great, the lifestyle exciting, the future potential almost limitless, but inside you're dying. What do you do? Cut off your foot and throw it away. Go back to being a worship leader in your old home church and say farewell to the great gospel career—if that's what you must do to maintain your relationship with the Lord.

Yes, in human terms, this is quite a price to pay, but falling away from God is far more costly. And that's what Jesus was trying to illustrate. Losing a hand or foot in this world is tragic. But losing your soul in the world to come is a million times more tragic.

The same principle applies to gouging out—and throwing away!—the eye that causes you to sin. Maybe you really love to go swimming. It's your favorite form of recreation and your number-one way to exercise. You've gone swimming several times a week for years, but you've moved to a new location now, and the only beach or pool near your home is always infested with virtually nude bathers. This is poison to your eyes, infecting your mind and causing spiritual decay to race through your soul. Those tantalizing images dance before you at night whenever you try to sleep, tempting you to fantasize and lust. So pluck out that eye and throw it away—in this case it would mean staying away from the beach or pool for good if need be—determining to lose something special in this natural life rather than diminish your spiritual life or even forfeit it entirely.

Yes, this is radical, but it's reasonable too. If we could look at things through the eyes of eternity, it would make perfect sense.

⌒

Because I do a lot of public speaking in locations around the world, I frequently stay in hotels, and it has been my custom for several years now to request that the TV be removed from my room. Why? First, it's all too easy to waste precious time—ministry time, prayer time, study time, or rest time—with a couple of hours of "harmless" late night television, like sports or news. Second, it's all too easy to accidentally catch a glimpse of something inappropriate while switching channels. Third—and I say this as one who has never dished out a dime to watch a pay-per-view movie in a hotel—it's all too easy to actually look for something sinful to watch, like pornographic movies, which are available for a fee at most hotels in America and Europe.

For me, it's a whole lot easier to ask the hotel to remove my television set than to put myself into a position where I might waste precious time, or worse yet, accidentally get polluted with a passing, unclean image, or even worse, have to resist a temptation to willfully sin. Sure, there are times when I could really enjoy an hour "winding down" with a late night snack and an exciting sports event, but it's a sacrifice I'm willing to make to keep myself from temptation.

If this seems extreme to you, perhaps you have never traveled on ministry or business, subject to a demanding and draining schedule. After saying good-night to your friends and coworkers, you find yourself alone in a room, thousands of miles from home, tired and worn out, with your only companion being that big-screen TV. The temptation to invite some company in—even if it is a newscaster on a Christian show—is great. The problem, of course, is that all too often, a few minutes of harmless or even edifying programming can end up turning into minutes or hours of harmful, destructive TV. In any case, when I travel, if the hotel won't remove the TV, I ask the front desk to disable any pay-per-view movies, both to make a statement to them and to keep myself safe.

One day, while thinking about this whole issue of televisions and hotels, I asked myself a question: "Why *wouldn't* I tell the hotel that I wanted the TV set removed? It would only be because I wanted to leave open the possibility of watching it when I got there!" From this I deduced a simple principle: If I have the opportunity to close the door on temptation in advance and I fail to do it, I'm asking for trouble. Or to put it another way, if I don't walk away from sin, I'm really walking right into it.

So, the way to avoid sin and overcome the pull of the flesh is often this: Determine to make lifestyle changes and difficult choices when you are clearheaded and sober. Then, when temptation comes, the door will be locked shut in advance.

For example, if you and your fiancée agree in advance never to go into your apartment alone together, this will make it much easier to refrain from sexual sin. The battle will be won before it even starts. Otherwise, if you know that it's not the wisest thing to hang out in that apartment together but you're not willing to make a commitment to stay out of it, you've already invited the tempter to join you.

And, if you end up spending a few hours with each other in that apartment, you might not have the will to resist the temptation to sin. After all, you have already weakened your will by overriding your convictions, and you have already said yes to the flesh by yielding to your carnal desires. You would have done far better to cut off the hand that caused you to sin—meaning, in this case, spending less time together in intimate surroundings.

Of course, we understand that hands, feet, and eyes don't cause us to sin. We sin because we yield to the desires of our hearts and minds. As Jesus said:

"For from within, out of men's hearts, come evil thoughts, sexual immorality, theft, murder, adultery, greed, malice, deceit, lewdness, envy, slander, arrogance and folly. All these evils come from inside and make a man 'unclean'" (Mark 7:21-23).

This truth reminds us again that we are not to literally chop off a hand that steals or gouge out an eye that envies. But the Lord wanted to get a point across to us in His teaching, and that point is that sin must be dealt with ruthlessly. Sever it from your life, amputate it from your soul, rip it from your heart—regardless of the cost or the consequences. We must be diligent and vigilant when it comes to dealing with sin. Slothfulness here can be malignant.

WE MUST PERFORM RADICAL SURGERY ON EVERYTHING THAT DEFILES US AND DRAGS US DOWN.

Think of it in natural terms. Gangrene, according to the dictionary, is "death and decay of body tissue caused by insufficient blood supply, usually following injury or disease."[1] In certain severe cases, failure to cut off that gangrenous limb may cause death and decay to spread through the whole body. Losing one's limb—a horrible, extreme prospect—can actually become an attractive alternative when compared to losing one's life. And in the light of eternity, the loss of one's livelihood or pleasures becomes insignificant when compared to the loss of one's soul.[2] Again, Jesus said, "It is better for you to enter life maimed or crippled than to have two hands or two feet and be thrown into eternal fire" (Matt. 18:8).

But it is up to us to do the spiritual maiming and crippling. We must perform radical surgery on everything that defiles us and drags us down. I hear the Savior saying again, "Cut it off, cut it out, and cast it away. I've given you power to overcome."

As Peter wrote:

> [God's] divine power has given us everything we need for
> life and godliness through our knowledge of Him who
> called us by His own glory and goodness. Through these He
> has given us His very great and precious promises, so that
> through them you may participate in the divine nature and
> escape the corruption in the world caused by evil desires
> (2 Pet. 1:3,4).

But Peter did not instruct us simply to sit back and claim the
blessings. Instead, he told us to "make every effort" (v. 5) to grow in
our walk with the Lord and to "be all the more eager to make [our]
calling and election sure. For if you do these things," he said, *"you
will never fall,* and you will receive a rich welcome into the eternal
kingdom of our Lord and Savior Jesus Christ" (2 Pet. 1:10,11).

There's that promise again—"you will never fall"—and once
again, there is something we must do. So it is written in the Word.

If we follow the Lord's guidelines and heed His laws, we don't
have to take any deadly spills. But we must make every effort—with
His help and grace—to stay clear of folly. We must make every effort
to prepare in advance for battle if we expect to win the war. (As it
has been said, being forewarned means being forearmed.) And
when the temptations and tests do come, we can stand our ground,
or resist the enemy, or cry out for relief, or simply flee. The way of
escape will be there!

We saw in the last chapter that it is sometimes necessary to "flee"
in the sense of taking an escape route during a time of temptation.
At other times it is necessary to "flee" in the sense of staying clear
from the *source* of temptation. That's part of cutting off the hand
and gouging out the eye. And sometimes the Lord warns us in
advance when we are heading in the wrong direction, just as He
supernaturally warned Jonah when he tried to run from the call of
God.[3] That's when we had better take heed in a hurry. That's when

we had better come to our senses and make an immediate about-face. Disaster is surely right around the corner. A Mack truck is racing through the intersection ahead, and the only thing standing between you and a deadly crash is a large, red stop sign. Learn to heed those signs!

༨

This warning needs repeating: One of the most important spiritual lessons you can ever learn is to recognize and respond to God's stop signs. Don't run them! Don't treat them lightly! They stand between you and spiritual suicide. There's an ambush of temptation waiting on the other side of that intersection. God's stop signs are all that stand between you and a date with the devil.

It is crucial that we grasp this principle. *We must never sin against revealed light.* In other words, if you have already been warned clearly by God, He may never warn you again. In fact, He *need not* ever warn you again if He has already made Himself clear.

If He has clearly spoken through His Word or Spirit, there's nothing to pray about. For example, because the Word says, "Do not commit adultery," you as a married person don't need to pray about the possibility of having a relationship with that really neat guy or girl you just met. You're married and adultery is forbidden. Don't sin against the revealed light of the clear will of God. For if you know what is right and fly in the face of it, you may find yourself in deep distress, your cries for help unheeded (see Prov. 1:22-33). And when your heavenly Father mercifully puts roadblocks in your path—like a talking donkey rebuking the prophet Balaam—you would do well to turn around and go back.

It is one thing to know the course that God wants you to take and to encounter supernatural resistance along the way. It is another thing to have a clear word from God not to go a certain way and then to meet supernatural resistance as you go. In the first case, it can be the devil (see 1 Thess. 2:18). In the second case, it can be the Lord. In one case it is Satan trying to stop you from doing the will of God; in the other case, it is God trying to stop you from doing the will of Satan!

When I was first saved, I loved to watch boxing, in spite of its violence and brutality. I would sit on the edge of my seat in front of the TV, waiting for the fight to start, my heart pounding. (It was really pathetic!) When Nancy and I got married, she used to leave the house when boxing came on. She hated to see how worked up I got watching this "sport." Yet I saw nothing wrong with it and continued watching fights for years.

In November of 1982, the Lord was working on my heart in a serious way, bringing me to a place of repentance and deep spiritual hunger. One night, as I watched a championship fight with a friend, our "hero" lost in a vicious match. His defeat crushed us! In fact, we were so down over the fight that we said to each other, "Maybe it's wrong that we even watch this anymore. It shouldn't have this kind of effect on us, completely dragging us down."

So we made an agreement not to watch the big fight that was being televised the next day, featuring the lightweight champ, Ray "Boom Boom" Mancini, and the challenger from Korea, Duk Koo Kim. Ray Mancini was a really nice young man, and I often wondered when he fought, "What would happen if he ever hurt anyone seriously in the ring? How would that affect him?"

Well, on this Saturday, I chose not to watch the match, praying instead, "Lord, are You trying to say something to me about boxing? Is this another area in my life that you are purging and refining?"

The next day, I arrived at church and began to talk to the other leaders, all of whom also watched boxing regularly. "What happened in the fight?" I asked.

One of the deacons responded, "They went toe to toe for fourteen rounds, and then Mancini knocked out Kim—and he was taken from the ring unconscious. He's brain-dead now."

My God! The news hit me like a ton of bricks. I was devastated. Of all days to pray about boxing! Of all days to ask the Lord how He felt about me watching the sport. Of all boxers to be involved. The conviction in my soul was overwhelming. I *knew* God wanted me to give up watching this. (The end of the tragic story is that Kim was kept on life support until his mother arrived to see him. Then he was disconnected and pronounced dead. A Christian friend in Korea told me that the fighter's death was a national tragedy. His mother returned home and drank laundry detergent, killing herself. Within a year, the referee in the match had also committed suicide, although reports said it was unrelated to the Mancini-Kim match.)

Now, from that time to this, God has never again convicted me about watching boxing. He doesn't have to! He has already spoken to me loud and clear. But there is something interesting in all this. Here and there, I have been around a TV where a fight was on, and I've seen a few minutes of boxing since 1982. I do not watch it anymore, nor does it have the grip on me that it once did. But the few times I have seen a round or two, I have not felt the slightest conviction about it. God dealt with me once about this, and He was absolutely decisive. Why do I need to be convicted again?

I would be a fool to think that the lack of conviction indicated a change in God's heart, just like a Christian thinking about stealing would be a fool to say, "Well, I guess the Lord has changed His mind about stealing, because I don't feel bad about doing it." Nonsense! When He speaks clearly on a subject, He need never speak again.

Think of Balaam. He had already received a definite word from God *not* to go curse Israel in Numbers 22:12. "Do not go with them," the Lord said. "You must not put a curse on those people, because they are blessed." That's pretty clear! But when he was offered more money to curse God's people, he asked the Lord again, as if a larger payoff would change His will. (That's why the New Testament calls him a mercenary prophet. See 2 Pet. 2:14-16; Jude 11.)[4] And when he prayed about it the second time, the Lord released him to go—but He was actually furious with him for it, sending an angel to stop him (see Num. 22:20-35).

What a mess we get ourselves into when we sin against revealed light! Instead of God's angels protecting us, they're opposing us.

Instead of helping us, they're hindering us. Why? Because we're going the wrong way! And when we begin to come up against these divine stop signs and supernatural roadblocks, right there, at that very moment, we know what we must do: Turn back now! There's danger ahead. Cut off that foot and throw it away. Get off the path of sin and take the loss and the shame, no matter how great. Don't ignore the stop signs!

Maybe, teenage employee, your boss really wrongs you one day, and in an angry rage, you decide to drive to his house and give him a piece of your mind . . . but for some reason, your brand-new car won't start. And when you finally manage to get it started by borrowing some jumper cables from your neighbor, you get two flat tires before you make it out of your neighborhood. You've just encountered God's roadblocks! Turn back now, before you do something you'll regret for years to come. Maybe the Lord saw that your anger would spill over into violence. Maybe it was going to be violence against you! That's why God so graciously intervened. (He didn't have to.) That's why He made it so difficult for you to sin. And that's why it is the height of folly, stubbornness, and carnality for us to choose to ignore these divine stop signs.

When we do, we're not asking for trouble, we're demanding it. The prospects of such reckless spiritual hardness are chilling.

Maybe, Christian leader, your family is away for the night and you're feeling a terrible pull to rent a sexually explicit video. You're about to get into your car when the phone rings, and to your surprise, you receive a call on your unlisted home number from someone you don't even know, telling you the sad news about another pastor who has just been caught in adultery. Danger! You could be next if you don't stop now.

Or maybe, young mother of three, you've come to your wits' end with your two-year-old son. You're about to punch him in the face and curse the day he was born when, out of the blue, the radio comes on by itself and it's Dr. James Dobson talking about the lasting effects of child abuse. Well, it may sound like Dr. Dobson's voice, but that's God speaking. Stop! You're about to start something ugly that will only get worse.

Thank God for His stop signs! Heeding them will spare us unspeakable grief. Heeding them will save our very lives—and the lives of many we touch. Fighting them can be fatal. We must not ignore the warnings! When the Lord repeatedly and unmistakably shows us that something is sinful or destructive, we must deal with it severely—before it deals severely with us.

In Amos 4, the Lord chided the people of Israel for not responding to His judgments. He had sent famine, blight, mildew, locusts, plagues, all kinds of destruction. Still they would not repent of their sins. He even resorted to some highly unusual happenings to get their attention:

> "I also withheld rain from you when the harvest was still three months away. I sent rain on one town, but withheld it from another. One field had rain; another had none and dried up. People staggered from town to town for water but did not get enough to drink, yet you have not returned to Me," declares the Lord (Amos 4:7,8).

These too are God's stop signs. These too are His holy alarms. Through them He says to us: "Wake up! Get with it! The way you've been living is displeasing and defiling. The tremors you feel are signs that an earthquake is near. Danger is around the corner. Turn back, make a change, get right. You're heading into a stiff wind, and soon it will blow you away. Stop! Your hand is causing you to sin. Your foot is leading you astray. Your eye is bringing death into your soul. Amputate now! Cut off, pluck out the offending members, before sin spreads like gangrene in your spirit, before pollution suffocates your very life."

Once more our glorious Savior tells us, "It is better for you to lose one part of your body than for your whole body to go into hell" (Matt. 5:30). I think He has made Himself clear.

CHAPTER TWELVE

IT'S ALL GRACE!

Love that goes upward is worship; love that goes outward is affection; love that stoops is grace.

DONALD GREY BARNHOUSE

During a British conference on comparative religions, experts from around the world debated what, if any, belief was unique to the Christian faith. They began eliminating possibilities. Incarnation? Other religions had different versions of gods appearing in human form. Resurrection? Again, other religions had accounts of return from death. The debate went on for some time until C. S. Lewis wandered into the room. "What's the rumpus about?" he asked, and heard in reply that his colleagues were discussing Christianity's unique contribution among world religions. Lewis responded, "Oh, that's easy. It's grace." After some discussion, the conferees had to agree.

PHILIP YANCEY

Some of you may still be reeling from the brutal reality of the last chapter. "Man," you say, "that's heavy stuff! I'm feeling a little bit overwhelmed right now. I think I need to hear about God's grace."

I couldn't agree with you more! There is nothing more encouraging, more heartening, more refreshing than the grace of God.[1]

In March of 1996, in the midst of a whirlwind ministry schedule in India, I participated in a baptismal service in the Bay of Bengal. It was a wonderful day, as new converts were immersed and older believers worshiped and prayed. All the ministers were overflowing with joy, and none of us were in a hurry to get out of the water. So we waded out deeper and jumped and frolicked and rode the waves, thoroughly enjoying the moment. I felt as if I had come all the way to India to get a few minutes of pure rest, as if I were swimming in a sea of grace—infinite, invigorating, powerful, peaceful. Words fail to express the beauty of the moment and the sense of God's love we experienced. But that is what God's grace is all about: It is more than words can express.

There is an ocean of grace waiting for us, inviting us to dive in and swim. There's no end to its depth or length, and even through the endless ages of eternity, we will stand in awe at the wonder of it all. The tragedy is that many preachers and teachers today have unintentionally misrepresented God's grace, practically turning it into a license to sin. And in doing this, they have cheapened its power and demeaned its value. They have polluted the holy waters flowing from the heavenly throne.

Can I be totally honest with you? I believe that grace is one of the most misunderstood subjects in the contemporary Church. On the one hand, there are legalists who seem to forget that salvation is by grace through faith and *not* by works. They turn Christianity into a lifeless religion plagued by futility and marked by always-failing human effort.[2]

On the other hand, there are leaders who seem to forget that salvation by grace includes *freedom* from sin as well as *forgiveness* of sin. They turn Christianity into a religion that "saves" but doesn't transform. Both positions are wrong. Dead wrong.

Naturally, if you're like me, you're wondering, "If so many fine teachers of the Word are wrong, how can I be sure of the truth? How can I come to the right position?"

Well, I'm going to be completely honest with you again. I don't believe that most believers—including ministers—have seriously studied the subject of God's grace for themselves, choosing instead to pass on what they have heard from others, either in books they've read or in lectures or sermons they've heard. They take one small part of the picture ("Grace means unmerited favor") and miss the rest.

Now, I could simply say, "I have studied the original Hebrew and Greek and I know what the Scriptures really say," but where would that leave you? What if you don't have the ability to check the accuracy of my study? How can you be sure for yourself? Let me help you. The fact is, anyone can do a good word study even if he or she doesn't know the original languages. In fact, you can make your study into a little game called "Fill in the Blank" or "Substitution."

I'll give you an example of how it works, using the English word "hard." This adjective can have several meanings, including "difficult" and "solid," but the context determines which meaning is correct. If we take the sentence, "The rock is hard," we can find out what "hard" means by filling in the blank with the appropriate synonym: "The rock is ____." What is the meaning of "hard" here? Obviously, the rock is not "difficult," the rock is "solid." But in the sentence, "The test is ____" (where the blank represents "hard") it is clear that the correct synonym is "difficult" as opposed to "hard."

So, you can identify the meaning of a word by seeing what synonym works as a substitute. Simple, right? The same kind of study can be done with biblical words. List the verses in which certain Hebrew or Greek words occur in your English translation, and you can see the different ways the words are used in different contexts.[3] Then, you begin to see the bigger picture, often enabling you to trace the ways that a word developed its different meanings.[4]

Some years ago, when I did a serious study of the concept of grace in the Bible, I opened up my Hebrew and Greek concordances and examined every reference where the key words for "grace" occurred.[5] Then, I arranged them in different categories and prayerfully analyzed their usage.[6] I was amazed by what I found, especially in the New Testament!

You see, grace is more than "unmerited favor" (although unmerited favor is nothing to snivel at). It is more than God's Riches At Christ's Expense, although that acronym sums up everything we will ever have or experience in God. God's grace is more than a noun or a concept, more than the manner in which God deals with us (as in, "I'm saved by grace, and everything I do is by grace"). It's more than that.

Grace is His merciful, enabling help, His ongoing empowerment, His continued working on our behalf. It speaks of the Lord's past, present, and future action, expressing what Jesus *does* for us and not just what He *did* for us. As expressed by A. M. Hunter, "Grace means primarily the free, forgiving love of God in Christ to sinners and the operation of that love in the lives of Christians."[7]

Let's take a closer look at grace. Are you ready to do some study?

We'll begin with verses where grace (in Greek, *charis*, rhyming with "Paris") does mean unmerited favor. Here are some clear examples:

"We believe it is through the grace of our Lord Jesus that we are saved, just as they are" (Acts 15:11). In context, salvation by grace is being contrasted here with salvation by works.

"I do not set aside the grace of God, for if righteousness could be gained through the law, Christ died for nothing!" (Gal. 2:21).

"The promise comes by faith, so that it may be by grace" (Rom. 4:16). In each of these verses, you could substitute "unmerited favor" for "grace" and the meaning would be the same. So we can see that we're on solid footing here.

It was this emphasis on grace that became a foundation of the gospel message (see John 1:17, "For the law was given through

Moses; grace and truth came through Jesus Christ"), and so the message became known as the gospel of grace.

> So Paul and Barnabas spent considerable time there, speaking boldly for the Lord, who confirmed the message of His grace by enabling them to do miraculous signs and wonders (Acts 14:3).

> However, I consider my life worth nothing to me, if only I may finish the race and complete the task the Lord Jesus has given me—the task of testifying to the gospel of God's grace (Acts 20:24; see also v. 32).

How glorious is this gospel of grace! As filthy as we were, as undeserving as we were, as damnable and ungrateful as we were, Jesus died for us. The Father set His love on us—even though we were rank rebels—and adopted us as His very own sons and daughters, actually making us *joint heirs* of the universe with His Son. Hallelujah! This is the most wonderful news a mortal ear could ever hear, and it expresses a goodness beyond human comprehension. We had huge, eternal debts that were damning our souls. Jesus, who owed us nothing, paid them all! That's why Paul could write that we "are justified freely by His grace" (Rom. 3:24). God can pronounce us "not guilty" because of what His own Son did.

But here is the surprising news: The New Testament word "grace" does *not* fundamentally mean "unmerited favor." Its basic meaning does include favor (of any kind) along with kindness, but it also includes enablement and gifting, important concepts we often miss.[8]

You see, God's grace not only did something amazing for us—forgiving us all our sins—but His grace *continues to do* something amazing for us: empowering us to live for Him.[9] In fact, there was nothing revolutionary in the New Testament concept of grace meaning "favor" or "gift." What was revolutionary was the degree of favor shown to us through the Cross and the ongoing effectiveness of that favor in our lives. Grace finishes what it starts.

Why is this so important to understand? Because many believers know that God saved them by His grace and that He continues to deal with them based on His grace, but they don't know that His grace is *presently at work* in them. It's one thing to say, "All that I do, I do by the grace of God," meaning I don't deserve any credit or honor (which is true). It's another thing to say, "The grace of God worked mightily in me," meaning I was supernaturally helped by God to do His work. Do you see the difference?

I AM ENABLED TO DO HIS WILL BECAUSE HE HIMSELF IS AT WORK IN ME.

It's one thing to say, "I come to God through His grace," meaning I have access to God through the blood of His Son (amen to that!). It's another thing to say, "I serve God daily through His grace," meaning I am enabled to do His will because He Himself is at work in me. There's a distinction here.

One believer says, "I'm not under the law, I'm under grace" (see Rom. 6:14), taking it (wrongly) to mean, "God understands my sins and doesn't condemn me for them. He receives me just the same regardless of how I live."

Another believer says, "I'm not under the law, I'm under grace," taking it (correctly) to mean, "Through grace, I'm not only forgiven for my sins but I can now live above sin. Whereas the law could only point out my shortcomings, God's grace can transform my nature." That is the power of grace![10]

Let's look again at the Scriptures. In fact, let me give you a biblical statistic: Of the 155 times that the word *charis* occurs in the New

Testament, less than half of the occurrences refer to "unmerited favor." So let's dig a little deeper in our study. We'll use the substitution principle we learned before, this time playing "Fill in the Greek." I'll give you a verse with the Greek word *charis* left untranslated, and you fill in the proper meaning:

1. "And the child [Jesus] grew and became strong; He was filled with wisdom, and the *charis* of God was upon Him" (Luke 2:40).

What does *charis* mean here? Simply "favor" (*NRSV*), in this case merited. The Father was pleased with the Son and showed Him special favor, and it is in this sense of "special favor" that we also use the word today (as in, "God really gave us grace with those people. They received us with open arms!")[11] So, sometimes *charis* simply means "favor," and that is part of what Paul had in mind when he invoked "grace and peace" on his congregations (e.g., see Rom. 1:7). He was saying: "May the favor of the Lord be yours!"[12]

2. "Now Stephen, a man full of God's *charis* and power, did great wonders and miraculous signs among the people" (Acts 6:8).

It's obvious that *charis* does not mean "unmerited favor" here. Not at all. Rather, it means "divine ability, enabling, gifting" and in this sense it is used throughout the New Testament.[13] Here are a few examples among many. According to Romans 1:5, Paul received *charis* (divine enabling) and apostleship through Jesus, and he writes to the Romans by the *charis* (ability, enabling) given to him (see Rom. 12:3), telling them that they have different gifts (*charismata*) according to the *charis* (ability, enabling) given to them (see Rom. 12:6).[14] So, grace sometimes refers to God's enablement and empowering (the gifts of the Spirit are His supernatural enablings), and this concept is sometimes tied in directly with the concept of favor: "With great power the apostles continued to testify to the resurrection of the Lord Jesus, and much *charis* [favor, empowerment] was upon them all" (Acts 4:33). Are you still with me? Good. Let's keep going.

3. "Let your conversation be always full of *charis*, seasoned with salt, so that you may know how to answer everyone" (Col. 4:6).

What does *charis* mean here? Simply "kindness," in the same sense that we would use the word "gracious." ("Be gracious to her. Show her a little kindness. She's a brand-new believer and she's got a lot to learn.") The thought that it could mean "unmerited favor" here is completely out of the question. Just try to fill in the blank with that phrase: "Let your conversation be always full of unmerited favor, seasoned with salt . . . ." It doesn't work!

Now, let's look at a longer passage. For the most part it has nothing to do with salvation from sin but it uses the word *charis* frequently. We'll read the first four verses to get the context:

4. "And now, brothers, we want you to know about the *charis* that God has given the Macedonian churches. Out of the most severe trial, their overflowing joy and their extreme poverty welled up in rich generosity. For I testify that they gave as much as they were able, and even beyond their ability. Entirely on their own, they urgently pleaded with us for the privilege of sharing in this service to the saints" (2 Cor. 8:1-4).

Paul is talking about the gracious, supernatural help (*charis*) that God gave to the churches in Macedonia, enabling them to give with great generosity in the midst of their poverty. And so he challenged the Corinthians to complete "this act of *charis*" (2 Cor. 8:6), urging them to "excel in this *charis* of giving" (v. 7), remembering the *charis* of Jesus, who gave up everything He had so that we could become rich through Him (see v. 9). And there's a promise attached to this sacrificial generosity too:

> God is able to make all *charis* abound to you, so that in all things at all times, having all that you need, you will abound in every good work (2 Cor. 9:8).

"Yes," Paul was saying, "God has given you Corinthians 'surpassing' *charis*" (v. 14). Do you see how rich this is?[15]

Of course, I realize that I've given you a lot to chew on. But a couple of things should be getting clear by now. First, many times the word *charis* does not mean "unmerited favor." Second, *charis* often refers to God's gracious help, to His merciful and powerful action on our behalf, to His enabling. That's why the Lord could say to Paul, "My *charis* is sufficient for you, for My power is made perfect in weakness" (2 Cor. 12:9). The Lord was saying to Paul, "If I am working in you, helping you, sustaining you, and showing you My favor, what more do you need? My grace is enough!"

With this foundation, it's time to make some practical application. If we had to sum up what we have learned so far, we could say this: God's *charis* is His *gracious help* on our behalf. With regard to our salvation, it refers to His helping the helpless (= unmerited favor). With regard to our walk with Him, it refers to His helping the helped (= favor and empowerment). Do you follow?

Let's consider these verses:

- "You then, my son, be strong in the *charis* that is in Christ Jesus" (2 Tim. 2:1). Timothy, be strong in the empowering of God!
- "Or do you think Scripture says without reason that the Spirit He caused to live in us envies intensely? But He gives us more *charis*. That is why Scripture says: 'God opposes the proud but gives *charis* to the humble'" (Jas. 4:5,6).

God gives grace—meaning help, empowerment, aid—to the humble. All of us need more!

- "Each one should use whatever gift [*charisma*] he has received to serve others, faithfully administering God's *charis* in its various forms" (1 Pet. 4:10). We are given divine gifts by the Spirit, and we must use this enabling well.

- "When [Barnabas] arrived and saw the evidence of the *charis* of God, he was glad and encouraged them all to remain true to the Lord with all their hearts" (Acts 11:23). Barnabas was glad to see the evidence of God's gracious activity in the hearts of these people, and so he encouraged them to continue in the faith. He could see "grace" at work in them!

Now, let's take our study one step further and apply it directly to the subject of salvation from sin. What exactly does God's grace do? Look carefully at Titus 2:11-14:

For the *charis* of God that brings salvation has appeared to all men. It teaches us to say "No" to ungodliness and worldly passions, and to live self-controlled, upright and godly lives in this present age, while we wait for the blessed hope—the glorious appearing of our great God and Savior, Jesus Christ, who gave Himself for us to redeem us from all wickedness and to purify for Himself a people that are His very own, eager to do what is good.

Notice what the text says: God's *charis* not only brings salvation, but it teaches us to say "No" to everything unholy and "Yes" to everything holy. This is in keeping with the Lord's purpose in dying for us: to redeem us from all wickedness and to purify for Himself a righteous and godly people. (Remember, Jesus is purifying a people for *Himself.* What kind of Bride does He want to marry?)

God's grace is comprehensive and complete. It saves and sanctifies, rescues and restores, transforming us from hell-bound sinners to holy-living saints. That's the grace of God! And just as it was the Lord's supernatural, infinite grace that saved us, it is His supernatural, infinite grace that *keeps* us. As I said before, it is an ocean of grace!

Look back and see how the Lord first began to deal with you. You were a hopeless slave to sin, a rejected wretch, a captive to the will of the flesh. "But because of his great love for us, God, who is rich in mercy, made us alive with Christ even when we were dead in transgressions—it is by *charis* you have been saved" (Eph. 2:4,5). Who can fathom God's grace?

But that is only the beginning. His grace is with us this very hour, helping us, keeping us, empowering us. That's why we can "approach the throne of *charis* with confidence, so that we may receive mercy and find *charis* to help us in our time of need" (Heb. 4:16).[16] What encouraging words! For His children, God's throne is a place of help, mercy, and favor, and at that throne, we find everything we need. Praise God for the stream of grace that flows from the throne of grace![17]

And yet there is more. We can also look ahead to future grace:

> And God raised us up with Christ and seated us with Him in the heavenly realms in Christ Jesus, in order that in the coming ages He might show the incomparable riches of His *charis*, expressed in His kindness to us in Christ Jesus (Eph. 2:6,7).

In light of this—who can imagine what it will be like?—Peter urges us to "set your hope fully on the *charis* to be given you when Jesus Christ is revealed" (1 Pet. 1:13). What a day that will be! Grace, more grace, and endless grace. That sums up our past, present, and future in Jesus. Do you realize what this means?

It means that we can rest confidently in the goodness of our God, knowing that the same blood that washed us in the beginning continues to wash us in this hour, and that the same grace that helped us in the past continues to help us in the present. God favored us by setting His love on us, and He favors us by keeping His love on us.

How were we saved? By grace through faith. How are we kept? By grace through faith. What is our eternal hope? Grace through faith. Revel in it, rejoice in it, delight in it, dive into it. The Lord is our strength, the Lord is our support, the Lord is our Sustainer, the Lord is our Savior. Yes, salvation is *of* the Lord, *through* the Lord, *by* the Lord, and *from* the Lord. From beginning to end, it's all grace.

But the Word doesn't stop there. There's more to be said, and again it is sobering. This wonderful concept can be abused. Remember when we looked at Romans 6 earlier? After Paul explained the meaning of grace in the fourth and fifth chapters of Romans, he asked, "What shall we say, then? Shall we go on sinning so that grace may increase?" (Rom. 6:1).[18] Absolutely not! God's grace separates us from sin. How could anyone think otherwise? Grace that doesn't make us holy is not worthy of the name.

And so Jude warns us strongly, "For certain men whose condemnation was written about long ago have secretly slipped in among you. They are godless men, who change the grace of our God into a license for immorality and deny Jesus Christ our only Sovereign and Lord" (Jude 4). Do you see the significance of this? Because a right understanding of grace means that salvation is *not* by works, "godless" men pervert the teaching of grace into a license for immorality and in so doing, deny the Lord Jesus.[19] This should tell us something about similar teaching today, even if it comes from godly men. This kind of teaching is dangerous, to say the least, and it leads to a denial of Jesus as the Lord of our lives.

And there is yet another strong warning about grace in the Scriptures: It can be missed!

Make every effort to live in peace with all men and to be holy; without holiness no one will see the Lord. See to it that no one misses the *charis* of God and that no bitter root grows up to cause trouble and defile many. See that no one is sexually immoral, or is godless like Esau, who for a single meal sold his inheritance rights as the oldest son. Afterward, as you know, when he wanted to inherit this blessing, he was rejected. He could bring about no change of mind, though he sought the blessing with tears (Heb. 12:14-17).[20]

New Testament commentator William Barclay hit the nail on the head when he wrote:

Grace is not only a gift; it is a grave responsibility. A man cannot go on living the life he lived before he met Jesus Christ. He must be clothed in a new purity and a new holiness and a new goodness. The door is open, but the door is not open to the sinner to come and remain a sinner, but for the sinner to come and become a saint.[21]

God's grace must be joined with a human response. When we heard the message of grace, we were required to believe. As Paul wrote, "Therefore, the promise comes by faith, so that it may be by grace" (Rom. 4:16).[22] Failure to believe would be damnable (e.g., see Acts 13:44-50).

The gospel message also comes with a call to repent (see Matt. 3:2; 4:17; Mark 6:12,13; Luke 5:31,32; 13:3; 15:7,10; 24:47; Acts 2:38; 3:19; 5:31; 11:18; 17:30; 20:21; 26:20; Heb. 6:1; 2 Pet. 3:9).[23]

"But how can sinners repent?" you ask. By grace! God gives them the power to turn from their sins.

"But isn't that salvation by works?" Of course not. Salvation by works says, "God will save me if I first become good," or "God will save me if I do enough good works to outweigh my bad works."

But salvation by grace through faith tells the sinner, "There's nothing you can possibly do to save yourself from God's judgment or make yourself acceptable to Him. Jesus is your only hope! Put your trust in Him, and turn from your sins by the power of His blood. He paid for all your misdeeds, dying for your sins, and He rose again to justify you. He'll forgive you, set you free, and change you. He'll make you a child of God and liberate you from slavery to Satan. Cry out for mercy now! Turn back and believe."

That's the gospel of grace!

But I tell you again: According to the Word, this grace can be missed. Let me give you an analogy. You're living in New York when you receive an urgent message that you must be in London within 24 hours. Obviously, you can't drive a car across the Atlantic Ocean (even if you could, it would take days) and no boat can sail there quickly enough. So, what can you do? You can get on a plane and be in London in plenty of time. The plane can do what you can't possibly do. It flies! It soars seven miles high at speeds of 600 miles per hour. It's breathtaking! But unless you get on the plane, it won't do you any good, and if you decide to jump off the plane in mid-flight, you're dead.

That's how it is with grace. Grace does what we can't possibly do. It frees us from sin! It pronounces us righteous! It soars, lifting us into the heavenlies, making us holy. But we have to cooperate with God's grace, believing and receiving empowerment to turn from our sins, and if we jump off in mid-flight, we're doomed.

You say, "But the way I was taught, if I can jump off, then it's not grace!"

May I respond candidly once again? You were taught incorrectly! Study every single verse dealing with grace in the Bible and find one that clearly supports your position. You can't. To the contrary, you'll find a verse like Hebrews 12:15, warning *believers* of the terrible consequences of scorning God's grace.

But the bottom line is this: If you really want to serve the Lord, you can rest secure in Him. Only a fool would jump off a jet in midair.

Only a fool would forfeit God's grace. Only a fool would throw the gift of eternal life and love into the face of the One who gave it.

As for me, I'm going to swim in the sea of grace as I long as I live, rejoicing in the unmerited kindness He has shown me, being refreshed daily by His favor and empowerment, and looking forward to that day when His grace will be fully revealed in me. Wow!

God's grace is His merciful help toward us, and His loving hand not only pulled us out of the pit, but it grasps us firmly every hour. Why not trust fully in the power of that grace until you see Him face-to-face, faultless and blameless on that day?

From first to last, it's all grace. You're saved by it. You're sustained by it. Now soar in it. His grace is sufficient for you.

CHAPTER THIRTEEN

HAVE YOU FORSAKEN YOUR FIRST LOVE ?

Show me a young convert, while his heart is warm, and the love of God glows out from his lips. What does he care for the world? Call up his attention to it, point him to its riches, its pleasures, or its honors, and try to engage him in their pursuit, and he loathes the thought. But let him now go into business, and do business on the principles of the world one year, and you no longer find the love of God glowing in his heart, and his religion has become the religion of conscience, dry, meager, uninfluential—anything but the glowing love of God, moving him to acts of benevolence. I appeal to every man in this house, and if my voice was loud enough I would appeal to every professor of religion in this city . . . . And if any one should say, "No, it is not so," I should regard it as proof that he never knew what it was to feel the glow of a convert's first love.

CHARLES FINNEY

*Surely they have but cold love to Jesus that do not
burn with desire to see the fair brow that was
crowned with thorns.*

ROBERT MURRAY M'CHEYNE

*One of the teachers of the law came and heard them
debating. Noticing that Jesus had given them a good
answer, he asked Him, "Of all the commandments,
which is the most important?"*
*"The most important one," answered Jesus, "is this:
'Hear, O Israel, the Lord our God, the Lord is one.
Love the Lord your God with all your heart and
with all your soul and with all your mind and with
all your strength.' The second is this: 'Love your
neighbor as yourself.' There is no commandment
greater than these."*

MARK 12:28-31

Nothing is more important than your relationship with the Lord. Nothing. Yet sin, in its very essence, is an assault on that relationship. That's why sin must be uprooted from your life. That's why sin's hold must be broken. That's why sin must be hated and rejected. Its goal is to steal the one thing that you cannot live without: intimate communion with God. Sin's goal is to separate you from your Savior. Don't let it succeed!

You can lose your friends and still be blessed. You can lose your possessions and still be rich. You can even lose your health and still be fruitful. But if you lose your relationship with Jesus, if you forfeit your communion with Him, all the friends, all the possessions, all the physical strength in the world won't buy you a moment's joy or true satisfaction. You will wither at the root! Soon, the leaves on your branches will dry up and die. Soon, your very branches will die. Soon enough, you will die. You have forsaken the Fountain of Life! And one day—God forbid it should come to this—when the winds of temptation blow, they will expose a house without foundations or a tree without roots. The house will fall with a crash, the tree topple with a sickening thud.

We were created to know and serve the Lord, to walk with Him, to love Him, to enjoy Him, to work for Him. But as a race, we have chosen instead to go our own way, looking to find satisfaction and fulfillment in money, achievements, food, sex, education, sports, music, arts, family, work, religion—the list is almost endless. But still there is a gaping hole in our spirits, a wound that cannot be healed, a heart cry that cannot be answered. Only God can fill it! Only God can mend it! Only God can answer it!

And so, in the infinite love of our Father, He sent His Son to seek and save us, giving His own life as the bridge that stretches across the gulf of our sins, making the way for us to come home to God. And we're almost all the way there! We have already been made His sons and daughters, we have already been grafted into the true Vine, we can already call the Creator of everything "Abba." Soon, we will leave the filth of this world and stand before our Maker, free forever, perfect for eternity, without blemish or spot through the coming ages. In Jesus, our destinies will be fulfilled. In Jesus, we will be complete—totally. The reality of it all feels so close I can practically reach out and touch it. It's nearer than we know!

But right now, we find ourselves locked into this world, and there's simply no way for us to fully escape its miserable condition. All of us struggle with more than enough hassles, problems, distractions, temptations, battles, and difficulties. That's just the way it is, like it or not, and the devil only leaves us alone until he can find a more opportune time to attack (see Luke 4:13; 1 Pet. 5:8,9). We won't get rid of him as long as we are in these bodies, and even though we can resist him and make him flee, sooner or later he'll be back. The war shows no signs of abating.

What then do we do? How then should we live? What should be our highest goal, our priority in life? The answer is simple: *We must pursue intimacy with the Lord.*

Knowing Him and walking with Him must be our highest goal, our number-one priority, the focus of our energy and attention.[1] All the ministry and all the spiritual activity and all the gifts and power cannot substitute for a solid relationship with God. In fact, ministry and "anointing" and service without intimacy is just so much performance or showmanship or religiosity or good works— if it doesn't flow from our heart for God. As Vance Havner said, "The primary qualification for a missionary is not love for souls, as we so often hear, but love for Christ."[2]

Everything we do—praying, studying, soul winning, discipling, worshiping, preaching, teaching, parenting, serving, giving—must flow out of our love for God. He is the Source, He is the Motivation, He is the Foundation.

Consider the Lord's rebuke of Ephesus in Revelation 2. Here was a congregation that excelled, a church that worked hard, a group of believers that hated false doctrine, an assembly that persevered. In many ways, they were a model church, rich in good works, attentive to the warnings of Paul, their spiritual father (see Acts 20:28-31; Rev. 2:2), and willing to endure hardship for Jesus' sake. And they did all this without growing weary. What more could the Lord want? The Ephesian believers certainly outclassed most of us.

"Yet," Jesus said to them, "I hold this against you: You have forsaken your first love. Remember the height from which you have fallen! Repent and do the things you did at first. If you do not repent, I will come to you and remove your lampstand from its place" (Rev. 2:4,5).[3] What a solemn warning!

Hard work was not enough. Sacrifice was not enough. Doctrinal purity was not enough. Fine pastoral oversight was not enough. Perseverance in the midst of suffering was not enough. This congregation had left its first love, and if it didn't repent—notice this is a corporate call—the Lord would actually remove it from its place. There would no longer be a church of Ephesus! *Do you see how important it is in the eyes of the Lord that we maintain our first love?*[4]

Just think:

It is possible for a church as a whole to backslide from intimacy and devotion to Jesus while working hard for Him and staying doctrinally and morally pure.

It is possible for individual believers to backslide from intimacy and devotion to Jesus while working hard for Him and staying doctrinally and morally pure.

The Lord speaks of our first love as a height—a glorious, wonderful height—from which we can fall. He calls us to return to that height![5]

We forsake—not "lose"—our first love, meaning that we leave that place of spiritual passion by the choices we make and the lifestyle we adopt. Our "first love" is not something that we accidentally misplace.[6]

The Lord calls us to repent of the sin of forsaking our first love, meaning that we can be restored to that place of spiritual passion by the choices we make and the lifestyle we adopt.

What then are those choices and what is that lifestyle? What must we do to be restored, to make that return, to regain our first love?

Jesus gives us the answer: "Repent"—meaning make an about-face—"and do the things you did at first" (Rev. 2:5). There are things we can do to restore the intimacy!

Have you ever read a Christian book on rekindling the spark of love in a failing marriage? In a book like this, you will not only be shown how to diagnose the nature of your marital problems, but you will also be given specific, practical steps that will help you to correct the problems.

For example, a book written to men might remind the husband about the early days of his relationship with his fiancée/wife. Back then, he used to call her several times a day, send her flowers once a week, take her on a special date every Saturday, be sensitive to her unspoken needs and desires, always put her first, leave her little love notes, and let her know how special she was. But all that was a long time ago—five children, three apartments, one house, four moves, six jobs, and about twenty pounds for him and forty pounds for her, to be exact! Things aren't quite the same anymore.

What then must this husband do? He needs to do the things he did at first. He must reignite the romance and make an effort to renew and deepen the relationship. He needs to set aside quality time with his wife and for his wife, making her happiness his number-one priority. He must let her know how important she still is to him and break away from his routine for her sake. He needs to love her again as his bride!

That's exactly what we need to do when our love for Jesus turns cold. We must renew our relationship with Him! How? We set aside blocks of quality time to meet with Him, pouring out our hearts to Him in prayer, sharing our innermost thoughts and burdens. We lift our voices to Him in worship and adoration, singing the songs and hymns that have been so precious to us through the years, expressing our love for Him with thanksgiving and praise. We saturate our minds and hearts with His Word, meditating on His truths, learning of Him, receiving from Him, growing in knowledge and grace. We think back to the awe and wonder of those early days, and we seek to recapture that sense of divine nearness. And whenever we feel prompted, we share our faith with those who don't know the Lord.

According to Matthew Henry, believers who have left their first love

> must return and do their first works. They must as it were begin again, go back step by step, till they come to the place where they took the first false step; they must endeavour to revive and recover their first zeal, tenderness, and seriousness, and must pray as earnestly, and watch as diligently as they did when they first set out in the ways of God.[7]

Then, over a period of time, as we do these things—not with a "time clock" mentality, not as a spiritual performance or out of religious habit, not to earn brownie points or somehow merit His favor, but rather because we love Him and long for Him and want to deepen our fellowship with Him—His Spirit will begin to flood our hearts, and before we know it, He will once again become the most precious One in our lives. He will become the reason for all we do, the center of our attention, the highest object of our affection. Then, all our good works—serving Him, sharing our faith, giving sacrificially—will become expressions of love, the overflow of hearts enamored with the Master.[8]

That's what it means to "do the things we did at first." That's what it means to return to the height from which we have fallen, to repent and return to our first love. God eagerly awaits our move back toward Him! He remembers what our relationship used to be like, and He expresses it in vivid terms as a mournful husband:

> The word of the Lord came to me: "Go and proclaim in the hearing of Jerusalem: 'I remember the devotion of your

youth, how as a bride you loved Me and followed Me through the desert, through a land not sown'" (Jer. 2:1,2).

And He expresses His longing toward us as a father, thinking back to the days of our infancy when we were totally dependent on Him. This is how God expressed His heart toward His people Israel:

When Israel was a child, I loved him, and out of Egypt I called My son. But the more I called Israel, the further they went from Me. They sacrificed to the Baals and they burned incense to images. It was I who taught Ephraim to walk, taking them by the arms; but they did not realize it was I who healed them. I led them with cords of human kindness, with ties of love; I lifted the yoke from their neck and bent down to feed them (Hos. 11:1-4).

But now they were far from Him! Yet the Lord continued to love them:

"How can I give you up, Ephraim? How can I hand you over, Israel? How can I treat you like Admah? How can I make you like Zeboiim? My heart is changed within Me; all My compassion is aroused . . . . Is not Ephraim My dear son, the child in whom I delight? Though I often speak against him, I still remember him. Therefore My heart yearns for him; I have great compassion for him," declares the Lord (Hos. 11:8; Jer. 31:20).

As He said through Jeremiah, "Turn back, O backturning children; I will heal your backslidings" (Jer. 3:22, my translation). That is the Word of the Lord!

On Monday, January 1, 1750, John Wesley made the following entry in his journal:

On several days this week I called upon many who had left their "first love," but they none of them justified themselves: One and all pleaded "Guilty before God." Therefore there is reason to hope that He will return, and will abundantly pardon.[9]

Yes, God will abundantly pardon. The Lord will receive you again, no questions asked.

Does anything hold you back? Does anything stop you from renewing your relationship with the Lord? He has promised to draw near to those who draw near to Him (see Jas. 4:8), and as John Bunyan quaintly put it, when we take a step toward God, He takes a step toward us—but His steps are larger than ours! Now is the time to pursue the Lord with all of our being.

It is in this pursuit that we become holy. As Oswald Chambers said, "Holiness is the characteristic of the man after God's own heart."[10] We were made for Him, and in Him we thrive. In fact, the ultimate factor that will keep us from sin is the nearness of the Lord in our lives. If God is near to us—and we are conscious of the fact—sin will be far from us. In this light, M. P. Horban could say, "True holiness is learning to enjoy friendship with God."[11]

That is the key to all our growth in grace, knowledge, obedience, and service. Everything flows out of knowing Him. In fact, *knowing God* is actually the essence of eternal life: "Now this is eternal life: that they may know You, the only true God, and Jesus Christ, whom You have sent" (John 17:3).

I think of the impassioned lyrics of Keith Green's song, "You Love the World and You're Avoiding Me," in which the Lord asks us, "If you end up losing Me, what will you do?" What *will* we do if we lose our closeness with the Lord? What is left for us in this world—or in eternity—if we leave the One we once loved?

If we know Him, we will serve Him. But if we try to serve Him without knowing Him, we insult the very purpose for which He created us and rob our service of its meaning. He did not make us to be robots or puppets but rather sons and daughters.

Yes, it is wonderfully true that forever we will serve the Lord and under His rule we will reign (see Rev. 22:3-5). But right in the middle of the passage that promises this, it is written:

> *They will see His face*, and His name will be on their foreheads. There will be no more night. They will not need the light of a lamp or the light of the sun, for the Lord God will give them light (Rev. 22:4,5).

He will be our all in all! He will be our portion. His face will be our light. As expressed so wonderfully by the saintly Robert Murray M'Cheyne:

> Christ Himself shall be the greatest reward of His people. . . . Any place would be heaven if we were with Christ. No place would be heaven without Him. . . . Oh, to talk with Him as Moses and Elijah did on the mount of transfiguration, to hear Him speak gracious words, to lean our head where John leaned his, to hold Him, and not to let Him go, to behold that countenance which is as Lebanon, excellent as the cedars, to have Him turning upon us His eyes of divine tenderness and holy love—that will be a reward.[12]

And so, everything we do in this world should ultimately be done in anticipation of that day when we will see Him face-to-face. That's really the purpose of it all. Do you live to see Him express approval to you when your eyes first meet? How glorious it will be to see Him smile!

There could be no higher joy possible and no greater satisfaction imaginable. In that indescribable moment—the moment to end all moments—all the pain, all the suffering, all the disappointment, all the hardship, all the labor, all the agony, all the questions will fade into oblivion—when we see the Savior's face. And that is what we must keep in mind every day of our lives: Soon we're going to meet the Lord in person, and we should be getting ready for that moment every hour that we breathe.

God Himself—not so much His reward, or His blessing, or His anointing, but the Lord Himself—must be our goal. Therefore, each of us must cultivate a relationship with Him. Each of us must settle in our hearts once and for all that anything of eternal good that we can do is birthed in Him, and anything truly good within us is birthed in Him.

So why are we spending so much of our time laboring and planning and running in our own strength and wisdom? Why aren't we communing more with Him in prayer and spending more time at His feet in worship and taking counsel with Him more through His Word? Why?

BECOMING LIKE HIM—THE ESSENCE OF HOLINESS—REQUIRES BEING WITH HIM AND COMING TO KNOW HIM.

And how can we even think about being holy without first knowing the Holy One? How can we have a measure or norm for holiness when we have forsaken the very Standard of holiness? And how can we receive strength to be holy when we have abandoned the Holy Spirit who empowers us? How can we even imagine that we can attain any kind of holiness without feeding on Him and learning from Him and becoming like Him? Becoming like Him—which is the essence of holiness—requires being with Him.

Tragically, we can have all the outward trappings of Christian zeal and service without having a vibrant relationship with the Lord. According to New Testament scholar Robert Mounce, "At Ephesus, hatred of heresy and extensive involvement in the works appropriate to faith had allowed the fresh glow of love to God and one another to fade."[13] In other words, "Every virtue carries within itself the seeds of its own destruction."[14]

So, it could be that our very zeal for truth and purity coupled with our penchant for hard work and sacrifice could rob us of our love, both for God and man. Charles Finney commented on this, explaining that even with a backslidden heart, a believer could remain active in Christian service.

For Finney, backsliding consisted in: (1) "taking back that consecration to God and His service, that constitutes true conversion"; (2) "the leaving, by a Christian, of his first love"; (3) "the Christian withdrawing himself from that state of entire and universal devotion to God, which constitutes true religion, and coming again under the control of a self-pleasing spirit."

Yet even in this state, Finney noted that

there may be a backslidden heart, when the forms of religion and obedience to God are maintained. As we know from consciousness that men perform the same, or similar, acts from widely different, and often from opposite, motives, we are certain that men may keep up all the outward forms and appearances of religion, when in fact, they are backslidden in heart. No doubt the most intense selfishness often takes on a religious type, and there are many considerations that might lead a backslider in heart to keep up the forms, while he had lost the power of godliness in his soul.[15]

Backsliding can be subtle, but its origins are always the same: Something has broken down in our relationship with the Lord. Somehow, our love has grown cold. Somehow, our devotion has waned.

"But," a troubled believers asks, "if I can seem to be on fire for God, keeping busy for the Lord and staying true to His Word, and yet be backsliding at the same time, how can I really know the state of my heart?"

Let me describe for you some symptoms of a backslidden heart, some tangible tests by which you can examine yourself. There's no reason to be in the dark when it comes to your own spiritual life. Here are some questions to ask yourself:

1. HAS MY *PERSONAL DEVOTION* TO JESUS DECREASED?

Perhaps your desire for intimate and private times with the Lord has waned, especially for prayer and worship, and your once-ravenous hunger and passion for the Word is now lacking. (According to John G. Lake, everyone who backslides first backslides in their lessening hunger for the Word, while Leonard Ravenhill often said that backsliding begins with backsliding in prayer.)

Remember, when you were hot, Jesus was everything! You couldn't wait to spend time with Him. Praising Him—even with the simplest little choruses—was pure joy. If there was a prayer meeting, you were there. You *devoured* the Word. You could relate to the words of Paul: "I consider everything a loss compared to the surpassing greatness of knowing Christ Jesus my Lord, for whose sake I have lost all things. I consider them rubbish, that I may gain Christ" (Phil. 3:8). But something happened. Something changed.

You spend time with the one you love. You share your heart with the one you love. You are jealous for the one you love. You think about the one you love. Do you love Jesus today as you once loved Him before?

You may enjoy the *forms* of worship—good music, singing, maybe dancing, being part of an exciting corporate experience—but what about the object of worship? What about the Lord? You may have a vision. You may be caught up in a movement. You may have a message or a burden. Theology may intrigue you. Spiritual issues may interest you. The ministry may consume you. But all these things are mere idols and distractions in comparison with coming into the light of God's presence and fellowshipping with Him. You only grow and bear fruit to the extent that you abide in the Vine (see John 15:1-9).

2. HAS MY *PERSONAL SATISFACTION* IN GOD DECREASED?

Do you feel the need for things other than God to gain fulfillment? Are you increasingly seeking social orientation in place of private devotions? Do you find that more and more you desire recognition and acceptance by persons of flesh and blood?

The Word says, "The desires for other things come in and choke the word, making it unfruitful" (Mark 4:19), and "If anyone loves the world, the love of the Father is not in him" (1 John 2:15). What do you desire? What brings you satisfaction? Do you love God, or do you love the world? "Remember those earlier days . . ." (Heb. 10:32-39).

At one time promotion on the job was not your primary source of satisfaction, nor was a big paycheck, a nice home, a new car, a special boyfriend or girlfriend, an exciting sports event, or even a happy family. (Yes! Even spouses and children can take away from your delighting in the Lord above all.) Walking with God used to satisfy you. Does it still satisfy you? Fully and completely? If not, you have left your first love.

M'Cheyne put it like this: "If ever you are so much engrossed with any enjoyment here that it takes away your love for prayer, or for your Bible, or that it would frighten you to hear the cry, 'Behold the bridegroom cometh'—then your heart is *'overcharged'* (Luke 21:34). You are abusing this world."[16]

3. HAS MY PASSION FOR *SPIRITUAL WORK* DECREASED?

This will be reflected by a decreased burden for the lost (both home and foreign "missions," both domesticated heathen and undomesticated heathen), a decreased burden for revival and visitation (often replaced by good works, and more subtly by good spiritual programs), and a penchant for *respectability* in place of *radicality*. "Unrefined" preaching of the gospel now embarrasses you. Holy zeal makes you uncomfortable and you are, slowly but surely, becoming ashamed of Jesus and His reproach.

How often do you share your testimony? You used to be a house on fire! You once sought out opportunities to talk about Jesus. Witnessing used to come naturally. But now, you almost avoid the subject. You simply don't care about the ones Jesus died for. You don't fully believe that they are lost. *Unbelief is always a result of backsliding somewhere, somehow.* Do you find yourself spiritually numb?

And what about revival and visitation? How would you feel if the Spirit fell in power? (Not necessarily in some "cultured"—and "containable"—way, but with intensity and suddenness and upheaval.) Are you willing to let *Him* be in control—of the service, of the leadership, of *you*? Are you hungry anymore for a real move of God? Or have you become satisfied with a comfortable seat in the theater while the show itself never goes on?[17]

Beware of a powerless spiritual sophistication. The world admires it, but it has no teeth.

4. HAVE MY *STANDARDS OF HOLINESS* BECOME LOWER?

Perhaps you have permitted things into your life, your family, or congregation that would have been unthinkable when you were on fire. You now find you are able to engage in certain activities, watch certain movies, enjoy certain sports and forms of entertainment, attend certain functions, etc., which the Lord at one time convicted you of—but now there is no conviction!

Beware! This type of backsliding is often done in the name of *spiritual maturity.* I warn you as one who once fell into this very error: It is a trap and a lie!

Absence of divine conviction does not mean absence of divine displeasure. It may actually point to a withdrawing of His presence. In fact, if the Holy Spirit is dealing with you even now, cry out to Him for restoring grace right where you are. Do not harden your heart against your Lord, your King, and your Friend. It is spiritual suicide. The fact that something doesn't "bother you" may be the loudest warning you will ever hear.

Can you sin freely without feeling grief? Then fall on your face and cry for mercy before it's too late. Otherwise you might disqualify yourself from receiving the prize. Do not be deceived: You are not experiencing the freedom that comes as a result of trust; you are experiencing the insensitivity that comes from hardness.

Have you actually deceived yourself by giving yourself a license to sin in the name of "liberty"? Have you despised the precious closeness you once enjoyed with Jesus by calling it "legalism"? Run back into His presence—with all the discipline and devotion that demands—while His arms are still open wide. Where godly sorrow is found, abundant grace is also found.

5. AM I BACKSLIDING IN *SPIRITUAL AUTHORITY* AND *PERSONAL VICTORY*?

Perhaps you are experiencing a lack of victory over the flesh, falling back into old habits and lusts, finding yourself unable to resist and drive out the devil from strongholds in your life or the lives of those to whom you minister.

Remember: You can fool others, but you can't fool the flesh— and you can't fool the devil. As Ravenhill often asked, "Are you known in hell?"[18]

Are you moving from victory to victory, or do you find yourself more and more entangled every day (or month, or year)? Peter taught that "a man is a slave to whatever has mastered him" (2 Pet. 2:19). You must ask yourself if Jesus is your Master, or if you are mastered by sin. Are you an overcomer or are you overcome? Is Jesus your Lord, or are you ruled by your belly, or your sexual lust, or your temper, or your greed, or your bitterness? Who, or what, governs you?

You once *chased* the devil; now you tremble at his shadow. You once cast off fear like a dog shakes off water; now you are paralyzed by anxiety and dread. You once forgave from the heart *instantly*; now you remember and hold a grudge. My friend, you are backsliding!

You once made effective inroads into the devil's kingdom. Now he's making inroads into you. What has become of your victory? You are backsliding from the place of spiritual authority! How tragic that Satan has paralyzed you, be it with theological questions, or with fear of failure, or with massive self-doubt. Press back in to Jesus! He is as victorious today as He ever has been! He will restore your faith.

I will never forget the words spoken one night by the pastor of the church in which I was saved. He said, "It may take a man twenty years to backslide" (referring to a complete apostasy from the Lord). This is a sobering thought. You grow old gradually. Your hair turns gray gradually. You can backslide just as gradually. Before you know it, you have wasted your whole life.

In which direction are you heading? Where is the present course and pattern of your life taking you? If you continued forever on the same path you have been on—be it of progress or regress— would you wind up in heaven or in hell? Are you moving toward the Lord or away from Him?

Again I ask you: Are you backsliding in your spiritual authority and personal victory? What makes you think that things will be better tomorrow? It will be only downhill from here, unless you humble yourself and turn back.

Let me share with you a little more from my own life experience. At one time in my walk—in the late 1970s and early 1980s—I began to backslide, but all the while I claimed to be growing and maturing. My prayer times decreased, and my devotional reading of the Word decreased (although my *linguistic* reading of the Scriptures may have increased). My fasting all but stopped; my witnessing dropped off. I became more interested in social action than in spiritual action. I had less and less control over the flesh. I virtually *never* took authority over the devil. (I really couldn't have done much anyway!)

I fell in areas that I had never fallen in before. Don't get me wrong. I never touched another woman or misused ministry funds or stole anything or even had a fleeting thought about going back to drugs or drinking, but still, I slipped up a few times in ways I never had before, and even though these slips were many months or more than a year apart, they scared me. I even became addicted to video games!

I felt the presence and joy of the Lord less frequently and less abundantly, yet all the while, I was an active leader in the church. I taught the Word with conviction, I preached with fervor (and even some anointing), I ministered actively, I remained an absolutely committed believer in Jesus my Messiah and Lord, I sought to keep a pure testimony before the world. I was considered by many to be zealous, and I was engaged in many good and even sacrificial works—yet I was backsliding!

I will be eternally grateful to my sister-in-law who, without my knowledge—in fact, if I had known, it would have been without my approval!—helped to pray me back on fire. How I praise God for His miraculous intervention, planting the first seeds on New Year's Day morning 1982, then lovingly rebuking me in March of that year, awakening me with a vision of a spiritual outpouring in May, showing me how far away I was drifting in September, calling me to lay everything on the altar in October, and then sending a visitation November 21, 1982. I have never been the same since.

I encourage you in the words of Psalms and Hebrews, today, if *you* hear His voice, do not harden your heart (see Ps. 95:7,8; Heb. 4:7).

Respond fully to the Lord today. Pour out your heart to Him. Pray through. Allow His Spirit to move freely. Don't be ashamed! He can—and will—fully restore. Obey whatever He speaks to you. Set a new pattern for your life beginning now. And then, every day, whenever you can, take another step closer to the Lord, one step at a time. Don't let the devil set you up for a fall by lying to you about what God requires.

Pray more and with more focus and direction, read His Word more, speak His Word more, share your faith more. Listen to tapes, watch videos, and read books that will help keep the fire burning.

Keep your conscience clear. If you know something is displeasing in God's sight, don't do it. Be sensitive. He understands your weakness, and He will give sufficient grace. But He will not put up with determined and willful hardness. Bow your knee to the Lord, and He will lift you up. Your future can be just as bright as the promises of God.

It's time to rekindle the flame!

CHAPTER FOURTEEN

BE HOLY

As obedient children, do not conform to the
evil desires you had when you lived in ignorance.
But just as He who called you is holy, so be holy in
all you do; for it is written: "Be holy, because I am
holy." Since you call on a Father who judges each man's
work impartially, live your lives as strangers here
in reverent fear. For you know that it was not with
perishable things such as silver or gold that you
were redeemed from the empty way of life handed
down to you from your forefathers, but with the
precious blood of Christ, a lamb without
blemish or defect.

1 PETER 1:14-19

God would not rub so hard if it were not to fetch
out the dirt that is ingrained in our natures. God
loves purity so well He had rather see a hole than a
spot in His child's garments.

WILLIAM GURNALL

*Our fathers disciplined us for a little while
as they thought best; but God disciplines us for our
good, that we may share in His holiness.*

HEBREWS 12:10

*Conspicuous holiness ought to be the mark
of the church of God. A holy church has God
in the midst of her.*

CHARLES H. SPURGEON

*Be merciful to those who doubt; snatch others
from the fire and save them; to others show mercy,
mixed with fear—hating even the clothing
stained by corrupted flesh.*

JUDE 22,23

Solomon's Temple in Jerusalem was the holiest site on earth, the only place in the world officially designated by God as His house of worship. It was built according to specific instructions, just as the Tabernacle of Moses was (see Exod. 25:9,40; 1 Chron. 29:11-19). Only then would it be acceptable to the Lord. All the materials, all the workmanship, all the details had to follow the divinely given pattern. Then—and only then—would God visit His people there. Then—and only then—would He pay attention to the prayers and sacrifices offered in that place. In light of this, it's no surprise that it took seven years to build the Temple of the Lord (see 1 Kings 6:38).

When it was time to dedicate this divine sanctuary, the Lord made Himself at home, giving a supernatural sign of approval by sending His fire to consume the sacrifices and His glory to fill the building (see 2 Chron. 7:1-3). This was the house of the Lord! Every inch of it was sacred, set aside for divine service. Every inch of it was holy. And it was to this holy place that the people of Israel came flocking from afar. There was no place on earth like the Temple of the Lord! What majesty, what splendor, what grandeur. This was sacred ground. But soon it would be defiled!

Within a few years, Solomon, the great Temple builder, was worshiping idols. Some 400 years later, the Temple had been defiled and cleansed, defiled and cleansed, and defiled once more. By the time of King Josiah, it was teetering on the verge of divine judgment. This is how far things had fallen:

> The king [Josiah] ordered Hilkiah the high priest, the priests next in rank and the doorkeepers to remove from the temple of the Lord all the articles made for Baal and Asherah and all the starry hosts. He burned them outside Jerusalem in the fields of the Kidron Valley and took the ashes to Bethel. He did away with the pagan priests appointed by the kings of Judah to burn incense on the high places of the towns of Judah and on those around

Jerusalem—those who burned incense to Baal, to the sun
and moon, to the constellations and to all the starry hosts.
He took the Asherah pole from the temple of the Lord to
the Kidron Valley outside Jerusalem and burned it there.
He ground it to powder and scattered the dust over the
graves of the common people. He also tore down the quarters
of the male shrine prostitutes, which were in the temple of
the Lord and where women did weaving for Asherah
(2 Kings 23:4-7).

How the holy Temple had become desecrated! The despicable
filth had to be purged. All the idolatrous articles had to be
destroyed; all the immoral temple personnel had to go; all the
polluted vessels had to be removed.

And so Josiah vigorously and aggressively went about demol-
ishing and destroying every abominable thing that had made its
way into the Temple, carrying out his purge through the whole
country. He burned the bones of the deceased pagan priests; he
ground every idol to powder; he pulverized the unauthorized altars.
"Josiah smashed the sacred stones and cut down the Asherah poles
and covered the sites with human bones" (2 Kings 23:14).

Housecleaning time had come, and Josiah cleaned up God's
house with a vengeance, hating every destructive remnant that sin
had left. Every trace of pollution had to be removed from the
sanctuary of the Lord. How could it be otherwise?

Male prostitutes in the Temple? Women weaving for Asherah
in the Temple? Articles made for Baal in the Temple? What an
abomination! What a perversion! What a tragedy! Honestly, now,
how do you feel when you read scriptures like these? Shocked and
outraged?

But there is something more shocking and outrageous than the
Temple in Jerusalem being polluted. According to the New
Testament, we are now the temple of the Lord, the house in which
the Spirit of God dwells, yet we allow ourselves to be polluted and

defiled. We allow unclean thoughts to dominate our minds; we allow sinful acts to contaminate our bodies; we allow impure words to proceed from our lips; we allow evil deeds to proceed from our hands. How can this be? *We* are now God's holy temple, His dwelling place of choice. You and I are now the earthly sanctuary in which the Spirit dwells!

Speaking of the corporate Church, Paul wrote:

Don't you know that you yourselves are God's temple and that God's Spirit lives in you? If anyone destroys God's temple, God will destroy him; for God's temple is sacred, and you are that temple (1 Cor. 3:16,17).

Yes, in Jesus, "the whole building is joined together and rises to become a holy temple in the Lord. And in Him you too are being built together to become a dwelling in which God lives by His Spirit" (Eph. 2:21,22).[1] The Lord takes this very seriously!

But it gets even more serious than this. Each of us *individually* are holy temples of the Lord. *God dwells in each of us!*

Do you not know that your bodies are members of Christ Himself? . . . Do you not know that your body is a temple of the Holy Spirit, who is in you, whom you have received from God? You are not your own; you were bought at a price. Therefore honor God with your body (1 Cor. 6:15,19,20).

Our bodies—meaning we ourselves—are members of Christ Himself, temples of the Holy Spirit, purchased at the high price of the blood of the Son of God.

Dare we take this lightly? Dare we pollute our bodies with sin? Dare we join Jesus to something unclean and defiling? "Do you not know that your bodies are members of Christ Himself? Shall I then take the members of Christ and unite them with a prostitute? Never!"

(1 Cor. 6:15). God's temple must not be defiled. The members of Messiah's Body must not be merged with the corruption of the world. Perish the thought!

Just think of how violently the Son of God purged the Temple in Jerusalem when He was on the earth:

> In the temple courts He found men selling cattle, sheep and doves, and others sitting at tables exchanging money. So He made a whip out of cords, and drove all from the temple area, both sheep and cattle; He scattered the coins of the money changers and overturned their tables. To those who sold doves He said, "Get these out of here! How dare you turn My Father's house into a market!" (John 2:14-16).

> And as He taught them, He said, "Is it not written: 'My house will be called a house of prayer for all nations'? But you have made it 'a den of robbers'" (Mark 11:17).

Yet this was just an earthly, man-made temple which cost God nothing to inhabit. Dwelling within *us* cost God the death of His own Son. This is quite a heavy thought! How jealous do you think the Lord is over His temple today?

Of course, you could always throw up your hands and say, "Really now, what's the use? After all, I fall so far short of the mark. The moment I think that I'm really doing well, I'm convicted of my pride and self-righteousness. The moment I think I'm covering all my bases—being as free from sins of commission as I know how to be—I realize how many sins of *omission* I'm overlooking! There's probably not a day that goes by in which I don't fail to love the Lord—at the least for a moment—with all of my being and to love my neighbor as myself. And that's on the best of my days. So why bother trying to attain to some high and lofty level of holiness? I'll never make it."

Thank God those are not *His* words! You see, the Lord is well aware of everything you're going through, and more than anyone else, He knows just how many times you and I blow it. For every sin of omission we see, He sees hundreds. For every sin of commission we resist, He sees others we do commit—some even unknowingly. And yet He is the one who calls us to holiness. He is the one who *commands* us to be holy. His focus is not on our frailty but rather on our devotion, our consecration, our exposing and expelling every known area of sin and pollution in our lives.

With full knowledge of who He is dealing with, He calls us to:

- Present our bodies as living sacrifices on His altar, holy and acceptable to Him (see Rom. 12:1).
- Purify ourselves from everything that contaminates body and spirit, perfecting holiness out of reverence for Him (see 2 Cor. 7:1).
- Be sanctified by avoiding sexual immorality and learning to control our own bodies in a way that is holy and honorable, not in passionate lust like the heathen, who do not know God (see 1 Thess. 4:3-5).
- Die to sins and live for righteousness (see 1 Pet. 2:24).
- Be kept blameless, through and through, body, soul, and spirit, until the coming of our Lord Jesus Christ (see 1 Thess. 5:23).

This is good news! Our Creator and Redeemer calls us to holiness, and therefore we can be holy. This is His clearly expressed will, and the closer we get to the Lord's return, the stronger the calling will be:

But the day of the Lord will come like a thief. The heavens will disappear with a roar; the elements will be destroyed by fire, and the earth and everything in it will be laid bare. Since everything will be destroyed in this way, what kind of people ought you to be? You ought to live holy and godly lives as you look forward to the day of God and speed its coming (2 Pet. 3:10-12).

There we have it in clear, definite terms: *We ought to live holy and godly lives.*

༈

How then do we deal with sin in our bodies—the holy temple of the Lord? We present ourselves to Him every day of our lives, completely and without reserve, offering each part of our bodies to our Master and Savior, and we hold nothing back from Him. We receive cleansing for all impurity, and we purpose in our hearts to keep all pollution far from us.

During my first few years in the Lord, I did this in a specific way at the end of my prayer time every night. It went something like this:

"Lord, my mind is Yours. May I not think any thoughts that are displeasing in Your sight but only that which glorifies You.

"My eyes are Yours. May they not look at anything forbidden or unclean.

"My ears are Yours. May they not hear gossip or anything unseemly.

"My mouth is Yours. May I not speak anything unwholesome or injurious but only that which is good.

"My hands are Yours. May I only touch that which is acceptable, right, and profitable.

"My heart is Yours. May it never get caught up in this world but rather in You.

"My feet are Yours. May I only go to the places to which You send me.

"Every part of my body is Yours, Lord. May I not use it for sinful gratification but rather for holiness."

Oh, how beautiful it is to be fully devoted to the Lord! How wonderful and wholesome and pure and healthy. To be His—spirit, soul, and body—is to really live. To play with sin is to die.

Let me give you something else to consider. Think about the ultimate consequences of taking either sin or righteousness to their logical conclusions. For example, a bad attitude, if allowed to develop and grow completely unchecked, will eventually lead to hatred, then violence, then murder. Sexual immorality, if unchecked and allowed to extend itself, will move from normal sexual acts to abnormal acts like homosexuality, child molestation, and even bestiality. What's to stop sin from festering if it's taken to its logical conclusion without restraint or limit?

But righteousness, taken to its ultimate end, produces righteousness; love produces love; truth produces truth. There is no downward spiral here, only infinite progress. We go from light to more light, while the wicked stumble in ever-increasing darkness. And that's how our lives should be: "The path of the righteous is like the first gleam of dawn, shining ever brighter till the full light of day. But the way of the wicked is like deep darkness; they do not know what makes them stumble" (Prov. 4:18,19).

Now stop for a moment and take it all in: Through Jesus, you have been made a temple of the Most High God, and He lives in you by His Spirit. "Be holy," He says. "Keep the temple clean. Keep the pollutants out." What a high and blessed calling, what a privilege, what an honor, what a joy. And what a responsibility! We are called to worship Him "acceptably with reverence and awe, for our 'God is a consuming fire' " (Heb. 12:28,29). This is serious business. This is sacred stuff.

But remember, we're not in it alone. The Spirit empowers us, the blood of Jesus washes us, the Word of God guides us, the grace of the Lord enables us, the Father helps and keeps us. You can be holy, my friend. You can live a godly life. You can shine. Only don't lose your sensitivity for the Lord, and don't lose your hatred for sin.

When David was convicted by God for his adultery and murder, he made a sweeping confession to his offended King, asking for total cleansing. Just look at how he prayed:

Have mercy on me ... blot out my transgressions .... Wash away all my iniquity and cleanse me from my sin .... Cleanse me ... wash me ... Hide Your face from my sins and blot out all my iniquity. Create in me a pure heart, O God, and renew a steadfast spirit within me .... Save me from bloodguilt, O God" (from Psalm 51).[2]

David left no stone unturned. He wanted everything unclean to go.

On a personal prayer retreat in July of 1998, I poured out my heart in similar terms to the Lord (although, thankfully, I wasn't repenting for adultery or murder). "God," I cried out, "wash me, scrub me, cleanse me, prune me, purge me, refine me, purify me! Make me—literally—as white as snow within. Let even the memory of sin be obliterated!"

WE CAN WALK IN SUCH A WAY THAT THE LORD HIMSELF CALLS US WORTHY. AND IT'S HIS DEFINITION—NOT MINE OR YOURS— THAT MATTERS.

There is nothing like being clean. As the Puritan John Flavel said, "What health is to the heart, that holiness is to the soul."[3]

Maybe you need to make a comprehensive confession to the Lord (or if you sinned in a serious way against someone else, you need to confess to that person too, making restitution where necessary). Maybe you need to get alone with Him and put the past behind you, once and for all. Charles Finney even advocated making a list of every sin you could remember committing in specific areas of your life—you'll need a lot of paper to do this!—renouncing each and every one of these sins before the Lord: "Never again, Father! I'm Your holy vessel, set apart for Your service alone. By Your grace, I will no longer defile myself or sin against You in these ways."[4]

But won't we still fall short for the rest of our lives, no matter what we declare or determine to do today? Well, if we define sin as J. C. Ryle defined it—"The slightest outward or inward departure from absolute mathematical parallelism with God's revealed will and character constitutes a sin, and at once makes us guilty in God's sight"[5]—then the answer is, yes, of course, we will always fall short.

But the fact is that we can make a definite, lifelong break with the enslavement of sin. We can live in sustained victory over fleshly lusts and desires, and we can walk in such a way that *the Lord Himself* calls us worthy. And it's His definition—not mine or yours—that matters.

Do you remember what Jesus said to the church of Sardis? "Yet you have a few people in Sardis who have not soiled their clothes. They will walk with Me, dressed in white, *for they are worthy*" (Rev. 3:4). This, too, is our calling, and this, too, is our potential. Paul often wrote about this to the congregations he fathered:

As a prisoner for the Lord, then, I urge you to live a life worthy of the calling you have received. Be completely humble and gentle; be patient, bearing with one another in love (Eph. 4:1,2).

Whatever happens, conduct yourselves in a manner worthy of the gospel of Christ (Phil. 1:27).

And we pray this in order that you may live a life worthy of the Lord and may please Him in every way (Col. 1:10).

For you know that we dealt with each of you as a father deals with his own children, encouraging, comforting and urging you to live lives worthy of God, who calls you into His kingdom and glory (1 Thess. 2:11,12).

With this in mind, we constantly pray for you, that our God may count you worthy of His calling, and that by His power

He may fulfill every good purpose of yours and every act prompted by your faith (2 Thess. 1:11).

As Spurgeon quaintly put it, "Our lives must be such that people may peep in doors and may see nothing for which to blame us."[6] That is living worthy of the Lord!

We are called to please Him in every way, and our love for Him should be the greatest incentive of all. Realize that "there is nothing destroyed by sanctification but that which would destroy us."[7] Everything holy is good; nothing unholy is good. Everything unholy is bad; nothing holy is bad. So let us pursue holiness with all of our hearts!

When Jesus returns, we will become like Him, for we will see Him as He is (see 1 John 3:2). How then should we live today?

> And now, dear children, continue in Him, so that when He appears we may be confident and unashamed before Him at His coming.
>
> How great is the love the Father has lavished on us, that we should be called children of God! And that is what we are! The reason the world does not know us is that it did not know Him. Dear friends, now we are children of God, and what we will be has not yet been made known. But we know that when He appears, we shall be like Him, for we shall see Him as He is.
>
> Everyone who has this hope in Him purifies himself, just as He is pure (1 John 2:28; 3:1-3).

That is the goal we strive for: to purify ourselves just as Jesus is pure. That's why we fill our minds with thoughts of "whatever is true, whatever is noble, whatever is right, whatever is pure, whatever is lovely, whatever is admirable [or] excellent or praiseworthy" (Phil. 4:8).

That's why we fill our hearts with "psalms, hymns and spiritual songs with gratitude" toward God (Col. 3:16). That's why we "clothe [ourselves] with the Lord Jesus Christ, and do not think about how to gratify the desires of the sinful nature" (Rom. 13:14). We are, after all, His holy temple. We are the earthly sanctuary which He inhabits, His representatives here in this world. How else can we possibly live?

It is God Himself who calls us to holiness, and He does it *because* He is holy. We cannot possibly coexist with Him without holiness. We cannot fulfill the purpose for which He created us without holiness. We cannot possibly be vessels used in His service without holiness. We cannot live truly blessed lives without holiness.

To be holy is to be like the Lord, in thought, word, and deed; in character, attitude, and action; in intellect, emotions, and will; in all that we are and all that we do. That is our wonderful calling!

Yes, the One who calls us is holy, the One "who alone is immortal and who lives in unapproachable light, whom no one has seen or can see" (1 Tim. 6:16). He is the very definition and description of holiness, the only source and the final destiny of holiness, the radiant One, the perfect One, the faultless One, the majestic One, the glorious One, the compassionate One, the gracious One, the just One, the God and Father of our Lord Jesus, the Giver of the Holy Spirit. And this is the One who calls us to be holy—because of His own holiness and in light of His own holiness.

Robert Murray M'Cheyne, known to his contemporaries as "Holy" M'Cheyne, thought long and hard on these themes. He even made this sobering statement:

> For we must all appear before the judgment seat of Christ; that every one may receive the things done in his body, according to that he hath done, whether it be good or bad (see 2 Cor. 5:10).
>
> Every man shall be rewarded according as his work has been. Some will be made rulers over five, some over ten cities. I have no doubt that every sin, inconsistency, backsliding and decay of God's children takes away something from their eternal glory. It is a loss for all eternity; and the

more fully and unreservedly we follow the Lord Jesus now, the more abundant will our entrance be into His everlasting kingdom. The closer we walk with Christ now, the closer will we walk with Him to all eternity.[8]

Can such teaching be fully supported by Scripture? Is it possible that sin in our lives here on earth will take away from our future, eternal glory? Maybe so!

This much is clear from the Word: Sin in our lives will take away from our effectiveness here in this world. Sin in our lives will displease the Lord and delight the devil. Sin in our lives will hurt many others—both in this world and in the world to come—and sin in our lives will hurt us too, perhaps forever.

But holiness will bring us nothing but good, in this world and in the world to come. So let us earnestly pursue holiness, without which none of us will see the Lord (see Heb. 12:14; Matt. 5:8), and let us endeavor to please Him in all that we say or do.

If anyone is worthy of our devotion, our love, our service, our sacrifice, our very lives, it is Jesus our Lord and Savior, without whom we would be eternally doomed and damned. And so, with His strength and support, let's determine to live for Him and love Him all the days of our lives, full throttle, nothing held back, until we meet Him face-to-face.

Let's refuse to be deterred by our shortcomings or weaknesses. Let's determine not to be sidetracked by Satan's wily ways. Let's decide never to be stopped by this world's attacks. God's grace is more than enough, and on the wings of that grace—remember, He is able to keep us and carry us!—we can be presented "before His glorious presence without fault and with great joy" (Jude 24). What a day that will be!

So prepare your mind for action, submit your body to the Master, and give your heart to Him without reserve. "Be holy," our God says to you and me. He will settle for nothing less.

WHAT ABOUT ROMANS 7?

Are you the kind of reader who goes right to a juicy sounding chapter—or in this case, straight to the appendix—rather than reading a book in the order in which it is presented?

Well, if that's you, I saw you coming and wrote this short study on your behalf. I didn't want you to be wondering about Romans 7—wondering if you can really live a holy life after all—while you worked your way through a book whose whole thrust is that you *can* live a holy life. So go ahead and read this appendix now. This way, you can get your questions answered up front.

As for those who are reading this appendix after finishing the whole book (good for you!), this will help to solidify your thinking and reinforce your convictions all the more.

Let's assume that you know that the Word of God consistently calls us to holiness, and let's assume that you really do want to live a godly, clean life, free from the bondage of sin. The problem is that you seem to have such a hard time walking in purity. You are engaged in constant, intense warfare and find great difficulty in living a truly consecrated life. And, you recall, it seems that Paul himself addressed this very issue, telling us that the things he wanted to do, he didn't do, while the things he didn't want to do, he did (see Rom. 7:14-25). Doesn't that describe our plight too?

Are we really free from sin? Have we truly died to it? Why then does the battle rage with such ferocity in our souls? What *does* the Word say, and what *can* we expect?

These questions must be addressed, since there is little use in reading a book about holiness if you're not convinced you can really live it out, if biblical teaching on sanctification is just a matter of ethereal, theological speculation and not a matter of concrete, attainable reality. Obviously, we all agree that the Word clearly calls us to holiness, but our experience (and maybe Paul's?) seems to render our situation hopeless.

So the real question is this: Does God require holiness from us—internally as well as externally—or is He resigned to the fact that we will consistently do the things we hate and fail to do the things we love? Can we or can we not stop the practice of habitual sin?

Before taking a careful look at Romans 7, let me give you a simple and logical principle of biblical interpretation. If you have fifty clear passages that are in total harmony on a given subject and one somewhat unclear passage that apparently contradicts the other passages, you never throw out or negate the fifty for the one. Either you interpret the single uncertain passage in light of the fifty certain passages, or you recognize a distinct, balancing aspect that the one passage offers the fifty. In either case, the interpretation of the fifty clear passages remains the same.

So, whatever you make of Romans 7—the one and only passage where Paul seems to speak about fighting a losing battle with sin and the flesh[1]—you can't dismiss the passages cited throughout this book (see Chapter Five, in particular), especially when you realize that Romans 7 is sandwiched between Romans 6 and 8, two of the clearest holiness passages in the Bible. In fact, if you were to read through the New Testament and mark down all the verses that call us to put away sin and give ourselves to purity, you would find virtually every book and every author saying the same thing: "Get the sin out of your life! Submit yourself to God. Be holy. Through the blood of Jesus, you can lead a new life."[2]

To give just the slightest hint at what you would discover in your study of the New Testament—and remember, this is just a tiny sampling from each book—in Matthew's Gospel there is the Sermon on the Mount, where we learn that even *thoughts* of adultery or hatred are abominations in the sight of God (see Matt. 5:21-30). In the Gospel of Mark, Jesus warns us not to let our eyes or hands lead us into sin, with hellfire the penalty for those who ignore the warning (see Mark 9:43-49). In Luke's Gospel, we read that if we don't repent we will perish (see Luke 13:1-5), while in the Gospel of John, we are called to abandon our evil deeds and walk in the light (see John 3:16-21; 8:23,24).

In Acts, sinners are rebuked—or even judged—on the spot (for example, Ananias and Sapphira in chapter 5, Simon the sorcerer in chapter 8, Herod in chapter 12, and Elymas the sorcerer in chapter

13), while in Romans, Paul tells the believers that the time for sinning is over (see Rom. 13:11-14). It's the same throughout the remainder of the New Testament—Gospel after Gospel, epistle after epistle, right through the Book of Revelation.

Now, read through the New Testament again, one chapter at a time, and look for verses saying that, as believers, we are destined to lead anemic, compromised, defeated lives that will never measure up to the norm. Where are the verses?

You say, "But weren't the Corinthians and Galatians rebuked by Paul because of sin or serious error in their midst? And wasn't that the case with five of the seven churches addressed by the Lord in Revelation 2 and 3?" Absolutely! But Paul and Jesus didn't say, "I understand your sin. No problem! Just do a little better if you can, OK?" Not at all. There were stern rebukes and sharp ultimatums for these straying saints. Such behavior is forbidden among the people of God.

In fact, holy living was such a consistent, underlying theme in the early Church that Paul instructed the Corinthians to "not associate with anyone who calls himself a brother but is sexually immoral or greedy, an idolater or a slanderer, a drunkard or a swindler. With such a man," he wrote, "do not even eat" (1 Cor. 5:11). Such persons, said Paul, are "wicked" (1 Cor. 5:13)—and unrepentant, wicked people have no place in the church. There is simply no compromise here.

That's why Paul could dogmatically state:

Do you not know that the wicked will not inherit the kingdom of God? Do not be deceived: Neither the sexually immoral nor idolaters nor adulterers nor male prostitutes nor homosexual offenders nor thieves nor the greedy nor drunkards nor slanderers nor swindlers will inherit the kingdom of God (1 Cor. 6:9,10).

On these verses, A. T. Robertson, the heralded Greek scholar, commented with chilling insight:

All these will fall short of the kingdom of God. This was plain talk to a city like Corinth. It is needed today. It is a solemn roll call of the damned even if some of their names are on the church roll in Corinth whether officers or ordinary members.[3]

"But wait!" you say. "What about all the *other* verses, the ones that bring balance to the extreme position you have taken? What about them?"

Sit down, my friend, you're in for a surprise. Not only is the position you call "extreme" actually the biblical norm, but those "other" verses you refer to don't exist! Aside from 1 John 1:8—2:2, beginning with the words, "If we claim to be without sin, we deceive ourselves and the truth is not in us," which is found in the beginning of a radical holiness book and which does *not* give us a license to sin,[4] and Romans 7, which is sandwiched between two glorious holiness chapters and to which we will turn shortly, the verses simply aren't there. Go through the Word and see for yourself!

Of course, you can point to Peter's pre-Pentecost denial of Jesus as an example of human weakness, but you certainly can't point to Peter—crucified upside down for his Master, according to Church tradition—as an ongoing example of human failing.

Or you can point to the apostle Thomas as an example of a disciple who doubted, but you certainly can't point to him as an example of continual doubt and unbelief. Tradition tells us he was speared to death in India for his testimony of Jesus!

And you can point to David as a man after God's own heart who blew it royally, but you certainly don't want to emulate his example: His adultery and murder cost him (along with future generations of Israel) untold agony and grief. Do *not* follow David in his sin!

Certainly, no one is denying that in ourselves we are hopelessly weak, that we are sometimes embarrassed by our words and deeds, that we are never completely and entirely "without sin." (If you think you are utterly sinless, you're probably guilty of pride, self-righteousness, self-deception or all three!) But the Word clearly teaches that we are not to be characterized by *our* weakness but by *His* strength, that the pattern of our lives should be obedience and not disobedience, that we should never again live as sin's captives but rather as the Lord's redeemed. Simply stated, rather than giving us a *cop-out* for our sinful nature, Jesus provides us with a *way out*.

You might say, "You've just stated the obvious. We are called by God to live in holiness, but we often battle with the flesh and fall short. Who doesn't know this?"

Ah, but it's the attitude that is crucial. Do you flee for refuge to Romans 7, finding an easy excuse for your all-too-persistent shortcomings and allowing yourself to accept your compromised condition as the expected status quo? Or to the contrary, do you find that subnormal condition to be completely unacceptable, determining by the grace of God to rise higher, considering yourself dead to sin and alive only to the Lord? What is your attitude in all this?

A lot also depends on what you mean when you say, "We often battle with the flesh and fall short." How often and how far short? Do you mean to say that you "just can't" keep your eyes off Internet pornography, or that looking at it "only" once a week is perfectly understandable? Do you mean to say that God understands the affair you had, even though you're a pastor? (Or could it be that, because you're a pastor, He knows how sorely Satan tempts you and how hard your lot is, making your sin even more understandable?) Do you mean that He overlooks your daily temper tantrums with your toddlers as you slap them and scream at them, assuring them they'll never amount to anything good?

Or do you mean that everyone has their "little" vices—like Christian ladies reading worldly romance novels (and putting their own names right in the middle of an adulterous fantasy), or like Christian men thumbing through lingerie catalogs, or like Christian salespeople telling "white lies" on their jobs, or like Christian teenagers fooling around sexually outside of wedlock? Or are you referring to those minor, "gray" areas like smoking cigarettes or watching videos with graphic and gratuitous violence (but without nudity or profanity, of course, making it "acceptable" for believers)? If so, you are sadly mistaken. The Word commands us to abandon all this. Failure to comply with the "house rules" carries serious ramifications.

Listen again to the Scriptures. Let's hear from just one biblical author in one short book:

> As obedient children, do not conform to the evil desires you had when you lived in ignorance. But just as He who called you is holy, so be holy in all you do; for it is written: "Be holy, because I am holy."
>
> Dear friends, I urge you, as aliens and strangers in the world, to abstain from sinful desires, which war against your soul. . . . He Himself bore our sins in His body on the tree, so that we might die to sins and live for righteousness; by His wounds you have been healed.
>
> Therefore, since Christ suffered in His body, arm yourselves also with the same attitude, because he who has suffered in his body is done with sin. As a result, he does not live the rest of his earthly life for evil human desires, but rather for the will of God. For you have spent enough time in the past doing what pagans choose to do—living in debauchery, lust, drunkenness, orgies, carousing and detestable idolatry (1 Pet. 1:14-16; 2:11,24; 4:1-3).

Yes, believers are to be armed with the attitude that says, "I'm done with sin! That was part of my former way of life. Now I live only to do the will of God." Peter's teaching really sums it all up.[5]

Peter also raises some issues regarding Romans 7, since the call to holiness in 1 Peter—in harmony with the rest of the Word—is absolutely clear, *presupposing* our ability in the Lord "to abstain from sinful desires." How then do we interpret Romans 7, which seems to say that we will also be slaves to sin in this life? Let's take a careful look at this much-disputed passage.[6]

To get the immediate context, we'll look again at Romans 6. There Paul explains to the Roman believers that through baptism, they have identified with Jesus in His death to sin and His resurrection to a glorious new life. These are a few of the expressions he uses:

> We died to sin . . . . We were therefore buried with Him through baptism into death in order that, just as Christ was raised from the dead through the glory of the Father, we too may live a new life. . . .
>
> For we know that our old self was crucified with Him so that the body of sin might be done away with, that we should no longer be slaves to sin—because anyone who has died has been freed from sin. . . .
>
> For we know that since Christ was raised from the dead, He cannot die again; death no longer has mastery over Him. The death He died, He died to sin once for all; but the life He lives, He lives to God (from Rom. 6:2-10).

Based on these glorious truths, Paul gives some practical exhortations:

> In the same way, count yourselves dead to sin but alive to God in Christ Jesus. Therefore do not let sin reign in your mortal body so that you obey its evil desires. Do not offer the parts of your body to sin, as instruments of wickedness, but rather offer yourselves to God, as those who have been brought from death to life; and offer the parts of your body to Him as instruments of righteousness.
>
> For sin shall not be your master, because you are not under law, but under grace (Rom. 6:11-14).

The issue, of course, is one of "servitude," because "when you offer yourselves to someone to obey him as slaves, you are slaves to the one whom you obey—whether you are slaves to sin, which leads to death, or to obedience, which leads to righteousness" (Rom. 6:16).

Peter referred to this too, quoting a common proverb of the day: "A man is a slave to whatever has mastered him" (2 Pet. 2:19). Thankfully, the Romans had made their choice, and they were freed from the tyranny of sin. Notice the italicized phrases:

> But thanks be to God that, though *you used to be slaves to sin*, you wholeheartedly obeyed the form of teaching to which you were entrusted. *You have been set free from sin and have become slaves to righteousness.* I put this in human terms because you are weak in your natural selves.
>
> *Just as you used to offer the parts of your body in slavery to impurity and to ever-increasing wickedness, so now offer them in slavery to righteousness leading to holiness. When you were slaves to sin, you were free from the control of righteousness.* What benefit did you reap at that time from the things you are now ashamed of? Those things result in death!
>
> *But now that you have been set free from sin and have become slaves to God,* the benefit you reap leads to holiness, and the result is eternal life. For the wages of sin is death, but the gift of God is eternal life in Christ Jesus our Lord (Rom. 6:17-23).

Any interpretation that still leaves the believer enslaved in sin is unacceptable. Agreed?

Now we turn to Romans 7. In the first six verses, Paul uses an analogy that describes the binding power of the law. A woman, he explains, is bound to her husband by the law as long as he is alive, but when he dies, she is "released from the law of marriage" and is free to marry another. But if she marries another man while her original husband is still alive, she is called an adulteress. Paul then applies this to the Church: "So, my brothers, you also died to the law through the body of Christ, that you might belong to another, to Him who was raised from the dead, in order that we might bear fruit to God" (Rom. 7:4).

What does this mean to the believers? Again, the application is clear:

> For when we were controlled by the sinful nature [literally, flesh], the sinful passions aroused by the law were at work in our bodies, so that we bore fruit for death. But now, by dying to what once bound us, we have been released from the law so that we serve in the new way of the Spirit, and not in the old way of the written code (Rom. 7:5,6).

And notice the verbal tenses here: We *were* controlled by the sinful nature, but now, we *have been released* from the law so that we *serve* in the new way of the Spirit.[7] Everything has changed!

But there is a logical question that Paul raises, and it is has to do with the nature of the law:

> What shall we say, then? Is the law sin? Certainly not! Indeed I would not have known what sin was except through the law. For I would not have known what coveting really was if the law had not said, "Do not covet." But sin, seizing the opportunity afforded by the commandment, produced in me every kind of covetous desire. For apart from law, sin is dead (Rom. 7:7,8).

And it is here that we arrive at the great interpretive dilemma of Romans 7: What period of Paul's life does he describe, his pre-conversion experience or his ongoing experience as a believer? And does he speak only of himself, or does he speak of himself as a picture of "everyman"? He writes:

Once I was alive apart from law; but when the commandment came, sin sprang to life and I died. I found that the very commandment that was intended to bring life actually brought death. For sin, seizing the opportunity afforded by the commandment, deceived me, and through the commandment put me to death (Rom. 7:9-11).

What does he mean when he says, "Once I was alive"? If he is speaking of his experience before his glorious conversion, there is no real problem, since the rest of the chapter, in which he describes his deep frustration over his inability to conquer sin, does not apply to his experience as a new creation in Jesus the Messiah. Therefore it does not apply to *us* as new creations in the Messiah (see 2 Cor. 5:17).

But if he is speaking in the present tense, referring to his consistently defeated life as a Spirit-filled child of God, then *all of us* are in trouble. We can expect the same!

How then do we understand these verses, and are there any other legitimate interpretations that take a "middle road"?[8] Let's keep reading the text before we come to any conclusions:

So then, the law is holy, and the commandment is holy, righteous and good. Did that which is good, then, become death to me? By no means! But in order that sin might be recognized as sin, it produced death in me through what was good, so that through the commandment sin might become utterly sinful.

We know that the law is spiritual; but I am unspiritual, sold as a slave to sin. I do not understand what I do. For what I want to do I do not do, but what I hate I do. And if I do what I do not want to do, I agree that the law is good. As it is, it is no longer I myself who do it, but it is sin living in me. I know that nothing good lives in me, that is, in my sinful nature. For I have the desire to do what is good, but

I cannot carry it out. For what I do is not the good I want
to do; no, the evil I do not want to do—this I keep on doing.
Now if I do what I do not want to do, it is no longer I who
do it, but it is sin living in me that does it (Rom. 7:12-20).

We see that Paul *does* speak in the present tense here, and all of
us, on one level or another, can relate to his frustration. ("For what
I want to do I do not do, but what I hate I do. And if I do what I do
not want to do, I agree that the law is good.") All honest believers
will admit that, at least sometimes, they think things, say things, or
do things that violate their own convictions, while the things they
truly believe in, they fail to do. But how far does this go, and how
consistent is this defeated pattern of behavior?

Is it the rule, or is it the exception to the rule? Is it the guiding
principle of life, or a passionate expression of momentary disappointment?[9] Is it a picture of who we really are—always failing,
always frustrated, always falling, always deviating from the path—or
is it more like a picture of a man walking down the road with little
dogs yapping at his heels? He is going somewhere, he is moving
forward, but there's always something pulling at him and trying to
distract him. Which picture describes the biblical norm?

In order to answer these difficult questions, let's consider what
we know for sure: First, Paul would not blatantly contradict what
he just wrote in Romans 6 and in 7:1-6 (especially when you
remember that there were no chapter divisions in the original text)
or what he is about to write in Romans 8 (we'll look at this in a
moment) or what he clearly wrote elsewhere in his letters; therefore, it
is impossible that Paul would speak of himself in his *present standing*
in the Lord as "unspiritual [or fleshly, carnal], sold as a slave to sin"
(v. 14). This cannot be![10]

Writing in the mid-1700s, John Wesley commented,

> The character here assumed is that of a man, first ignorant
> of the law, then under it and sincerely, but ineffectually,

striving to serve God. To have spoken this of himself [i.e., Paul], or any true believer, would have been foreign to the whole scope of his discourse; nay, utterly contrary thereto, as well as to what is expressly asserted [in] Romans 8:2.[11]

Writing in the late 1900s, Prof. Douglas Moo, after carefully reviewing all the major interpretive options, stated even more fully,

In chapters 6 and 8 [of Romans], respectively, Paul makes it clear that "being free from under sin" and "being free from the law of sin and death" are conditions that are true for every Christian. If one is a Christian, then these things are true; if one is not, then they are not true. This means that the situation depicted in verses 14-25 [of Romans 7] cannot be that of the "normal" Christian, nor of an immature Christian. Nor can it describe the condition of any person living by the law because the Christian who is mistakenly living according to the law is yet a Christian and is therefore not "under sin" or "a prisoner of the law of sin."[12]

Paul had just gone to great lengths to remind the Romans they had *died to sin*, that they are *no longer slaves to sin*, and that they now lead a *new life* in Jesus. How then could he speak of himself as "sold as a slave to sin"? Was Paul *really* a slave to sin?

As for the term "unspiritual" (Greek, *sarkinos*), Paul uses this word two other times in his epistles: in 1 Corinthians 3:1, where he rebukes the Corinthians for this unacceptable mode of behavior ("Brothers, I could not address you as spiritual but as worldly [*sarkinos*]—mere infants in Christ"), and again in 2 Corinthians 3:3, where it simply means "fleshly" as opposed to "stone" (see also Heb. 7:16, where it means "human, physical"). Would Paul, the apostle to the Corinthians, rebuke them for acting like infants, calling them carnal [*sarkinos*], and then describe himself with that very term? Hardly![13]

Also the conclusion to his discussion in Romans 7 raises some serious questions if Paul is speaking of our normal, ongoing experience in the Lord:

> So I find this law at work: When I want to do good, evil is right there with me. For in my inner being I delight in God's law; but I see another law at work in the members of my body, waging war against the law of my mind and making me a prisoner of the law of sin at work within my members. What a wretched man I am! Who will rescue me from this body of death? Thanks be to God—through Jesus Christ our Lord! So then, I myself in my mind am a slave to God's law, but in the sinful nature a slave to the law of sin (Rom. 7:21-25).

Now, take out your Bible and keep reading, right through Romans 8, right up to its glorious end, and then read on through Romans 12, where Paul sets a wonderfully high standard for our conduct in Christ. Then read passages like Ephesians 1 and 2, celebrating the unsearchable riches of our Savior, with whom we—the chosen and elect, trophies of the grace of the God—are seated in heavenly places. Then read through 2 Corinthians 3, where Paul writes,

> We, who with unveiled faces all reflect the Lord's glory, are being transformed into His likeness with ever-increasing glory, which comes from the Lord, who is the Spirit (3:18).

And then ask yourself this question: Could this same Paul, the author of these very passages, say of himself—and, by implication, of us too—"What a wretched man I am!" How could this be? And how could he end his discourse by simply resolving to be a slave to God's law in his mind while still being a slave to the law of sin in his flesh? As the influential New Testament scholar C. H. Dodd commented, "It would stultify [Paul's] whole argument if he now confessed that, at the moment of writing, he was a 'miserable wretch, a prisoner to sin's law.'"[14]

It is for reasons such as these that the early Greek Church fathers, along with respected leaders through the centuries, interpreted the entire passage with reference to Paul's life *before* meeting the Messiah.[15] But does this really solve all the problems in the text? If Paul was speaking only of his pre-conversion life, why does he move to the present tense, stay in the present tense, end in the present tense, and speak in such passionate, personal terms?[16] It is for reasons such as these that the Reformers, along with many modern commentators, generally interpreted the passage with reference to Paul's post-conversion experience.

Either way, there are problems to face, but, to be scripturally sound, we must admit that the problems we encounter when we interpret Romans 7 with reference to Paul's ongoing experience as a believer are insurmountable. It is simply impossible to think of Paul totally contradicting *all* his other writings—especially those in the immediate, surrounding context—and denying the overall, consistent, clear testimony of the Word. Perish the thought!

On the one hand, it seems inaccurate to say that Paul spoke *only* of his past life, although some of the verses could well refer to that. On the other hand, it is impossible to believe that Paul spoke as a perpetually defeated (and that means *disobedient*) believer, resigned to being a slave to sin in this life.[17]

So, if you want to believe that we will never have a struggle with sin, basing yourself on the "pre-conversion" reading of Romans 7, you'll have problems to face, both with the biblical text and with your own life. But if you use the "post-conversion" reading of Romans 7 as an excuse for consistent sin in your life, you'll find yourself facing God's rebuke. The Word is against you!

⌒

"Well," you ask, "are there any other possible interpretations to the chapter?" Of course! In fact, there are many.[18] But here are just two insights to the chapter that may help clarify things:

1. *Paul writes as a victorious believer still aware of our never-ending battle as long as we live in this world, and he expresses himself as one who knows the heat of the battle.* A similar sentiment is reflected in verses such as Galatians 5:17: "For the sinful nature desires what is contrary to the Spirit, and the Spirit what is contrary to the sinful nature. They are in conflict with each other, so that you do not do what you want."

Yes, there *is* an ongoing battle, but, as Paul continues to explain to the Galatians in chapter 5, believers have now crucified their sinful tendencies through the Cross. So, you might think of the non-believer as a jet plane that is stuck on the runway and cannot fly, whereas the believer is a jet plane in flight, but fighting turbulence and needing a good pilot in order to get to the destination. Sometimes there is a mighty buffeting, but the plane doesn't come down!

2. *Paul speaks of the unwinnable battle with the fleshly, sinful nature, a nature that will **never** change in this life* (see Rom. 7:25).[19] To the extent that we continue to allow ourselves to live under the influence of this nature, and to the extent that we seek to fight the flesh by the Law and not by the Spirit, we will be engaged in a war that we cannot win—and it will be a hellish war.

The wonderful revelation is that, through Jesus, we are delivered from the power of that nature! This is the great theme of Romans 8, where the law of the Spirit of life in Messiah Jesus sets us free from the law of sin and death:[20]

> Therefore, there is now no condemnation for those who are in Christ Jesus, because through Christ Jesus the law of the Spirit of life set me free from the law of sin and death. For what the law was powerless to do in that it was weakened by the sinful nature, God did by sending His own Son in the likeness of sinful man to be a sin offering.
>
> And so He condemned sin in sinful man, in order that the righteous requirements of the law might be fully met in

us, who do not live according to the sinful nature but according to the Spirit (Rom. 8:1-4).

Paul continues to expand on this in the following verses, calling believers to set their minds on what the Spirit desires, resulting in life and peace, in contrast with fleshly people who have their minds set on what the sinful nature desires, resulting in death (vv. 5,6). Yes, "the sinful mind is hostile to God. It does not submit to God's law, nor can it do so. Those controlled by the sinful nature cannot please God" (vv. 7,8).

Once again, we see how utterly impossible it is to think that Paul could have just described *himself* as controlled by the sinful nature—and consequently "hostile to God." Never! Instead, he affirms to the Romans, "You, however, are controlled not by the sinful nature but by the Spirit, if the Spirit of God lives in you" (v. 9). Glory!

Yes—

If Christ is in you, your body is dead because of sin, yet your spirit is alive because of righteousness.

Therefore, brothers, we have an obligation—but it is not to the sinful nature, to live according to it. For if you live according to the sinful nature, you will die; but if by the Spirit you put to death the misdeeds of the body, you will live, because those who are led by the Spirit of God are sons of God (Rom. 8:10,12-14).

Praise be to God, we *are* led by the Spirit—led to put to death the misdeeds of the body, led to live in holy obedience to the Master, led to do the will of God.

Is there a battle in the flesh? You bet! But we have been given victory in Jesus over the flesh! Will we experience conflicts and difficulties in this world? Absolutely (see John 16:33; Acts 14:22; 2 Cor. 6:6-10). But we are overcomers, by life or by death (see Rom. 8:35-39; 2 Cor. 2:14; 1 John 2:13,14; 4:4; 5:4). Being defeated by the devil and bound by the flesh are *not* the expected norm. We are not slaves; we are free (see 1 Pet. 2:16)!

So stand fast in your freedom, and rather than looking to Romans 7 as an excuse for sinful living, read *everything* Paul wrote in Romans 6–8, and recognize that while the battle in the flesh can rage, we are no longer controlled by the flesh but rather by the Spirit. And the Spirit-filled, Spirit-led, Spirit-empowered life is glorious. Don't let anyone talk you out of it!

ENDNOTES

CHAPTER ONE

1. Evangeline Booth expressed this passionately: "Drink has drained more blood, hung more crepes, sold more homes, plunged more people into bankruptcy, armed more villains, slain more children, snapped more wedding rings, defiled more innocence, blinded more eyes, twisted more limbs, dethroned more reason, wrecked more manhood, dishonored more womanhood, broken more hearts, driven more to suicide and dug more graves than any other poisonous scourge that ever swept its death-dealing waves across the world." Cited in Albert M. Wells, Jr., *Inspiring Quotations: Contemporary and Classical* (Nashville: Thomas Nelson, 1988), p. 6, #14.

2. According to a beautiful, but completely homiletical interpretation of the ancient rabbis (see Genesis Rabba 35:3, end), this verse was interpreted to mean the following: "When you walk, they will guide you"—meaning in this world; "when you sleep, they will watch over you"—meaning in the hour of death; "when you wake up, they will speak to you"—meaning in the Resurrection to come.

3. See *Oswald Chambers: The Best from All His Books*, Volume I, compiled by Harry Verploegh (Nashville: Oliver Nelson, 1987), p. 197.

CHAPTER TWO

1. For a brief scriptural study on the joy of the Lord and its relationship to holiness and revival, see Michael L. Brown, *From Holy Laughter to Holy Fire: America on the Edge of Revival* (Shippensburg, PA: Destiny Image, 1996), pp. 104-118 ("Joy Unspeakable and Full of Glory").

2. God promises "true happiness" to His people, and the most accurate way to translate the Hebrew word *'ašrey*, found, for example, at the beginning of Psalm 1, is "truly happy." See my article on *'ašrey* in Willem VanGemeren, ed., *The New International Dictionary of Old Testament Theology and Exegesis* (Grand Rapids: Zondervan, 1997), pp. 1:570-572. (This dictionary will henceforth be referred to as *NIDOTTE*.) The same probably holds true for the Greek word *makarios*, found, for example, in the beatitudes (i.e., "Truly happy are the poor in spirit," etc.).

3. It was D. Martyn Lloyd-Jones who drew attention to the fact that there is no more gentle and kindly depiction of Jesus than that of "the Lamb," yet in Revelation 6:12-17, people plead with the mountains and rocks to fall on them and hide them from the face of Him who sits on the throne and from the wrath of the Lamb.

4. My colleague Steve Hill, the evangelist of the Brownsville Revival, has preached a powerful sermon entitled "When the Gavel Falls." It is available on video through Destiny Image Publishers. See also Michael L. Brown, *It's Time to Rock the Boat: A Call to God's People to Rise Up and Preach a Confrontational Gospel* (Shippensburg, PA: Destiny Image, 1993), pp. 98-108 ("The Wrath of God"); idem, *How Saved Are We?* (Shippensburg, PA: Destiny Image, 1990), pp. 51-57 ("Whatever Happened to the Fear of God?"). A videotaped message entitled "Whatever Happened to the Wrath of God?" preached at a leadership conference at the Brownsville Revival in November, 1996, is available through ICN Ministries.

5. Thomas Brooks, *Precious Remedies Against Satan's Devices* (Carlisle, PA: Banner of Truth, 1987), p. 31.

6. Of course, some would argue that Islam, in its true essence, can readily be somewhat monstrous! For some frightening documentation, see Amir Taheri, *Holy Terror: Inside the World of Islamic Terrorism* (Bethesda, MD: Adler & Adler, 1987); Victor Mordecai, *Is Fanatic Islam a Global Threat?* (Springfield, MO: n.p., 1996); see also Emanuel Sivan, *Radical Islam: Medieval Theology and Modern Politics* (New Haven: Yale University Press, 1985).

CHAPTER THREE

1. *Precious Remedies Against Satan's Devices*, p. 39.

2. This quote originated with Carey Robertson, associate pastor of the Brownsville Assembly of God, who passed it on to me directly.

3. *Precious Remedies Against Satan's Devices*, p. 36.

4. According to Franz Delitzsch, *Commentary on the Epistle to the Hebrews*, English translation (Minneapolis: Klock & Klock, 1978), vol. 2, p. 188, the Greek word *katapato*, translated here with "trample," "is not merely to reject or cast away as something unfit for use which men carelessly tread upon (Matt. 5:13; Luke 8:5), but to trample down with ruthless contempt as an object of scorn or hatred (Matt. 7:6)." In light of this, Deliztsch exclaims, "To trample Him under foot—the gracious and almighty Heir of all things, who is now seated at God's right hand—what a challenge to the Most High to inflict the severest and most crushing penalty!" Similarly, William Lane, *Hebrews 9-13*, Word Biblical Commentary (Dallas: Word, 1991), p. 294, states, "The paradoxical notion of treating with disdain one who possesses transcendent dignity commands attention."

5. For discussion of the Greek word *enubrizo*, here translated with "insult," see Harold W. Attridge, *The Epistle to the Hebrews*, Hermeneia (Philadelphia:

Fortress, 1989), pp. 294, 295; cf. also Lane, ibid., p. 295, who notes that the Greek could be rendered with, "having insulted," "having outraged," "having displayed contempt with injury." Delitzsch, ibid., p. 190, observes, "To contemn or do despite to . . . this Holy Spirit is to blaspheme the whole work of grace of which one has once been the subject, and to exhibit it as a deception and a lie. It is profanely to contradict the very truth of God, and draw down upon oneself a vengeance which cannot fail."

6. For a revealing yet sympathetic look at the rise and fall of some of the leaders in the so-called "healing revival" (1947-58), see D. E. Harrell, Jr., *All Things Are Possible: The Healing and Charismatic Revivals in Modern America* (Bloomington: Indiana University Press, 1975).

7. I would encourage those of you who are convinced that it is completely impossible for a true believer to lose his or her salvation to read David Pawson, *Once Saved, Always Saved?* (London: Hodder & Stoughton, 1996) and, more fully, Robert Shank, *Life in the Son* (Minneapolis: Bethany, 1961). There are also some relevant chapters on this subject in my book *It's Time to Rock the Boat* (see especially pp. 24-38, 84-96). See also below, chapter 7, endnote 8. For recent defenses of the "once saved, always saved" position, see R. T. Kendall, *Once Saved, Always Saved* (Chicago: Moody Press, 1983); Charles Stanley, *Eternal Security* (Nashville: Thomas Nelson, 1990).

CHAPTER FOUR

1. The letters "kh" represent the equivalent of "ch" in the Scottish word "loch."

2. For its varied usages in the Old Testament, see Andrew Hill, *'aḥarît*, in *NIDOTTE*, vol. 1, p. 361, 362, with references to other, more full treatments of the word on p. 362. In Exodus 33:23, the related word *'aḥôr* occurs in a plural form with reference to God's "back"; in Ezekiel 8:16, it refers to the backs of people.

3. Note Isaiah 46:10, "I make known the end from the beginning," where the word for end is *'aḥarît*, derived from the word for "that which comes after; back." The word for beginning is *re'šît*, derived from the word for "head."

4. I have translated this literally to bring out the force of the original; for the Hebrew word *mûsar*, meaning "discipline; instruction," cf. Eugene H. Merrill, "*ysr*," in *NIDOTTE*, vol. 2, pp. 479-482, especially 480, 481.

5. Commentators through the centuries have noted that the somewhat abrupt, staccato Hebrew verbs used here are reflective of Esau's character. See recently Nahum M. Sarna, 182, *Genesis*, The JPS Torah Commentary (Philadelphia: Jewish Publication Society, 1989), who notes, "The abrupt succession of five

short Hebrew verbs effectively reproduces the chilling, sullen atmosphere in which Esau silently devours the meal."

6. Cited in I. D. E. Thomas, ed., *The Golden Treasury of Puritan Quotations* (Carlisle, PA: Banner of Truth, 1989), p. 267.

7. William C. McKane, *Proverbs: A New Approach*, Old Testament Library (Philadelphia: Westminster, 1970), p. 248, translates this verse with, "Its sequel is like a snake bite, or a viper's prick." For his commentary on 23:29-35, see pp. 393-396, where he equates the *'aḥarît* with the "hang-over" (pp. 394, 395).

8. This well-known fact was also confirmed to me independently by two of his family members, a son of his and an in-law.

9. We should remember the *'aḥarît* of Job: "The Lord blessed the latter part ['*aḥarît*] of Job's life more than the first" (Job 42:12). See also James 5:11, "As you know, we consider blessed those who have persevered. You have heard of Job's perseverance and have seen what the Lord finally brought about [literally, you have seen the end—Greek, *telos*—of the Lord]. The Lord is full of compassion and mercy."

CHAPTER FIVE

1. Barnabas Lindars, *The Gospel of John*, New Century Bible (Grand Rapids: Eerdmans, 1995), p. 305, notes, "The story itself tells how Jesus was able to deal compassionately with a woman, whose guilt rendered her liable to the death penalty. He neither condones her sin nor denies the validity of the law; nevertheless, he gives her an incentive to make a new start in life."

2. For discussion of the textual integrity of John 8:1-11, see Bruce M. Metzger, *A Textual Commentary on the Greek New Testament* (London/New York: United Bible Societies, 1975), pp. 219-223; for the wider interpretive issues, see George R. Beasley-Murray, *John*, Word Biblical Commentary (Waco, TX: Word, 1987), pp. 144-147.

3. See *John Wesley's Notes on the Whole Bible: The New Testament* from the Sage Digital Library CD-ROM (Albany, OR: Sage Software), p. 281.

4. See the comments of Adam Clarke: "Our Lord, intending to discover to this man who he was, gave him two proofs of the perfection of his knowledge. 1. He showed him that he knew the secret of the past—sin no more: thereby intimating that his former sins were the cause of his long affliction. 2. He showed him that he knew the future—lest a worse thing come unto thee: if thy iniquity be repeated, thy punishment will be increased." See *Adam Clarke's Commentary on the Bible* from the Sage Digital Library CD-ROM (Albany, OR: Sage Software), Volume 5, p. 103.

5. Matthew Henry noted here: "Had she not been taken in this act, she might have gone on to another, till her heart had been perfectly hardened; but sometimes it proves a mercy to sinners to have their sin brought to light, that they may *do no more presumptuously*. Better our sin should *shame* us than *damn* us, and be set in order before us for our conviction than for our condemnation." See *Matthew Henry's Commentary on the Bible* (Peabody, MA: Hendrickson, 1991), on the Logos CD-ROM, ad loc.

6. Charles Spurgeon, *Morning and Evening* from the Sage Digital Library CD-ROM (Albany, OR: Sage Software), May 30, A.M., to Song of Solomon 2:15.

7. It is interesting to note that in the original, correct wording of Charles Wesley's classic hymn, "Oh for a Thousand Tongues," one of the stanzas read, "He breaks the power of cancell'd sin, He sets the prisoner free; His blood can make the foulest clean, His blood avail'd for me," whereas some later hymnals changed it to read, "He breaks the power of ruling sin," thereby watering down the force of Wesley's original wording. When the change was first made, it was, of course, made intentionally, because of theological differences. For the background to the hymn, as well as its 18 (!) stanzas, see John R. Tyson, ed., *Charles Wesley: A Reader* (New York: Oxford, 1989), pp. 107-109. For an edifying study of Charles Wesley, see Arnold A. Dallimore, *A Heart Set Free: The Life of Charles Wesley* (Westchester, IL: Crossway, 1988).

8. John Owen, *Temptation and Sin* (Grand Rapids: Sovereign Grace, 1971), p. 8.

9. Most translations are even more challenging; cf., e.g., the *KVJ, NKJV, NASB*.

10. For an entirely different understanding of these verses, see Charles G. Finney, *Principles of Sanctification*, compiled and edited by Louis Gifford Parkhurst, Jr. (Minneapolis: Bethany, 1986), pp. 104-106, who understands John to be saying, "If we say that we are not sinners, that is, say we have no sin and no need of the blood of Christ, and that we have never sinned and consequently need no Savior, we deceive ourselves. For we have sinned, and nothing but the blood of Christ cleanses us from sin or procures our pardon and justification. If we will not deny but confess that we have sinned, 'He is faithful and just to forgive us our sins, and to cleanse us from all unrighteousness.'" Thus, Finney does "not understand the Apostle as affirming anything in respect to the present moral character of anyone, but as speaking of the doctrine of justification."

11. In the words of another Puritan, Joseph Caryl, "Perfect holiness is the aim of the saints on earth, and it is the reward of the saints in heaven." Cited in Thomas, *The Golden Treasury of Puritan Quotations*, p. 142.

12. Readers from a Reformed (i.e., Calvinistic) background might find Anthony A. Hoekema's summary of the Reformed view of sanctification somewhat

surprising (although it is, no doubt, quite accurate). After acknowledging that believers are in a constant battle against sin, he notes, "Yet, though the struggle against sin is very real, believers are no longer enslaved to sin. The crucifixion of the old self with Christ, Paul teaches, implies that we have been freed from the slavery of sin (see Rom. 6:6); because we are not under law but under grace, sin shall no longer be our master (see v. 14). 'The sin which still inheres in the believer and the sin he commits does not have dominion over him.' [This quote is taken from John Murray, *Principles of Conduct*.] Summing up, we may say that believers are no longer old persons but new persons who are being progressively renewed. They must still battle against sin and will sometimes fall into sin, but they are no longer its slaves. In the strength of the Spirit they are now able to resist sin, since for every temptation God will provide a way of escape." Hoekema's essay is found in Melvin Dieter, idem, et al., *Five Views on Sanctification* (Grand Rapids: Zondervan, 1987), pp. 61-90, the quote cited here taken from p. 82.

13. John Wesley, *A Plain Account of Christian Perfection, as believed and taught by the Reverend Mr. John Wesley, from the year 1725, to the year 1777*, in *The Works of John Wesley* (Grand Rapids: Baker, 1986), vol. 11, p. 366. For the entire account, see vol. 11, pp. 366-446.

14. On these verses, B. B. Warfield, a strident opponent of "perfectionist" teaching, still commented, "There is no feature of Christianity more strongly emphasized by those to whom its establishment in the world was committed, than the breadth and depth of its ethical demands. The 'salvation' which was promised in the 'Gospel' or 'Glad Tidings' which constituted its proclamation was just salvation from sin and unto holiness. In other words, it was moral revolution, and in 'sanctification' the very essence of our salvation is made to consist. 'This is the will of God' for you, says the Apostle to his readers in this very epistle, 'even your sanctification.' A great part of this epistle is given, accordingly, to commending the new converts for the progress they had already made in this sanctification, and to urging them onward in the same pathway. No moral attainment is too great to be pressed on them as their duty, no moral duty is too minute to be demanded of them as essential to their Christian walk." See Benjamin Breckenridge Warfield, *Perfectionism*, ed. Samuel G. Craig (Nutley, NJ: Presbyterian and Reformed, 1974), p. 457. In light of the fact that there tends to be a great deal of misunderstanding as to exactly what both proponents and opponents of perfectionism actually believe, interested readers would benefit from a study of the material presented in *Five Views on Sanctification*, referred to in note 12, above. For detailed discussion

of the opposite ends of the spectrum, Warfield's *Perfectionism*, and Finney's *Principles of Sanctification* should be consulted. (Note that the current subtitle given to Finney's volume—which is a compilation of some of his teachings on the subject—reads, "Studies on Biblical Sanctification and its distinction from 'perfectionism.'" See further the introductory comments of Parkhurst, ibid., pp. 9-14, with reference to other writings of Finney that further clarify his actual position, which has often been somewhat caricatured and misrepresented.) Note also John Wesley's *A Plain Account of Christian Perfection* (cited above in note 13, with an extensive question-and-answer section, in which he addresses most of the major sources of confusion and misunderstanding). In a shorter message on perfectionism, Wesley noted, "Whosoever preaches perfection, (as the phrase is,) that is, asserts that it is attainable in this life, runs great hazard of being accounted by them worse than a heathen man or a publican." See *The Works of John Wesley*, p. 6:1. Of course, a key issue is the meaning of the Lord's exhortation in Matthew 5:48, "Be perfect, therefore, as your heavenly Father is perfect." For a devotional study based on this text, see Andrew Murray, *Be Perfect* (Springdale, PA: Whitaker).

15. See *The Works of John Owen* (Carlisle, PA: Banner of Truth, 1977), vol. 3, pp. 574, 575.

CHAPTER SIX

1. Commenting on this verse, Douglas J. Moo, *The Epistle to the Romans*, New International Commentary on the New Testament (Grand Rapids: Eerdmans, 1996), p. 778, states, "Paul might here be urging Christians to maintain a strong and emotional commitment to the Lord in their own spirits." Moo, however, believes that "Paul is exhorting us to allow the Holy Spirit to 'set us on fire': to open ourselves to the Spirit as he seeks to excite us about the 'rational worship' [Rom 12:1] to which the Lord has called us." In either case, the meaning is virtually the same: We are challenged to be set on fire *in* our spirits *by* the Spirit.

2. Charles H. Spurgeon, *Morning and Evening*, March 11, A.M., to Romans 7:13 ("Sin . . . exceeding sinful").

3. The Greek word *argos*, translated "careless" (cf. "idle" in the *KJV*) includes the meanings of "useless, unproductive." See the standard Greek lexicons for references.

4. For the meaning of the Hebrew word *bote'*, translated "reckless" in the *NIV*, as well as discussion of Proverbs 12:18 and related verses in Proverbs, see Michael L. Brown, *Israel's Divine Healer*, Studies in Old Testament Biblical

Theology (Grand Rapids: Zondervan, 1995), pp. 157-164 (in particular 163, 164).

5. For a remarkable testimony of the conversion of an influential, liberal German New Testament scholar, see Eta Linnemann, *Historical Criticism of the Bible: Methodology or Ideology*, English translation (Grand Rapids: Baker, 1990).

6. *Morning and Evening*, May 30, A.M., to Song of Solomon 2:15.

7. The *NIV* correctly brings out of the force of the Greek here, which simply says, "But we"—in contrast with "they"—the words "do it" forming the logical end of the thought.

8. Charles Bridges, *Proverbs* (Carlisle, PA: Banner of Truth, 1987), p. 483, to Proverbs 25:28, "He that hath no rule over his own spirit is like a city that is broken down, and without walls."

9. Ibid.

CHAPTER SEVEN

1. Many readers will be familiar with the differences in Greek manuscripts of Romans 8:1, some of which read, "Therefore, there is now no condemnation for those who are in Christ Jesus" (so *NIV*), and others of which read, *"There is therefore now no condemnation to them which are in Christ Jesus, who walk not after the flesh, but after the Spirit"* (so *KJV*). In reality, however, even if the shorter version of Romans 8:1 is accepted, the overall context of Romans 8:1-16 makes it clear that believers are being addressed as those who walk in the Spirit, not in the flesh. For discussion of the textual issues, cf. Metzger, *Textual Commentary*, p. 515, and see the commentaries.

2. For discussion of these verses, see Brown, *Israel's Divine Healer*, pp. 193, 194.

3. Note the interesting observation of Thomas Brooks, *Precious Remedies Against Satan's Devices*, p. 67: "It is impossible for that man to get the conquest of sin, that plays and sports with the occasions of sin. God will not remove the temptation, except you turn from the occasion. It is a just and righteous thing with God, that he should fall into the pit that will adventure to dance upon the brink of the pit, and that he should be a slave to sin, that will not flee from the occasions of sin."

4. I imagine that both Christians who believe "once saved, always saved" and Christians who reject "once saved, always saved" sometimes struggle with negative thinking and "feeling condemned."

5. For a study of *katakrima* and its related nominal and verbal forms, see Walter Schneider, *"krima,"* in Colin Brown, ed., *The New International Dictionary of New Testament Theology* (Grand Rapids: Zondervan, 1986), vol. 2, pp. 362-367

(henceforth cited as *NIDNTT*). According to James D. G. Dunn, *Romans 1-8*, Word Biblical Commentary (Dallas: Word, 1988), p. 280, *"krima* can mean 'judgment' in the sense of 'condemnation' (see Rom. 2:2 and 3:8), but here [viz., Rom. 5:16] it is complemented by the stronger word *katakrima* where the idea of 'condemnation' includes the carrying out of the sentence."

6. According to some teachers, Romans 8:1 theoretically gives us a license to sin without limit, since according to this theology, our sin cannot affect our eternal standing with the Lord. Rather, it can only hurt our present relationship with Him or possibly cause us to lose some of our heavenly reward. For a typical statement, with specific reference to Romans 8:1, cf. Robert P. Lightner, Th.D., *Sin, the Savior, and Salvation* (Nashville: Thomas Nelson, 1991), pp. 222, 224, "The Lord Jesus Christ bore the condemnation of man's sins. Therefore those sins no longer condemn the sinner who trusts the sin bearer. There is no more condemnation for those who are 'in Christ Jesus' (Rom. 8:1). Sin disrupts the believer's fellowship with God, but not his family relationship as a child of God." See also above, chapter 3, note 7. While I am sure that Dr. Lightner would strongly disavow himself from any teaching that overtly gave believers a license to sin, there is no question but that the contemporary, once-saved, always-saved doctrine does, in fact, open the door to license.

7. See above, chapter 5, and note also the discussion in the appendix.

8. One of my faculty members, Steve Alt, supplied me with the following citations from two leading Calvinistic teachers, John Owen from the seventeenth century and Arthur Pink from the twentieth century, both of whom repudiate the notion that once a person is truly saved, he or she can sin freely and still enter heaven. First the quote from Pink: "There is a deadly and damnable heresy being widely propagated today to the effect that, if a sinner truly accepts Christ as his personal Saviour, no matter how he lives afterwards, he cannot perish. That is a satanic lie, for it is at direct variance with the teaching of the Word of truth. Something more than believing in Christ is necessary to ensure the soul's reaching heaven." Quoting John 10:27,28, he says, "It is not honest to generalize the principle of verse 28: It must be restricted to the characters in verse 27!" That is, not all sheep, but only "those who plainly evidence themselves to be of his 'sheep' by yielding to his authority and following the example which he has left them—and none others." See Iain H. Murray, *The Life of Arthur W. Pink: His Life and Thought* (Edinburgh: Banner of Truth, 1981), pp. 248, 249. Pink then cited Owen (ibid., p. 249), regarding abuses in the doctrine of perseverance (commonly found among those who hold to the "once saved, always saved" position):

"Doth this doctrine promise, with the height of assurance, that under what vile practices so ever men do live, they shall have exemption from eternal punishment? Doth it teach man that it is vain to use the means of mortification because they shall certainly attain the end, whether they use the means or no? Doth it speak peace to the flesh, in assurance of blessed immortality, though it disport itself in all folly in the meantime? . . . The perseverance of the saints is not held out in the Scriptures on any such ridiculous terms: carry themselves well, or wickedly miscarry themselves; but is asserted upon the account of God's effectual grace preserving them in the use of the means and from all such miscarriages."

9. See also Pawson, *Once Saved, Always Saved?*, p. 103, who makes a similar observation.

10. *Precious Remedies Against Satan's Devices*, p. 32.

11. For the background to this hymn, cf. the works cited in note 7 to chapter 6, above.

12. The message of Israel's prophets is summed up in 2 Kings 17:13; Zechariah 1:2-4; cf. also Jeremiah 25:1-6.

13. For a systematic theological exposition, cf. the sermon of Jonathan Edwards, "Pardon for the Greatest Sinners," reprinted in *Jonathan Edwards on Knowing Christ* (Carlisle, PA: Banner of Truth, 1990), pp. 266-276. He states there (p. 267): "If we truly come to God for mercy, the greatness of our sin will be no impediment to pardon."

14. Cited in Jack Hywel-Davies, *The Life of Smith Wigglesworth* (Ann Arbor: Vine Publications, 1988), p. 83.

15. I heard an amusing story about a minister who was going through terribly difficult times and found himself continually rebuking Satan for all his troubles. After some weeks like this, the Lord spoke to him, saying, "Son, you and I would get along together much better if you stopped calling me Satan!"

16. For discussion of the Greek word *elencho*, "convict," see Hans-Georg Link, "*elencho*," *NIDNTT* pp. 2:140-142; for John 16:8-11, a key section on the Holy Spirit's work in conviction, see Brooke Foss Westcott, *The Gospel According to St. John* (Grand Rapids: Baker, 1980), pp. 219-223. He notes that, "He who 'convicts' another places the truth of the case in dispute in a clear light before him, so that it must be seen and acknowledged as truth. He who then rejects the conclusion which this exposition involves, rejects it with his eyes open and at his peril. Truth seen as truth carries with it condemnation to all who refuse to welcome it" (p. 219).

17. See note 5, above.

18. Matthew Henry, commenting on Romans 8:1, writes: "It is the unspeakable privilege and comfort of all those that are in Christ Jesus that there is therefore now no condemnation to them. He does not say, 'There is no accusation against them,' for this there is; but the accusation is thrown out, and the indictment quashed." See *Matthew Henry's Commentary on the Bible*, ad loc.

19. The Greek word for "saint, holy one" is *hagios* (see Colin Brown and Hans Seebass in *NIDNTT*, vol. 2, pp. 224-232). It is used with reference to believers in the New Testament in, e.g., Romans 1:7; 1 Corinthians 1:2; 2 Corinthians 1:1. In many English translations of the Bible, the related verb *hagiazo* is translated with "sanctified" (i.e., made holy); see, e.g., 1 Corinthians 6:11. According to Seebass, ibid., vol. 2, p. 230, "Holiness is a condition of acceptance at the *parousia* [i.e., the return of Jesus] and of entering upon the inheritance of God's people (see Col. 1:12; Acts 20:32; 26:18)."

20. In his book, *Putting Amazing Back Into Grace* (Grand Rapids: Baker Books, 1991), Michael Horton entitles one chapter, "Righteous Sinners" (pp. 165-204), arguing that, "Even on a good day, the average Christian is wicked" (pp. 166, 167). He finds support for this position in the Reformation teaching that believers at best are *simul iustus et peccator* (Latin for "simultaneously justified and sinful"). While Horton is careful not to turn this doctrine into an excuse for sinful behavior, and while he certainly advocates holiness of heart and conduct, there is no question that this particular Reformation teaching is not in real harmony with the overall testimony of the Word. Therefore it can potentially be more destructive than constructive. After all, the belief that we are now "righteous sinners" and at best "wicked" (!) does provide an escape route for believers in their pursuit of sanctification. See also my concluding thoughts in chapter 14, "Be Holy."

21. The *NIV* should not put "sinners" in quotes here (as it does, with perhaps more justification, throughout the Gospels).

22. For discussion of Galatians 2:17, cf. Ronald Y. K. Fung, *The Epistle to the Galatians*, New International Commentary on the New Testament (Grand Rapids: Eerdmans, 1988), pp. 119, 120.

23. On 1 Timothy 1:15, cf. below, note 1 to the appendix.

24. Of course, in times of revival, it is quite common for believers to become completely undone through their dramatic encounter with a holy God, and they will often cry out for mercy *as sinners*. See Brown, *From Holy Laughter to Holy Fire*, pp. 90-103; idem, *It's Time to Rock the Boat*, pp. 62-82. According to Charles G. Finney, *Revivals of Religion* (Grand Rapids: Baker Books, 1993), p. 7, "A revival always includes conviction of sin on the part of the Church.

Backslidden professors cannot wake up and begin right away in the service of God, without deep searchings of heart. The fountains of sin need to be broken up. In a true revival, Christians are always brought under such conviction; they see their sins in such a light that often they find it impossible to maintain a hope of their acceptance with God. It does not always go to that extent, but there are always, in a genuine revival, deep convictions of sin, and often cases of abandoning all hope." An informal survey I conducted in September, 1998, with about 650 of our students in the Brownsville Revival School of Ministry (in a class on the history and characteristics of revival) bore this out: Among those students who first attended the revival as believers, the great majority of them experienced deep conviction over their sins, as many as half of them even questioning their salvation for a short period of time, or actually fearing whether God would ever forgive them. Thankfully, they truly repented of their sins and experienced a deep sense of forgiveness, assurance, and the love of God.

CHAPTER EIGHT

1. Cited in Thomas, *The Golden Treasury of Puritan Quotations*, p. 140.
2. Ibid., p. 142.
3. Ibid., p. 140.
4. See *Oswald Chambers: The Best from All His Books*; see also William Barclay, cited in Wells, *Inspiring Quotations: Contemporary and Classical*, p. 87, #1116, "The aim of reconciliation is holiness. Christ carried out His sacrificial work of reconciliation in order to present us to God consecrated, unblemished and irreproachable."
5. In the words of Ralph Finlayson, "The sum of all God's attributes, the outshining of all that God is, is holiness." I have no source for this quote, other than the holiness calendar in the room of our ministry's former administrator!
6. Cited in *12,000 Religious Quotations*, compiled and edited by Frank S. Mead (Grand Rapids: Baker, 1989), p. 227. According to Jerry Bridges, "Holiness is nothing less than conformity to the character of God." See his important study *The Pursuit of Holiness* (Colorado Springs, CO: NavPress, 1978), p. 26. For further thoughts on holiness from Bridges, cf. idem, *Transforming Grace* (Colorado Springs, CO: NavPress, 1991); *The Discipline of Grace: God's Role and Our Role in the Pursuit of Holiness* (Colorado Springs, CO: NavPress, 1994).
7. Charles R. Swindoll, *The Grace Awakening* (New York: Walker and Co., 1990), pp. xv-xvi.
8. Ibid., pp. 89-123 ("Squaring Off Against Legalism"). For further discussion of the dangers of legalism, see H. Foster, "The Perils of Legality," reprinted in

David Wilkerson and Leonard Ravenhill, eds., *The Refiner's Fire*, Volume II, pp. 25-27. See further J. B. Stoney, in ibid., pp. 34-36, for contrasts between legalism and lawlessness.

9. For an excellent, graciously written exposé, see James R. White, *The King James Only Controversy: Can You Trust the Modern Translations* (Minneapolis: Bethany, 1995). It is important to distinguish those who hold to "King James Onlyism" from believers and scholars who hold that the *KJV* is the best translation or is simply their translation of choice.

10. Max Lucado, *In the Grip of Grace* (Dallas: Word, 1996), p. 12.

11. See chapter 13, "Have You Forsaken Your First Love?" for more on the danger of Christians backsliding from their intimacy and devotion to the Lord.

12. In the famous words of the Mishnah, compiled around A.D. 200, "Put a hedge around the Torah" (Pirkei Avot, 1:1). For an example of this in practice, see the Mishnah, Berakhot 1:1.

13. R. Kent Hughes, *Disciplines of a Godly Man* (Wheaton: Crossway, 1991), p. 206, cited in J. I. Packer, *Rediscovering Holiness* (Ann Arbor: Servant, 1992), pp. 114, 115.

14. Harry Verploegh, ed., *Oswald Chambers: The Best from All His Books*, Volume II (Nashville: Oliver Nelson, 1989), p. 175.

15. The reader will have to judge whether any of the books cited below in chapter 12, note 1, are guilty of this peril to any degree, or whether they safely steer clear of this other, opposite extreme.

16. When Kent Hughes expressed a similar sentiment in his quote cited by Packer (see above, note 13; his specific comment was that legalism was "less a statistical danger than passivity" for the typical American male), Packer could not help but second this comment with his own parenthetical remark, viz., "You can say that again, Dr. Hughes!" (ibid., p. 114). Amen to both of them!

17. See the chapter, "A Warning and a Promise," in Brown, *From Holy Laughter to Holy Fire*, pp. 250-266.

18. *Oswald Chambers: The Best from All His Books*, Volume I, pp. 196, 197.

19. For a helpful listing of verses—in both the Old and New Testaments—that speak of the value and authority of the Law, see Bruce R. Booker, *A Call to Holiness* (1994), pp. 69-84. The author is a Messianic Jew with an irenic approach to the question of the believer's relationship to the Law.

20. It might be said that, for Paul, through the New Covenant, the ultimate goal of Moses and the prophets opens up to us in transforming effect, and the Law is now written on our hearts.

21. Note A. T. Robertson's comment on these verses, cited below, appendix.

22. Cited in Albert Wells, *Inspiring Quotations: Contemporary and Classical*, p. 107, #1399.

CHAPTER NINE

1. Cf. Richard E. Averbeck, *"thr,"* in *NIDOTTE*, vol. 2, pp. 338-353, with references to other, related articles in *NIDOTTE* on p. 352; see also David P. Wright, "Day of Atonement," in David Noel Freedman, ed., *The Anchor Bible Dictionary* (New York: Doubleday, 1992), vol. 2, pp. 72-76.

2. By the way, when I speak of a momentary blemish or temporary spot I do *not* mean suddenly murdering someone in cold blood, or suddenly committing rape, or suddenly robbing a bank. No, those kinds of things happen only after the heart has gone through a lengthy process of being hardened, since numerous restraints and checks would have to be overridden before a child of God could commit such acts.

3. The following verses from Psalm 26 are relevant here (although reading the whole psalm is even more forceful): "Vindicate me, O Lord, for I have led a blameless life; I have trusted in the Lord without wavering. Test me, O Lord, and try me, examine my heart and my mind; for Your love is ever before me, and I walk continually in Your truth. I do not sit with deceitful men, nor do I consort with hypocrites; I abhor the assembly of evildoers and refuse to sit with the wicked. I wash my hands in innocence, and go about your altar, O Lord . . . . But I lead a blameless life; redeem me and be merciful to me" (Ps. 26:1-6,11).

4. The principal Hebrew root for "blameless" (*tamam*) basically means "complete; whole; sound"; the Greek words for blameless primarily mean "without spot" and "without blemish" (*aspilos* and *amomos*; note that the Greek prefix, *a*, is used here in the sense of "without; not" as in English "apathetic," i.e., without pathos or feeling).

5. References: Genesis 3:8 (the Lord in the garden); Genesis 13:17 (walk back and forth in the land; cf. Joshua 18:4,8!); Genesis 24:40 (Abraham looking back at his life); Genesis 48:15 (Jacob referring back to his forefathers); Exodus 21:19 (an injured man getting back on his feet and walking around); Leviticus 26:12; Deuteronomy 23:14 (God walking in the camp); Isaiah 38:14 (Hezekiah's plea).

6. It was M. Basilea Schlink who wrote the book entitled, *Repentance: The Joy Filled Life*, English translation (Minneapolis: Bethany, 1984). So much for the notion of true repentance being morbid! See also the chapter entitled, "Repentance: The Missing Jewel," in Michael L. Brown, *Whatever Happened to*

the Power of God: Is the Charismatic Church Slain in the Spirit or Down for the Count? (Shippensburg, PA: Destiny Image, 1991), pp. 101-108; see also idem, *The End of the American Gospel Enterprise* (Shippensburg, PA: Destiny Image, 1989), pp. 23-33 ("The Lost Art of Repentance" and "Repentance Prepares the Way"); idem, *How Saved Are We?*, pp. 21-27 ("Were You Ever Lost?").

7. As expressed concisely in Proverbs 28:13 (just seven words in the Hebrew!), "He who conceals his transgressions will not prosper, but he who confesses and forsakes them will obtain mercy" (*RSV*).

8. See *Matthew Henry's Commentary on the Bible*, ad loc.

9. Ibid.

10. In Revelation 3:5, Jesus states, "He who overcomes will, like them, be dressed in white. I will never blot out his name from the book of life, but will acknowledge his name before My Father and His angels." This clearly implies two things: (1) Our names can be blotted out of the book of life once they are written in it; (2) It is a significant, momentous event if someone's name is blotted out, as opposed to being an everyday (or every month) occurrence. For discussion of this verse, see David E. Aune, *Revelation 1-5*, Word Biblical Commentary (Dallas: Word, 1997), pp. 223-225, who correctly observes (p. 223) that, "The possibility of having one's name erased from the Book of Life suggests that fidelity to God rather than any type of predestinarian system is the reason for having one's name inscribed in the Book of Life in the first place (see Rev. 17:8)."

CHAPTER TEN

1. I believe this is what is meant by Proverbs 24:16, "For though a righteous man falls seven times, he rises again, but the wicked are brought down by calamity." The context (Prov. 24:15-18) speaks of temporary advantages the wicked may have over the righteous, pictured as the righteous falling seven times but getting back up. In contrast the wicked fall and do not rise. In any case, the context is not talking about righteous people taking serious moral falls—and seven times, at that!—but rather of the righteous temporarily "falling" before the wicked.

2. According to Johannes P. Louw and Eugene A. Nida, eds., *Greek-English Lexicon of the New Testament Based on Semantic Domains* (New York: United Bible Societies, 1988), vol. 1, p. 240, #21.16, the Greek word *ekbasis* is "a means by which one may escape from some danger or difficulty—'a means of escape, a way of escape.'"

3. The *NIV* misses the full force of Exodus 14:16, translating, "Raise your staff and stretch out your hand over the sea *to divide* the water so that the Israelites

can go through the sea on dry ground" (my emphasis), whereas the Hebrew should be rendered, "As for you, raise your staff, stretch out your hand, and divide the water . . . ." See Brown, *It's Time to Rock the Boat*, p. 181.

4. For a discussion of Luke 10:19 in its original context, cf. John Nolland, *Luke 9:21–18:34*, Word Biblical Commentary (Dallas: Word, 1993), pp. 564, 565.

5. It is interesting to note that there is considerable overlap in some of the Hebrew and Greek words for "tempt" and "try," so that the exact translation can only be determined by context. For example, in Genesis 22:1, the *KJV* reads, "God did tempt Abraham," whereas the *NIV* (correctly) renders, "God tested Abraham." Another good example is found in James 1:12-15, where the same Greek words are alternately (and properly) translated with "try" and "tempt" in most English versions. Of course, there are Hebrew and Greek words that specifically mean "test" and do not overlap in any way with the concept of "tempt," while there are words for "tempt" that do not overlap with "try."

6. Their historic rate of success is better than 80 percent (meaning that more than 80 percent of those who graduate from the Teen Challenge program do not return to drugs). For the original, classic story, see David Wilkerson with John Sherrill, *The Cross and the Switchblade* (Grand Rapids: Baker Books, 1981). For a recent update, cf. Don Wilkerson, *The Cross Is Still Mightier than the Switchblade* (Shippensburg, PA: Destiny Image, 1996).

7. This specific, historic aspect of the Brownsville Revival was pointed out to me by Prof. Vinson Synan, Dean of the Regent University School of Divinity, and Mr. Richard Ostling, religion editor for *Time* magazine. For a lively and informative account of the revival, see Steve Rabey, *Revival at Brownsville* (Nashville: Thomas Nelson, 1999).

8. It is a dictum of Rabbinic Judaism that "one does not depend on a miracle" (see Babylonian Talmud, Pesachim 64b), in other words, "Don't stand in a place of danger and say 'A miracle will happen to me!'" (Babylonian Talmud, Shabbat 32a). For additional, related sayings in Hebrew or Aramaic with English translation, see Reuven Alcalay, ed. and trans., with Mordekhai Nurock, *Words of the Wise* (Israel: Massada, 1970), pp. 322, 323.

CHAPTER ELEVEN

1. "The American Heritage® Concise Dictionary," *Microsoft® Encarta® 97 Encyclopedia. The American Heritage® Concise Dictionary, Third Edition*, Copyright © 1994 by Houghton Mifflin Company. Electronic version licensed from and portions copyright © 1994 by INSO Corporation. All rights reserved.

2. Contrast this with the *gain* of knowing Jesus, even if one suffers the loss of all things; see Philippians 3:7-12.

3. Although scholars have debated the exact location of Tarshish, Leslie Allen's comment on Jonah's disobedience—he was called to Nineveh but sailed for Tarshish—is excellent. First, Allen translates the Lord's command in Jonah 1:2 with, "Go off and visit the vast city of Nineveh and denounce it," translating 1:3 with, "Jonah did go off—in the direction of Tarshish, running away from Yahweh." He then observes that, "Jonah does the exact opposite of what he is told. The narrator makes him act out a defiant 'no' to Yahweh's call to Nineveh. *Tarshish* was at the other end of the world from Nineveh." See Leslie C. Allen, *The Books of Joel, Obadiah, Jonah, and Micah*, New International Commentary on the Old Testament (Grand Rapids: Eerdmans, 1976), pp. 202, 204. (See pp. 204-205, note 10, for an extensive discussion of the precise location of Tarshish.)

4. We learn from other portions of Scripture (specifically, Numbers 31:8,16; Deuteronomy 23:4,5; Joshua 13:22; Revelation 2:14) that Balaam, having failed to curse the Israelites himself, counseled Balak to use Moabite women to seduce the Israelites into immorality and idol worship, thereby bringing them directly under God's curse. Significant references to Balaam have also been found in ancient, extra-biblical inscriptions. For a recent summary, see Jo Ann Hackett, "Balaam," *Anchor Bible Dictionary*, vol. 1, pp. 569-572.

CHAPTER TWELVE

1. In the last few years, a number of insightful books by best-selling Christian authors have been written on the subject of grace, although the call to holiness is not central in their themes. These books include Philip Yancey, *What's So Amazing About Grace?* (Grand Rapids: Zondervan, 1997); Max Lucado, *In the Grip of Grace* (Dallas: Word, 1996); Charles R. Swindoll, *The Grace Awakening* (New York: Walker and Co., 1990). On a more theological level (specifically, Reformed) there is Michael Horton, *Putting Amazing Back into Grace* (Grand Rapids: Baker Books, 1991). Cf. also Warren Wiersbe, ed., *Classic Sermons on the Grace of God* (Grand Rapids: Kregel, 1997).

2. See chapter 8, " 'The Letter Kills': The Peril of Legalistic Religion."

3. Readers with almost no background in Hebrew or Greek can still benefit from tools like *The Englishman's Hebrew Concordance* and *Greek Concordance*, since for each Hebrew or Greek word used in the Bible, a list of all occurrences from the *KJV* (in English) then follows. This means that the reader can see just how one particular word was translated and used in its various contexts.

Interested students of the Scriptures can also use the numbering systems in concordances like *Strong's* and *Young's*, although the dictionary in the back of *Strong's* (especially for the Hebrew and Aramaic) must be used with caution.

4. For discussion on the relationship between semantics, etymology, and biblical interpretation, cf. the introductory articles in *NIDOTTE*, Volume 1; and see the references in Michael L. Brown's *"Kipper* and Atonement in the Book of Isaiah" in *Ki Barukh Hu: Ancient Near Eastern, Biblical, and Judaic Studies for Baruch A. Levine*, R. Chazan, W. W. Hallo, and L. H. Schiffman, eds. (Winona Lake, IN: Eisenbrauns, 1998).

5. The most important Hebrew words are *hen* and *hesed* (note that *hesed* has been the subject of a good deal of scholarly discussion; cf. the literature cited in *NIDOTTE*, vol. 2, p. 218, especially N. Glueck, K. D. Sakenfeld, and G. R. Clark. The key Greek word is *charis*, from whence we get the words "charisma" and "charismatic," i.e., gracious gifts (from God).

6. These different categories are called semantic domains; cf. above, note 4, and see Louw-Nida, *Greek English Lexicon*, vol. 1, pp. vi-xxiii. The important five-volume reference work, *NIDOTTE*, includes a breakdown into semantic domains of all words treated in the dictionary, approaching an Old Testament equivalent of Louw-Nida's New Testament work.

7. Cited in Wells, *Inspiring Quotations: Contemporary and Classical*, p. 83, #1044.

8. According to Louw-Nida, *Greek-English Lexicon*, vol. 2, p. 262, the New Testament usages of *charis* can be summed up as: kindness; gift; thanks; good will.

9. One interesting dictionary definition of *charis* in the New Testament is: "a special manifestation of the divine presence, activity, power, or glory." According to Horton, *Putting Amazing Back into Grace*, p. 168, "As in the medieval church, grace is once again spoken of as the assistance of the Holy Spirit in helping us live the 'victorious Christian life.' When we fall, he picks us up again and gives us the power to keep going."

10. See chapter 5, "Go and Sin No More: What Does the Bible Say?" and the appendix, where verses from Romans 6 are discussed.

11. The Old Testament frequently uses the word "grace" in this sense (see, e.g., Prov. 3:3,4); cf. above, note 5.

12. For epistolary greetings, see Romans 1:7; 1 Corinthians 1:3; 2 Corinthians 1:2; Galatians 1:3; Ephesians 1:2; Philippians 1:2; Colossians 1:2; 1 Thessalonians 1:1; 2 Thessalonians 1:2; Titus 1:4; 1 Peter 1:2; 2 Peter 1:2; Revelation 1:4; for epistolary closings, see 1 Corinthians 16:23; 2 Corinthians 13:14; Galatians 6:18; Ephesians 6:24; Philippians 4:23; Colossians 4:18; 1 Thessalonians 5:28;

2 Thessalonians 3:18; 1 Timothy 6:21; 2 Timothy 4:22; Titus 3:15; Philemon 25; Hebrews 13:25; 2 Peter 3:18; Revelation 22:21. For a discussion of the verse "With the help of Silas, whom I regard as a faithful brother, I have written to you briefly, encouraging you and testifying that this is the true grace of God. Stand fast in it" (1 Pet. 5:12), interpreted with reference to our sharing in Christ's suffering, see Joseph Ton, *Suffering, Martyrdom and Rewards in Heaven* (Lanham, MD: University Press of America, 1997), pp. 257-268.

13. According to H. H. Esser, "Grace," in *NIDNTT*, vol. 2, p. 119, "In Acts grace is that power which flows from God or from the exalted Christ, and accompanies the activity of the apostles giving success to their mission (see Acts 6:8; 11:23; 14:26; 15:40; 18:27)."

14. I believe it was John Wimber who coined the term "gracelets."

15. Note the following renderings for *charis* in these passages in the *New Living Translation*: kindness (2 Cor. 8:1); ministry (v. 6); gracious ministry (v. 7); full of love and kindness (v. 9); generous[ly] (2 Cor. 9:8); grace (9:14).

16. According to the Puritan George Swinnock, cited in Thomas, *The Golden Treasury of Puritan Quotations*, p. 167, "The Law is a court of justice, but the Gospel a throne of grace."

17. For devotional thoughts on Hebrews 4:14-16, see Andrew Murray, *The Holiest of All* (Springdale, PA: Whitaker, 1996), pp. 163-174.

18. Note also Romans 6:15: "What then? Shall we sin because we are not under law but under grace? By no means!"

19. Chuck Swindoll, following the well-known argument of D. Martyn Lloyd-Jones, points out that if people do not (wrongly) accuse us of giving a license to sin through our preaching of grace, then we are probably not really preaching grace (see *The Grace Awakening*, pp. 41-46). This is based on the fact that Paul anticipated this very kind of response when writing to the Romans (see Rom. 6:1, "Shall we go on sinning so that grace may increase?" and 6:15, "Shall we sin because we are not under law but under grace?"). This, of course, is an important point, since no one would accuse a "graceless" legalist of giving people a license to sin. However, we should be careful not to take this too far since, (1) In Romans 6:1, Paul is countering a wrong response to the fact that where sin abounded in the past, grace abounded all the more (see Rom. 5:20)—as if we should sin more to bring more grace, clearly a preposterous notion that Paul completely rejects—while in Romans 6:15, he is countering the wrong response to the fact that we are no longer under the law but under grace (see Rom. 6:14)—as if this gave us liberty to sin, whereas his whole point in 6:14 is that because we are under grace, sin shall no longer be our master!

So, as we teach all of Paul's message, we can keep people from misunderstanding grace. (2) Elsewhere the New Testament connects grace with holy living (see below to Titus 2:11 and Heb. 12:18), and we should make this part of our message too. There is no need for imbalance here! We can declare God's amazing grace and at the same time warn people of the danger of scorning that grace.

20. The Greek for "misses" in Hebrews 12:15 might also be rendered, "forfeits, falls short of, fails to obtain." Note also 2 Peter 3:17,18, where after the apostle exhorts us not to fall from our "secure position," he exhorts us instead to "grow in grace." K. Berger, "*charis*," in in Horst Balz and Gerhard Schneider, eds., *Exegetical Dictionary of the New Testament* (Grand Rapids: Eerdmans, 1993), vol. 3, p. 458, points out that the noun *charis* is used with various verbs in the New Testament: stand in grace (see Rom. 5:2; 1 Pet. 5:12), grow in grace (see 2 Pet. 3:18), become strong in grace (see 2 Tim. 2:1), continue in grace (see Acts 13:43), fall from grace (see Gal. 5:4), fail to obtain God's grace (see Heb. 12:15), and insult the Spirit of grace (see Heb. 10:29); cf. also Galatians 2:21 with "frustrate the grace of God," not cited by Berger. He makes the significant point that the use of these verbs indicates that, "Grace acquires special significance for Christian existence, and not just at its beginning."

21. William Barclay, cited in Wells, *Inspiring Quotations: Contemporary and Classical*, #1117, p. 87.

22. Note that this verse also proves that faith is not a work; see also Romans 4:1-5, and cf. Robert Shank, *Elect in the Son* (Minneapolis: Bethany, 1989), p. 125, for some insightful observations concerning the relationship between faith, grace, and election.

23. In August of 1997, during a discussion with a young theologian visiting the Pensacola area, I quoted the words of the late revival historian James Edwin Orr, viz., that "Repent is the first word of the gospel." To my surprise—in spite of the scriptural evidence that I presented—this Christian brother responded, "No, 'repent' is law. 'Believe' is gospel"—making a distinction that, I am quite sure, would be foreign to the New Testament authors. For these men, repentance and faith went hand in hand. (I would encourage those who question this statement to simply review the verses cited in the text, above, remembering that the fundamental concept of repentance is "making an about-face," not merely "changing one's mind.") In any case, this same theologian, when a guest on a Christian radio program, actually commented that the leaders in the Brownsville Revival didn't understand what the gospel was! David Pawson, *Once Saved Always Saved*, also points out that, biblically speaking, repentance is not a "work."

CHAPTER THIRTEEN

1. This is a central theme of Mike Bickle's *Passion for Jesus* (Orlando: Creation House, 1993). Sammy Tippit, *Fire in Your Heart* (Chicago: Moody Press, 1987), links together the themes of personal revival, devotion to the Lord, and holiness.

2. Cited in Leonard Ravenhill, *Why Revival Tarries* (Minneapolis: Bethany, 1959), p. 114.

3. Robert H. Mounce, along with many other commentators, defines the Ephesians' "first love" primarily with respect to loving one another, in other words, brotherly love; see idem *The Book of Revelation*, New International Commentary on the New Testament (Grand Rapids: Eerdmans, 1977), p. 88. However, he notes that, "The expression includes both love of God and love of mankind at large," correctly observing that, "A cooling of personal love for God inevitably results in the loss of harmonious relationships within the body of believers" (ibid.).

4. Alan Johnson, "Revelation," in the *Expositor's Bible Commentary* (Grand Rapids: Zondervan, 1981), vol. 12, p. 435, cites John R. W. Stott (*What Christ Thinks of the Church*, p. 27) in support of the view that the Lord's reference to "first love" in Revelation 2:4 speaks of the believers' "inner devotion to Christ that characterized their earlier commitment, like the love of a newly wedded bride for her husband." Johnson, however, also notes that, "Loving devotion to Christ can be lost in the midst of active service, and certainly no amount of orthodoxy can make up for failure to love one another" (ibid.). Adam Clarke states simply, "They did not retain that strong and ardent affection for God and sacred things which they had when first brought to the knowledge of the truth, and justified by faith in Christ." See *Adam Clarke's Commentary on the Bible*, vol. 6, p. 1025, to Revelation 2:4.

5. The *NIV's* usage of the word "height" is an attempt to bring out the meaning of the Greek which simply says, "Remember from where you have fallen."

6. Although the *King James Version* correctly translates the Greek verb *aphiemi* as "left" in Revelation 2:4, it is common for Christians to misquote the verse as if Jesus said that the Ephesians *lost* their first love. Alan Johnson, "Revelation," vol. 12, p. 435, notes that the Greek verb means to forsake or let go. Recently, however, David Aune translated with "lost," without explanation or comment. See his *Revelation 1-5*, pp. 133, 146. Although Aune is a top New Testament scholar, there is absolutely no lexical support for his translation.

7. *Matthew Henry's Commentary on the Bible*, to Revelation 2:5, ad loc.

8. See Brown, "Jesus, the Pearl of Great Price, the Center of Revival," in *From Holy Laughter to Holy Fire*, pp. 186-195; cf. also idem, *Whatever Happened to the*

Power of God?, pp. 117-124 ("Jesus the King: The Center of the Kingdom of God").

9. *The Works of John Wesley*, vol. 2, p. 170.
10. *Oswald Chambers: The Best from All His Books.*
11. Cited in Wells, *Inspiring Quotations: Contemporary and Classical*, p. 88, #1121.
12. *Watching Unto Prayer* (Glasgow: Free Presbyterian Publications, 1988), p. 7.
13. Mounce, *Revelation*, p. 88.
14. Ibid.
15. Charles G. Finney, *Revivals of Religion*, p. 467.
16. *Watching Unto Prayer*, p. 4.
17. See the chapter entitled "The Disruptive Messiah" in Brown, *From Holy Laughter to Holy Fire*, pp. 68-79; see also my (tongue-in-cheek) "Prayer for a Nice Revival" along with Spurgeon's prayer for "a season of glorious disorder" in Michael L. Brown, *Let No One Deceive You: Confronting the Critics of Revival* (Shippensburg, PA: Destiny Image, 1997), p. 180 and p. 156, respectively.
18. This was the closing challenge from Leonard Ravenhill, *Why Revival Tarries*, pp. 162-168.

CHAPTER FOURTEEN

1. See also 1 Peter 2:1-5, where we are described as both a spiritual building and a holy priesthood.
2. Cf. Brown, *Whatever Happened to the Power of God?*, pp. 106, 107, with reference to Psalm 51. Hebrew scholars have sometimes pointed out that an inventive, hyper-literal translation of the Hebrew verb *hitte'* in Psalm 51:7 would be "Unsin me!" Cf., e.g., David Baron, *The Visions and Prophecies of Zechariah* (Grand Rapids: Kregel, 1972), p. 461. Also see Mitchell Dahood, *Psalms 51-100*, Anchor Bible Commentary (Garden City, NY: Doubleday, 1968), p. 5.
3. John Flavel, cited in Thomas, *The Golden Treasury of Puritan Quotations*, p. 138.
4. See Finney, *Revivals of Religion*, pp. 45-47.
5. J. C. Ryle, *Holiness* (Durham, England: Evangelical Press, 1979), p. 2.
6. Charles H. Spurgeon, calendar.
7. William Jenkyn, cited in Thomas, *The Golden Treasury of Puritan Quotations*, p. 139.
8. This quote was supplied to me by my dear friend and co-worker Chuck Cohen.

APPENDIX

1. Some would also cite 1 Timothy 1:15, where Paul writes, "Here is a trustworthy saying that deserves full acceptance: Christ Jesus came into the world to save sinners—of whom I am the worst." Of course, the context is speaking of

his past sins, before his conversion (just read 1 Timothy 1:12-14, 16, which are perfectly clear), in which case his description of himself as the worst of sinners would simply be a reference to his murderous, persecuting past. But, if Paul was referring to his present life, he was using great hyperbole, speaking of himself in light of the majestic holiness of God, a holiness that makes the holiest human being appear vile. In other words, when you are as close to God as Paul was, you can easily consider yourself the "worst sinner"! But would anyone who cites this verse as an excuse for ongoing, personal sin think for a moment that Paul, as compared to other sinners was really the worst—worse than a pedophile, worse than a rapist, worse than a mother killer, worse than an idol worshiper? God forbid. He served the Lord with all his heart and soul (cf. 2 Tim. 4:6-8; Phil. 3:7-14) and expected us to do the same. Note also that Paul called Timothy to high standards of personal purity (see 1 Tim. 4:12; 5:1), that he insisted that overseers and deacons be godly and above reproach (see 1 Tim. 3:1-13; Titus 1:5-9), and that he always used his own life as an example to be followed (see, e.g., Phil. 4:9; 1 Cor. 11:1; 2 Tim. 3:11). The man who could write to the Thessalonians—without exaggeration—"You are witnesses, and so is God, of how holy, righteous and blameless we were among you who believed" (1 Thess. 2:10) was hardly the worst of sinners!

2. I could make the same argument for the Old Testament as well, but I'll base all my arguments on the New Testament, lest someone make the bogus claim, "That's only for Old Testament Israel!"

3. Archibald Thomas Robertson, *Word Pictures in the New Testament* (Grand Rapids: Baker Books, 1981), Vol. IV, The Epistles of Paul, p. 119.

4. See chapter 5 for discussion of these verses.

5. Paul also offers a "summary" prayer in 2 Corinthians 13:7: "Now we pray to God that you will not do anything wrong." That certainly covers things!

6. For discussion on some of the interpretative difficulties in the text, see the references to key commentaries in notes 8, 10, 13 and 18 below.

7. J. Sidlow Baxter also makes special reference to the completed aspect of the verb tenses used here, but draws the wrong conclusion, viz., that the actions spoken of are merely judicial and not experiential: "In Romans 6, Paul is not discussing how God sanctifies you and me *inwardly* or experientially, but how God dealt once for all *judicially* with sin as an hereditary evil in man, by putting way the whole Adam humanity representatively on the Cross" (*A New Call to Holiness* [Grand Rapids: Kregel, 1993], p. 77, his emphasis). Baxter also finds support for his position based on the overall contextual placement of Paul's arguments in Romans 6. His overstated position here, however, forces him to

claim that in Romans 6:6, when Paul wrote that our "old man" was crucified with Jesus, he actually meant *the whole human race* in Adam (ibid., p. 91, his emphasis). For his complete discussion, see ibid., pp. 72-104. Needless to say, Baxter does call believers to holiness and not license, but his misreading of Romans 6 undercuts the force of some of his arguments.

8. For a typical, middle-of-the-road approach, cf. E. F. Harrison, "Romans," in *The Expositors Bible Commentary* (Grand Rapids: Zondervan, 1976), pp. 84, 85. Cf. also A. M. Hunter, cited in Matthew Black, *Romans*, The New Century Bible Commentary, 2nd ed. (Grand Rapids: Eerdmans, 1989), p. 95, as holding to a compromise view when he suggests that verses 14-25 of Romans 7 "therefore depict not only the man under the law, but the Christian who slips back into a legalistic attitude towards God. The present tenses describe not merely a past experience, but one which is potentially ever present." This interpretation certainly has merit.

9. It could be said that defeat or lack of desire to overcome evil is the normal state for the unsaved, but the abnormal state for the believer, who is no longer bound by sin but rather striving toward perfection. Cf. the reflections of John Wesley, shortly after his new birth: "Herein I found the difference between this and my former state chiefly consisted. I was striving, yea, fighting with all my might under the law, as well as under grace. But then I was sometimes, if not often, conquered; now, I was always the conqueror" (*The Works of John Wesley*, pp. 1:103, 104); see also below, note 15.

10. Cf. the clear and comprehensive discussion in Moo, *Romans*, pp. 442-451.

11. John Wesley's *Notes on the Whole Bible: The New Testament*, pp. 465, 466. Note that Wesley was an Arminian.

12. *Romans*, p. 448. Note that Moo is a Reformed (i.e., Calvinist) scholar.

13. In order to defend the view that Paul was speaking of his ongoing experience in the Lord—and thus, the ongoing experience of all believers, C. E. B. Cranfield, *The Epistle to the Romans, Volume 1*, International Critical Commentary (Edinburgh: T & T Clark, 1974), p. 357, had to argue that Paul "does not regard the Christian as being carnal in the same unqualified way that the natural man is carnal." This is because Paul's language in Romans 8 is just too clear and strong.

14. Cited in Black, *Romans*, p. 95. Black rightly finds this to be "a convincing point." For an opposing view, cf. Cranfield, *Romans*, pp. 346, 347.

15. Harrison, "Romans," pp. 83, 84, conveniently lists the main arguments for the pre-conversion interpretation. Wesley's description of his own pre-conversion experience is taken from Romans 7 imagery: "In this vile, abject state of